English-Medium Instruction Translanguaging Practices in Asia

Wenli Tsou · Will Baker
Editors

English-Medium Instruction Translanguaging Practices in Asia

Theories, Frameworks and Implementation in Higher Education

 Springer

Editors
Wenli Tsou 🆔
National Cheng Kung University
Tainan, Taiwan, ROC

Will Baker
University of Southampton
Southampton, UK

ISBN 978-981-16-3003-3   ISBN 978-981-16-3001-9   (eBook)
https://doi.org/10.1007/978-981-16-3001-9

This Springer imprint is published by the registered company Springer Nature Singapore Pte Ltd.
The registered company address is: 152 Beach Road, #21-01/04 Gateway East, Singapore 189721,
Singapore

Foreword

Re-focusing on the Dynamic Meaning-Making Processes of Multilingual Teachers and Students

The spread of English Medium Instruction (EMI) programs in higher education in Asia might come as a mixed blessing. On the one hand, we can see more flows of cultures, knowledges, skills, and perspectives in Asia through using English as a lingua franca. On the other hand, EMI higher education in Asia can easily witness a trend of importing Anglo-dominated academic cultures, curriculums, pedagogies, epistemologies, and language-in-education policies without critical re-designs that take into consideration the specificities of different sociolinguistic, sociocultural, and sociopolitical contexts in Asia. The scholarship in our field has also traditionally been dominated by various deep-rooted beliefs, as critically reviewed by Kubota:

> …I will review insights generated by previous research and discuss how we can think differently and critically for change. Specifically, I will focus on language ideology constituted by beliefs about (1) legitimate varieties of English, (2) native speakerness, (3) whiteness, (4) Euro- and US-centrism, (5) cultural essentialism, (6) English as an international language, (7) English competence for economic success, (8) early learning of English, (9) the monolingual approach to pedagogy, and (10) the ideal learner and learning. (Kubota, 2019, p. 10)

In this pioneering body of works brought together by Tsou and Baker, we see how researchers in various Asian contexts speak to the need to deconstruct some of these deep-rooted ideological beliefs in EMI programs. For instance, the "E" in EMI should not be seen as "native English varieties" from Anglophone countries (Lin, 2020; Lin & Motha, in press); instead, it should be seen as English as a Multilingual Franca (EMF) (see Tsou; Baker; Ishikawa, this volume). With this re-conceptualization of "EMI," there are important ramifications in the design of language-in-education policies, curriculums, and pedagogies. These various themes are picked up and elaborated by the different chapters in this volume. Below I will just highlight two important implications, among others:

(1) Monolingual English should not become the pedagogical norm in EMI higher education in Asia:

While traditional TESOL pedagogy has often stipulated an "English-only" monolingual principle, and even the bilingual education policies of some Asian governments often privilege "native English speaker" teachers, the authors in this volume have spoken strongly of changing this deep-rooted ideological belief. For instance, at this critical moment in the history of Taiwan, when it wants so much to have a greater global presence, participation and influence, it is also at this historical moment that the official bilingual education policy is most susceptible to reproducing and perpetuating the colonialist, monolingual, dominant "native English speaker" ideologies in the language-in-education policy and practice of Taiwan and many Asian countries. It is timely at this historical moment that scholars and researchers in Asia "diffract" (Hill, 2017) and counter these monolingual, "native English speaker" ideologies for the long-term benefits of students and teachers in Asian societies; i.e., both providing access to a broader school population, and affirming a true, egalitarian bilingualism, not an "English-dominant bilingualism" as witnessed in many so-called "post-colonial" societies in Asia (Lin, 2015; Lin & Motha, in press).

(2) Re-focusing on the dynamic, complex, meaning-making processes of multilingual teachers and students:

The many chapters in this volume speak to the importance of researching the design of viable and context-responsive curriculums, pedagogies, and policies in different higher education contexts in Asia; specifically, the different authors in this volume have drawn on and innovated with the insights and ideas of translanguaging theories and pedagogies, English as Multilingual Franca awareness, dynamic complex systems and student agency (Larsen-Freeman, 2019). In all of these studies, we see the significant potential of shifting the traditional lens of pedagogical monolingualism to a dynamic translanguaging and trans-semiotizing lens, valuing the multifarious translingual and transcultural resources that teachers and students bring to the classroom to make meaning and knowledge together (Baker & Tsou, this volume; Lin, 2020).

While this is just a beginning and there is still much research work to do, I am honored and thrilled to write the foreword for this ground-breaking volume, witnessing the wonderful contribution of a whole new generation of researchers to the scholarship of egalitarian bi/multilingual education.

December 2020   Angel M. Y. Lin
                                                                                  Simon Fraser University
                                                                                     Burnaby, Canada

References

Hill, C. M. (2017). More-than-reflective practice: Becoming a diffractive practitioner. *Teacher Learning and Professional Development*, 2(1), 1–17.

Kubota, R. (2019). A critical examination of common beliefs about language teaching: From research insights to professional engagement. In F. Fang & H. P. Widodo (Eds.), *Critical perspectives on global Englishes in Asia: Language policy, curriculum, pedagogy and assessment* (pp. 10–26). Bristol, UK: Multilingual Matters.

Larsen-Freeman, D. (2019). On language learner agency: A complex dynamic systems theory perspective. *The Modern Language Journal, 103*, 61–79. https://doi.org/10.1111/modl.125360 026-7902/19/61–79.

Lin, A. M. Y. (2015). Egalitarian bi/multilingualism and trans-semiotizing in a global world. In W. E. Wright, S. Boun, & O. García (Eds.), *The handbook of bilingual and multilingual education* (pp. 19–37). West Sussex, UK: Wiley Blackwell.

Lin, A. M. Y. (2020). From deficit-based teaching to asset-based teaching in higher education in BANA Countries: Cutting through 'either-or' binaries with a heteroglossic plurilingual lens. In S. Preece, & S. Marshall (Eds.), Special Issue: Plurilingual approaches to teaching and learning in Anglophone higher educational settings. *Language, Culture and Curriculum*, 1–10. https://doi.org/10.1080/07908318.2020.1723927.

Lin, A. M. Y., & Motha, S. (in press). "Curses in TESOL": Postcolonial desires for colonial English. In R. Arber, M. Weinmann, & J. Blackmore (Eds.), *Rethinking languages education: Directions, challenges and innovations*. New York: Routledge.

Acknowledgments

The editors would like to take this opportunity to give their compliments and express their gratitude to the anonymous reviewers for their supportive and intellectual comments. Their sincere thanks are also due to all chapter contributors and to the Springer editorial team for their professional and generous encouragement. The editors and the chapter authors would also like to thank the financial supports from National Cheng Kung University, the Ministry of Science and Technology, Taiwan, ROC. Finally, hearty thanks and love are sent to Dr. Angel M. Y. Lin for her insightful foreword of this book.

Contents

Editors and Contributors

About the Editors

Wenli Tsou is a Full Professor in the Department of Foreign Languages & Litera-ture, and currently Director of the Foreign Language Center at National Cheng Kung University, Taiwan. She received her Ph.D. in Foreign and Second Language Educa-tion from the State University of New York at Buffalo, US. She is the project leader of the National Cheng Kung University ESP and EMI programs. She is also the leading figure of the bilingual education in Taiwan, helping with its teacher training and curriculum design. Her research interests include teacher training, ESP, English as a Lingua Franca, Content and Language Interacted Learning, and English as a Medium of Instruction. Her current research projects have focused on the links between trans-diciplinary teaching and translanguaging of bilingual education and EMI. She chairs various international conferences including the 13th International Conference of English as a Lingua Franca and has co-edited the following books: *English as a Medium of Instruction in Higher Education: Implementations & classroom practices in Taiwan* (2017, Springer), *Exploring CLIL: A Resource Book* (2018, Bookman) and *Resources for Teaching English for Specific Purposes* (2014, Bookman).

Will Baker is an Associate Professor of Applied Linguistics and Director of the Centre for Global Englishes at the University of Southampton, UK. His research interests are English as a Lingua Franca, Intercultural and Transcultural Commu-nication, English medium instruction, Intercultural education, Intercultural Citi-zenship, and ELT, and he has published and presented internationally in all these areas. His current research projects have focused on the links between Intercultural Citizenship, Internationalization of HE, and EMI including the recently completed "From English language learners to intercultural citizen" https://www.teachinge nglish.org.uk/article/english-language-learners-intercultural-citizens. Recent publi-cations include Baker, W., & Ishikawa, T. *Transcultural Communication and Global Englishes: Exploring intercultural communication through English in a multilin-gual world.* (2021, Routledge), co-editor of the *Routledge Handbook of English as a Lingua Franca* (2018), author of the monograph *Culture and Identity through English* *as a Lingua Franca* (2015, DGM), and co-editor of the book series *Developments in English as Lingua Franca* (DGM).

Contributors

Will Baker   Centre for Global Englishes, University of Southampton, Southampton, UK

Fay Chen   National Cheng Kung University, Taiwan, Republic of China

Yi-Ping Huang   National Chengchi University, Taipei, Taiwan, ROC

Simon Humphries   Faculty of Foreign Language Studies, Kansai University, Osaka, Japan

Tomokazu Ishikawa   Center for English as a Lingua Franca, Tamagawa University, Tokyo, Japan

Shin-Mei Kao   National Cheng Kung University, Taiwan, Republic of China

Phuong Le Hoang Ngo   Faculty of English, University of Foreign Languages, Hue University, Hue, Vietnam

Jaewon Jane Ra   Research Institute for Languages and Cultures of Asia, Mahidol University, Nakhon, Thailand

Wenli Tsou   National Cheng Kung University, Tainan, Taiwan, Republic of China

Rining (Tony) Wei   Department of Applied Linguistics, Xi'an Jiaotong-Liverpool University, Suzhou, China

Tomoko Yashima   Faculty of Foreign Language Studies, Kansai University, Osaka, Japan

Yi Zhang   Department of Applied Linguistics, Xi'an Jiaotong-Liverpool University, Suzhou, China

Part I
Introduction

Chapter 1
Translanguaging as a Glocalized Strategy for EMI in Asia

Wenli Tsou

Abstract This introductory chapter makes the case for the research focus on translanguaging in English medium instruction (EMI) in Asia's higher education. This chapter first describes the features of EMI programs, and how the phenomenon of English as a lingua franca (ELF) has introduced new directions and insights in English education. This is followed by an overview of the opportunities and key challenges of EMI at the policy and implementation levels. Then, related concepts and the use of translanguaging as a glocalized strategy in Asia's ELF contexts are discussed. Finally, an overview of the chapters by researchers contributing to this volume is provided.

Keywords Asia · Translanguaging · English as a Lingua Franca (ELF) · English Medium Instruction (EMI) · Content and Language Integrated Learning (CLIL) · Higher education

1 Introduction

In 2017, two volumes were published on English medium instruction in Asia. They were *English Medium Instruction in Higher Education in Asia–Pacific*, a collection edited by Ben Fenton-Smith, Pamela Humphreys, and Ian Walkinshaw and *English as a Medium of Instruction in Higher Education: Implementations and Classroom Practices in Taiwan*, edited by myself and Shin-Mei Kao. These two books differ in scope, with the former addressing a wide range of EMI issues in policy making, research, and practices, and the latter focusing on discipline-specific EMI classroom practices in Taiwan. We collected data from EMI classrooms in international business, mechanical engineering, environmental science, medical science, tourism, and professional writing. With two books covering EMI implementation and issues in different Asian contexts and academic disciplines, why do we need more?

W. Tsou (✉)

Department of Foreign Languages & Literature, National Cheng Kung University, Tainan, Taiwan, ROC

e-mail: wtsou@ncku.edu.tw

The publication of this current volume testifies to the important role that EMI programs play in the internationalization in higher education, and the need to update our understanding of EMI with emerging concepts and trends in language education. In this volume, we focus on implications of the reconceptualization of the English as a lingua franca (ELF) phenomenon as a multilingual franca, and the extended scope of ELF discussion to include emerging and related thoughts in multilingualism, translanguaging, multimodality, and multiliteracies (Jenkins, 2018). This introductory chapter begins with a brief introduction to EMI programs, implications of ELF on English education, and related challenges in Asia's EMI programs. Then I discuss translanguaging as a glocalized strategy in bilingual education. This chapter concludes with an overview of the contributors and their chapters.

2   CBI, CLIL, EMI and ICLHE

Due to the internationalization of higher education, there has been a growing presence of programs in which English is used as a medium to teach academic content courses in contexts where English is learned as an additional language. The trend has ushered in an array of approaches, most notably CBI (content-based instruction), CLIL, EMI and ICLHE. Risking simplification, respective features of these four approaches could be illustrated with a continuum with content-driven approaches on the one end and language-driven instruction on the other.

On this continuum, CBI generally focuses more on language learning outcomes, with content as a vehicle for authentic input and a means to engage learners in meaningful language use (Brown & Bradford, 2017; Edsall & Saito, 2012). In the English as a foreign language (EFL) contexts, CBI usually follows a theme-based model, with subject-content topics introduced and discussed to facilitate language learning.

In contrast, CLIL programs are developed with explicit content and language goals in mind. It denotes "a dual-focused educational approach in which an additional language is used for the learning and teaching of both content and language" (Coyle et al., 2010: 1). With its European secondary school origins, CLIL has been adopted widely since the 1990s (Marsh, 2002) and in higher educations in many EFL contexts (Arno-Macia & Mancho-Bares, 2015; Wei, 2013; Yang, 2017). In Taiwan, to facilitate learning of college students from universities of science and technology, students who need scaffolding due to lower English proficiency, lecturers have adopted CLIL to provide language skill training. Some of the scaffolding may include pre-teaching vocabulary or instructions of language learning strategies (Yang, 2017).

Although EMI, as the name suggests, refers to classes where English is the instructional language, the approach differs from CBI and CLIL in its aim to deliver professional and discipline-specific content, and its primary focus on subject-content mastery (Brown & Bradford, 2017). EMI lecturers, through experience sharing, may at times advise students on studying skills or genre-related instruction such as how to write a lab report or compile case studies in English; however, language instruction is not typically a regular feature. Like subject-content courses delivered in universities around the world in students' first languages, EMI lecturers have a strict syllabus and tight schedule to follow; there is seldom time for language instruction. Most EMI lecturers are specialists in their content areas; they do not view themselves as having the responsibility, or the expertise, to teach language (Tsou & Kao, 2017).

While EMI programs' primary aim is to teach content in English, they are usually supported by English for specific purposes (ESP) classes (Tsou & Kao, 2014). These classes provide the necessary training for students to succeed in EMI classrooms. The training focuses on academic and studying skills such as listening comprehension, note-taking, discussion skills, presentation, etc. Most universities encourage EMI and ESP teachers to work together so that language training is aligned with the demand of EMI courses. As a result, ESP courses in a variety of disciplines such as business administration, science and engineering, management, and medicine are commonly developed to support EMI programs in higher education.

In Taiwan, to meet the increasing demands of local law students who aspire to pursue international law, most universities have offered ESP in legal studies and EMI courses (Chou, 2017). Because very few language teachers had related legal background, many law professors were asked to teach both legal English and subject-content EMI courses (Tsai, 2014). In Taiwan, Chou (2017) showed that even though many law professors studied in the U.S. and thus were fluent in English, they professed a lack of pedagogical content knowledge required to conduct either ESP or EMI courses.

Finally, it is worth noting that in some contexts EMI is discussed alongside of ICLHE, which stands for Integrating Content and Language in Higher Education. ICLHE practices have rapidly gained in popularity in the European contexts and consequently given rise to a growing number of research topics from language policies, teacher–student interactions, to academic performance of students (Dafouz, 2014). It is generally agreed that EMI, as discussed above, is mainly driven by content learning and related research has focused on how English is used to facilitate instruction, whereas research of ICLHE may foreground both the teaching and learning process and how teachers and learners co-construct meanings in classrooms. However, it is difficult to clearly distinguish the two models because there are many overlapping features (Smit & Dafouz, 2012).

3   EMI and ELF

EMI programs have gained popularity is Asia due to internationalization of higher education, which was mainly driven by globalization and, equally important, the phenomenon of ELF. To fully appreciate ELF, it would be helpful to first present the related terms that have been used to describe the nature and role of English being used and transformed as a result of globalization. According to Rose and Galloway (2019), Global Englishes (GE) is an umbrella term inclusive of research in the diverse but overlapping fields of World Englishes, ELF, English as an international language

(EIL). Research of Global Englishes has focused on the linguistic and sociocultural dimensions of global uses and users of English (Centre for Global Englishes, 2020), and their implications on language teaching (Galloway & Numajiri, 2020).

ELF researchers have highlighted the pragmatic strategies and English language use observed in global communication. As a means of communication in global contexts, ELF is "used as a contact language among speakers from different first languages" (Jenkins, 2009:143). ELF is also commonly referred to as "any use of English among speakers of different first languages for whom English is the communicative medium of choice and often the only option" (Seidlhofer, 2011:7).

ELF may be observed in conversations among non-native speakers, or between non-native and native speakers. As such, Hülmbauer et al. (2008, p. 26) identified ELF as a trend commonly observed in Europe, "a phenomenon which is a part of the linguistic repertoire utilized on a daily basis by a large number of plurilingual individuals in Europe." Although ELF is observed and its features analyzed with corpus data (Cogo & Dewey, 2012), it is not a foreign language or a variety of English to be learned. It is fluid and dynamic, better described as competence in terms of communication skills and strategies. In contrast to the traditional understanding of American or British versions of English, ELF is often "defined functionally by its use in intercultural communication rather than formally by its reference to native-speaker norms" (Hülmbauer et al., 2008).

The ELF trend has had many implications on English education. The phenomenon has called on English language teaching (ELT) researchers and practitioners to critically reflect on how ELF and multilingualism relate to their own contexts. For instance, issues such as ownership or custodianship deserve further investigation. In ELF contexts, where the number of non-native speakers outnumbers the native speakers, ownership of English should be reconceptualized.

It is generally agreed that ELF awareness has contributed to the positive identify forming of its users. It has allowed non-native speakers to value their linguistic repertoire and multilingual abilities. In Asia, English education has always been greatly valued due to several reasons. The ability to communicate in English is a prerequisite to establishing international trade and a practical tool of empowerment. However, due to colonial heritage or political and economic ties, English education has followed the native-speakerism model where sounding like a native-speaker is a primary goal, and any deviation is viewed as deficient.

ELF research has called attention to the difference between native-speaker norms and intercultural communicative competence and awareness (Baker, 2011, 2015; Fang, 2018). Studies have shown that to prepare EFL students to become effective communicators in global contexts, the goals of English education should be reexamined. While traditional ELT classrooms have focused on linguistic goals such as achieving native-like proficiency and appreciating Anglophone cultures, ELF-informed language training reconceptualizes communicative competence to include (1) intercultural communicative skills to achieve intelligibility, and (2) the ability and flexibility to adapt in multilingual communicative contexts (Baker, 2011, 2015). Implications of ELF highlight the importance of focusing on the process, rather than the product, of intercultural communication.

ELF is an important concept in the current discussion because the "E" in EMI is ELF. It is fair to say that ELF is the classroom language in EMI programs because these programs were almost always designed for academic internationalization and attended by international and local students. To better reflect the multilingual and multicultural reality of today's global communication context, ELF received an update in 2015: English as a multilingual franca (EMF). The working definition of an EMF scenario is: "Multilingual communication in which English is available as a contact language of choice, but is not necessarily chosen" (Jenkins, 2015, p. 73). As EMI classes in Asia are usually attended by local and international students from several countries, it is common that, in addition to English, several languages are being spoken in any given class.

4 Opportunities and Challenges of EMI in Asia

As the ELF trend ushers in a pragmatic view of communicative competence, it has allowed non-native speakers to claim their own unique way of using English as long as the intended communicative purpose is served. In academic settings, ELF also means that EMI programs in Asia, with many lectures provided by local academics who teach in English as an additional language, could compete with universities in the Anglophone countries as a more accessible alternative to global talent development (Tsou & Kao, 2017). While each country in Asia has its own unique socio-historical context, as a region Asia has experienced rapid growth in economic development. To substantiate the growth momentum, many countries have introduced ambitious plans for talent development. Where possible, policy makers have called for the internationalization of all stages of education from primary to higher education. Take Taiwan as an example, Taiwan's EMI programs began around 2013, when the Ministry of Education (MOE) announced two major policies to attract international students to study in Taiwan's universities (Hou et al., 2013). In 2018, the Ministry announced its commitment to launch bilingual education in compulsory education (MOE Taiwan, 2018).

Similar internationalization efforts have been introduced in other Asian countries. In 2008, the Japanese Ministry of Education, Culture, Sport, Science and Technology (MEXT) introduced two initiatives (Hashimoto, 2013). The national Course of Study for Foreign Languages, introduced in 2008, mandated that senior high schools were to "conduct English classes in English" and to focus on communicative skill development. A second initiative aimed to attract international students to study in Japan's universities. The Ministry offered scholarships and encouraged 13 core universities to introduce "English-only" degree programs (MEXT, 2017).

Likewise, the Chinese Ministry of Education promoted EMI as a policy priority (MOE China, 2001). A large-scale survey reported that in 2006, there were 132 Chinese universities providing EMI courses, which translates into an average of 44 EMI courses per university (Wu et al., 2010, quoted in Hu, 2019). Moreover, aiming to provide an alternative to overseas degrees in English, Chinese higher education institutes have actively collaborated with Western universities to launch branch campuses in China where English is the working language. Since 2006, as many as 12 U.S. universities and 4 British institutions have partnered with local Chinese universities (Precht, 2017). Similar cooperative models are found in countries like Vietnam, Malaysia and Japan, where American, British, and Australian universities formed local partnerships to introduce degree-bearing EMI programs (Bernard, 2014).

While the Asian governments have invested a great deal of resources to promote bilingual education (details to be reported in the chapters of this volume), key challenges of these EMI programs have been extensively reported and examined (Barnard & Hawim, 2018; Fenton-Smith et al., 2017; Tsou & Kao, 2017). One of the major obstacles has to do with stakeholders' misunderstanding of the "E" (English) in the EMI programs. Studies have shown that most bilingual education policies are not informed by ELF (Chen et al., 2020; Jenkins & Mauranen, 2019; Lin & Lo, 2018; Murata, 2018). The traditional ELT principles, developed for immigrants and international students studying in the English-speaking countries, follow the native-speakerism, or English as a native language (ENL), model (Lin & Lo, 2018; Widdowson, 2013). The ENL model has aimed at helping the newcomers achieve near-native proficiency in places where English is the dominant language. When applied in the ELF context, the ENL ideology has the undesirable effect of equating internationalization with Englishization. Although the ENL model has guided the curriculum development in EFL classrooms for many years, it is much established that English education policies should be updated from the monolingual approach to incorporate the multilingual reality in today's ELF context.

An overview of the ELF phenomenon and the English education history in Taiwan showed that national language policies often reflect language hierarchies influenced by ENL, privileging the native norms and native-speaking English teachers over local multilingual teachers (Chen, et al., 2020). Similarly, many Asian regions, having close political or economic ties with the U.K. or the U.S., subscribe to the monolingual ideology (Bernard, 2014; García, & Lin, 2018). In Japan, many Japanese still consider English to belong to native speakers in North America, who serve as the single most important, and often unattainable, role model (Ishikawa, 2017). Similar monolingual ideology is observed in the current language policy in China, which is still largely native-oriented, and the native versus non-native dichotomy is still salient, especially in foreign English teacher recruitment (Fang, 2018).

Given the ideological dominance, it is not surprising that policy makers advocate the immersion model, believing that creating an "English-only" or "all-English" environment taught by native speakers of English is the best approach. As discussed earlier in this chapter, the limitations of the ENL model is that the learning emphasizes meeting the standards established by native speakers, whereas critical communicative skills such as leveraging learners' resources like their L1 and the use of accommodation strategies, important to the ELF context, are not the primary learning goals.

The second challenge is related to the twin-peak nature of students' language proficiency. Although EMI programs were created to attract international enrolment, many local students enroll in these programs, thus contributing to the EMI classroom context where the majority of students and the teachers share the same L1. Most college students in Asia study English as a subject for college admission. While many EFL students have obtained high scores in standardize tests, because the tests almost always focused on reading and listening comprehension in General English, most students lack the ability to use English as a working language or learning tool in EMI. Furthermore, most students lack domain-specific vocabulary and specialist knowledge on register and genre (Lin & Lo, 2018). Students need English for Academic Purposes (EAP) training, such as English for business or English for engineering, to be prepared for EMI. In Asia, where EMI programs attract international students, many are attended by college students from other Asian regions (FICHET, 2020). Most of these international students also use English as an additional language. They too need additional training in studying skills such as listening comprehension and note-taking in English.

Another challenge has to do with college lecturers' beliefs and abilities. Not all professors are willing to change their instructional language, believing that EMI creates language barriers and thus affects students' comprehension and the amount of content covered. The language barriers often have a negative impact on delivery and classroom interactions. In Taiwan's EMI classrooms, the majority of students and the teacher share the same L1, if there are no international students in the class, most lecturers find it easier to give instruction in Chinese rather than spending time to scaffold students (see Chaps. 5 and 6 of this volume).

Although these issues have been previously discussed (Hu, 2019; Tsou & Kao, 2017; Walkinshaw, et al., 2017), recent theoretical development in multilingualism, translanguaging and multimodality has introduced new insights into Asia's EMI implementation. For instance, Angel Lin's (2015) Multimodalities/Entextualization Cycle (MEC) showed how lecturers could leverage translanguaging and multimodality to facilitate learner engagement and support language output (see Sect. 6).

5   Glocalization and English Education

Before we move on to discuss translanguaging as a glocalizing strategy, a brief overview of glocalization is presented here. As a concept, glocalization describes the natural and inevitable result of globalization. Robertson (1995, p. 25) defines it as the "simultaneous coexistence of generalization and specialization." When a global concept is first introduced in a specific context, the practice must adapt to local needs and characteristics. Through this adaptation process, the concept is transformed and carried forward locally, resulting in a mixture, diversity, and creativity. Glocalization is commonly observed in international business. Taking a global fast-food chain expanding to Taiwan as an example, the providers have introduced Taiwanese-style bread in the breakfast menu, or chicken marinated with the Sichuan spicy flavor to the lunch menu.

In higher education, Brooks and Normore (2010) have also documented the importance of glocalization as a concept. They believe it is necessary to incorporate a global perspective in the formulation of education policies and urged educators around the world to actively respond to the trends by implementing meaningful practices in curriculum planning and education sites. Brooks and Normore (2010) highlighted specific areas that most need a local perspective: politics, economy, culture, morality, education, information, organization, spirituality and religion, and contemporary literature. In specific relation to EMI, Dafouz and Smit (2020) included glocalization as one of the elements of their ROADMAPPING framework. They highlighted the difficulties in "how to strike a balance between issues of curricular harmonization for the sake of student and staff mobility while maintaining curricular diversity and local institutional academic practices" (2020: 58).

With the rapid speed of internationalization of Asia's higher education, how to effectively adapt theories developed by international scholars and convert the experiences of many countries around the world into a model suitable for the local classrooms has become an important topic of academic and educational research. In other words, how the bilingual education policy promotes the cultivation of international competition and cooperation ability under the trend of globalization, and the sustainable development of the local subjectivity is the focus of today's education planning (Tsou & Kao, 2017).

An example of importing global trends without localization can be observed in many private schools or after-school language programs in Taiwan. Traditionally, parents have been paying a premium for English-only after-school programs taught by native English speakers. Most of these classes are led by foreign teachers, with local teachers as assistants. Students' first language is viewed as interference and not permitted in class. These schools advertise as "American-style" schools, where learners are exposed to English in all class periods and across all subjects. The unintended consequence is that students view native-speaking English teachers more favorably, and devalue their own and local teachers' bilingual skills. In 2018, when MOE announced that bilingual education will be a policy priority in Taiwan, many policy makers and parents envisioned local schools to begin offering American school-style classes where English is the only language for instruction and communication.

6   Translanguaging as a Glocalizing Strategy

Translanguaging as a term was coined by Cen Williams in 1994 to refer to the work of teachers in bilingual education in Wales, U.K. Initially, Williams used the Welsh term, *trawsieithu*, meaning "translinguifying," which was later changed to "translanguaging" (Williams, 1994, 2002). It describes the practice of using two languages in classrooms. Its original purpose was pedagogic, but it has since been extended from the classroom context to refer to the use of bilingual or multiple languages to achieve communicative effectiveness in any context. Thus it could be described as "*multiple discursive practices* in which bilinguals engage in order to *make sense of their bilingual worlds*" (García, 2009, p. 45, original emphasis). In other words, instead of a separation of languages, one language reinforces the other so that the learner can understand and use both languages. In translanguaging, both languages are used in a dynamic and integrated way to organize and mediate mental processes in understanding, speaking, literacy, and learning.

Translanguaging as a concept is often compared with code-switching. The latter views languages as separate systems where speakers engage in the process of changing from one to the other. In contrast, translanguaging as a phenomenon "goes beyond what has been termed code-switching" and "includes it, as well as other kinds of bilingual language use and bilingual contact" (García, 2009, p. 45). Theorists of translanguaging highlight the fluidity and dynamic nature of language relationships, and how multilingual speakers construct their language repertoire. As Canagarajah (2011, p. 8) observed, "The semiotic resources in one's repertoire or in society interact more closely, become part of an integrated resource, and enhance each other. The languages mesh in transformative ways, generating new meanings and grammars."

In language classrooms, translanguaging could be theorized as a "social space" for the multilingual users "by bringing together different dimensions of their personal history, experience and environment, their attitude, belief and ideology, their cognitive and physical capacity into one coordinated and meaningful performance" (Li Wei, 2011, p. 1223). The act of translanguaging then is transformative in nature, creating a space where learners' multilingual resources are valued and leveraged for learning.

Translanguaging is thus an effective scaffolding strategy in bilingual education. According to Lin (2020: 5–6), "Spontaneous translanguaging pedagogies take place without planning or design as the bi-/multilingual teacher spontaneously translanguages (or allows students to spontaneously translanguage or both) to scaffold students' learning in the ongoing dynamic interaction." However, translanguaging as an effective scaffolding strategy requires teachers or curriculum developers to have an "intimate knowledge of learners' multilingual linguistic resources" and demand "careful and strategic planning" (Lin, 2020, p. 6). In other words, translanguaging pedagogy as a global concept must be localized to reflect the multilingual contexts and learners' multilingual resources and needs.

In 2018, Li Wei expanded and went beyond the "language" aspect of translanguaging to propose a multilingual, multisemiotic, multisensory, and multimodal practice with an emphasis on the notion of "trans." This resonates with Lin's (2015) "trans-semiotizing," who in turn was informed by Halliday's (2013) "trans-semiotic" view. This trend broadens the focus to analyze language as entangled with many other semiotics (e.g. visuals, gestures, bodily movement) in meaning-making. Wu and Lin's (2019) study demonstrated how translanguaging and trans-semiotizing could be leveraged in bilingual education to support and engage learners in making sense of a topic, and to scaffold students in presenting their experience and understanding.

In this book, we follow this trend and espouse translanguaging to include related concepts such as multimodality and trans-semiotizing. Whenever possible, we looked at translanguaging from both verbal and non-verbal aspects, and different modes of communication (i.e. body language, print, digital resources) are included under the umbrella term of translanguaging. We understand that each term is a specialized concept; however, a broader definition of translanguaging will help facilitate a discussion in Asia's EMI in higher education and enable the discussion to focus on how to *glocalize* these emerging concepts.

7   Overview of the Chapters

The above overview shows that much has changed in terms of theories and practices since the 2017 publication of the two EMI collections mentioned in the introduction of this chapter. Publications on EMF have enriched, and further complicated, the discussion of the role of English in today's international communication. Similarly, research on translanguaging has problematized traditional ideologies and introduced new perspectives in classroom practice. Since 2020, with Covid-19 affecting the number of outbound students for overseas degrees, now seems to be a critical time for Asia's EMI programs to actively improve the quality of instruction so more local students would stay. As studies in EMF and translanguaging have shown, there is no "one size fits all" paradigm for global trends in education. As the following chapters will show, each context is at a different stage of going *glocal*. The chapters will also show that all players of EMI programs including policy makers, program directors, teachers, and students must find a way to adopt the glocal mindset. Although government policies are lagging behind practices, the data show that teachers and students of each context have found their own way of making learning in an EMI classroom more effective. We hope that the lessons learned in each context can serve as information exchange and help generate more innovations for EMI implementation excellence.

To compile this book, we examined EMI programs in 5 different contexts. Together the chapters present policy documents, classroom observations, field notes, and interviews with key stakeholders related to how languages are used in EMI programs and classrooms. Through data analysis and synthesis, cases were compiled to critique current practice and to recommend pedagogical strategies in translanguaging. This book consists of four parts. Part 1 provides an overview of theory, research and policy in Asia (Chaps. 1–4). Part 2 presents case studies from lecturers' practices and perspectives (Chaps. 5–6). Part 3 focuses on students' practices from their perspectives (Chaps. 7–9), and we conclude, in Part 4, by summarizing key findings and relating them to other EMI research and contexts (Chap. 10).

All the chapters in Parts 2 and 3, the "practical" sections, analyze samples of spontaneous translanguaging, rather than planned or structured translanguaging. The empirical evidence provided in these studies demonstrates the fluid, dynamic nature of language while highlighting how translanguaging differs from code-switching and mixing theories. In these chapters, detailed classroom analyses were conducted to illustrate the key role played by translanguaging practices in meaning-making and discursive construction in EMI education.

To present a unified research approach for the case studies, Dafouz and Smit's (2020) ROAD-MAPPING framework has been adopted to structure the practical chapters (6–9). Moreover, a synthesis of the findings is conducted in the final chapter to highlight the key themes that emerged from the studies in this collection. This conceptual framework consists of six dimensions, respectively, RO-AD-M-A-PP-ING, together forming its name. The six parts are Roles of English (RO), Academic Disciplines (AD), Management (M), Agents (A), Practices and Processes (PP), Internationalization and Glocalization (ING) (Dafouz & Smit, 2020: 46).

The ROAD-MAPPING framework was first used in the European context, where Dafouz and Smit saw a need to provide a conceptual framework of reference at the metalevel as they investigated the region's EMI programs. It has been proven as a valuable research approach because of its ability to accommodate the complexity and diversity of EMI in Europe. It has allowed researchers to investigate Europe's EMI contexts by making a systematic and meaningful comparison. Given its success in Europe, the authors in this volume agreed that the framework has the potential to provide valuable insights into our studies. The following briefly introduces the sections and chapters in this collection.

In this chapter, Wenli Tsou provides an overview of CBI, EMI, CLIL, ICLHE and translanguaging pedagogy in Asia's higher education, and interrogates macro-level EMI policies and implementation from the ELF perspectives. Following the discussion, Will Baker explores the implications of ELF on EMI pedagogy in Asia while developing a theoretical framework of "translanguaging pedagogy." Both chapters have focused on theory and research, and conclude with a discussion on translanguaging and how the concept contributes to EMI in Asia.

Chapter 3 builds a bridge between theory and pedagogy. In "Translanguaging and English-within-multilingualism in the Japanese EMI context," Tomokazu Ishikawa reconceptualizes the "E" and the "M" in EMI, and discusses the implications of English as a multilingual franca (EMF) on Japan's EMI context. Specifically, Ishikawa proposes to revitalize the "I" by incorporating EMF awareness as a pedagogic intervention.

Chapter 4, "Translanguaging and language policy in Thai higher education EMI programs," shifts the focus to the policy level. Jaewon Jane Ra and Will Baker investigate explicit and implicit language policies in EMI in Thailand and explore to what extent multilingualism and translanguaging are recognized by major Thai universities and government education departments.

Part 2 of this volume focuses on classrooms and lecturers. In Chap. 5, "Translanguaging strategies for EMI instruction in Taiwanese higher education," Shin-Mei Kao, Wenli Tsou, and Fay Chen examine the different ways with which multiple languages are deployed by EMI instructors in engineering, business, and professional writing classrooms. Similarly, in Chap. 6, "Strategic use of L1 in EMI classrooms: A translanguaging perspective," Yi Zhang & Rining (Tony) Wei investigated the strategic use of L1 to facilitate good EMI practices in China. The authors identified different scenarios and purposes in which lecturers used L1 in EMI classrooms.

Part 3 reports on three EMI contexts where students were the focus. In Chap. 7, "Translanguaging practices in EMI settings from the perspective of student agency:

An example from Vietnamese higher education," Phuong Le Hoang Ngo compares findings from two EMI classes, one monolingual and another multilingual and found many benefits when students were encouraged to utilize their multilingual resources to actively construct their disciplinary knowledge.

In Chap. 8, "'I forgot the language': Japanese students' real multilingual selves and translanguaging challenges as English majors in Taiwan," Simon Humphries & Tomoko Yashima studied a unique situation where English majors studied in the country of their third language (Chinese). Rather than English dominating or replacing Chinese, it helped facilitate students' development of their third language. In Chap. 9, "Translanguaging in EMI higher education in Taiwan: Learner perception and agency," Yi-Ping Huang analyzes data from an international business program in Taiwan and suggests that the use of translanguaging could help enact and enhance learner agency.

The concluding chapter summarizes key themes from the chapters, and makes use of the ROADMAPPING framework (Dafouz & Smit, 2020) to link the findings here to wider EMI research outside the regions, and also provide suggestions for further research.

Drawing together viewpoints and research findings of scholars and practitioners in Asia, this book is the first to combine ELF, EMI and translanguaging as the explicit focus. The book will be of particular interest to policy makers and EMI researchers interested in either a specific context or the Asian region as a whole, as well as educators and teacher trainers in higher education seeking resources to teach in academic English. Given the common phenomenon in Asian EMI classrooms where multilingualism and multiculturalism are a reality, translanguaging in EMI classrooms will mean empowerment of both instructors and students, and a critical pedagogical strategy in the highly multilingual and multicultural contexts in Asia.

References

Arno-Macia, E., & Mancho-Bares, G. (2015). The role of content and language in Content and Language Integrated Learning (CLIL) at university: Challenges and implications for ESP. *English for Specific Purposes, 37*, 63–73.

Baker, W. (2011). Intercultural awareness: Modelling an understanding of cultures in intercultural communication through english as a lingua franca. *Language and Intercultural Communication, 11*(3), 197–214.

Baker, W. (2015). *Culture and identity through english as a lingua franca: Rethinking concepts and goals in intercultural communication.* De Gruyter Mouton.

Bernard, R. (2014). English medium instruction in Asian universities: Some concerns and a suggested approach to dual-medium instruction. *Indonesian Journal of Applied Linguistics, 4*(1), 10–22.

Barnard, R., & Hawim, Z. (Eds.). (2018). *English medium instruction programmes: Perspectives from South East Asian Universities.* Routledge.

Brooks, J. S., & Normore, A. H. (2010). Educational leadership and globalization: Literacy for a glocal perspective. *Educational Policy, 24*, 52–82.

Brown, H., & Bradford, A. (2017). EMI, CLIL, & CBI: Differing approaches and goals. In P. Clements, A. Krause, & H. Brown (Eds.), *Transformation in language education*. Tokyo: JALT.

Canagarajah, S. (2011). Translanguaging in the classroom: Emerging Issues for research and pedagogy. *Applied Linguistics Review, 2*, 1–28.

Centre for Global Englishes. (2020). About us. https://www.southampton.ac.uk/cge/index.page.

Chen, F., Kao, S. M., & Tsou, W. (2020). Toward ELF-informed bilingual education in Taiwan: Addressing incongruity between policy and practice. *English Teaching & Learning, 44*(2), 175–191.

Chou, J. T. (2017). Use of authentic materials in law school. In W. Tsou & S.-M. Kao (Eds.), *English as a medium of instruction in higher education* (pp. 131–145). Springer.

Cogo, A., & Dewey, M. (2012). *Analysing English as a lingua franca: A corpus driven investigation*. Continuum.

Coyle, D., Hood, P., & Marsh, D. (2010). *CLIL: Content and language integrated learning*. Cambridge University Press.

Dafouz, E. (2014). Integrating content and language in European higher education: An overview of recurrent research concerns and pending issues. In Psaltou-Joycey, E. Agathopoulou & M. Mattheoudakis (Eds.), *Cross-Curricular approaches to language education* (pp. 289–304). Cambridge: Cambridge Scholars

Dafouz, E., & Smit, U. (2020). *ROAD-MAPPING English medium education in the internationalised university*. Palgrave Macmillan.

Edsall, D., & Saito, Y. (2012). The motivational benefits of content. *OnCue Journal, 6*(2), 66–94.

Fang, F. (2018). Native-speakerism revisited: Global Englishes, ELT and intercultural communication. *Indonesian Journal of English Language Teaching, 13*(2), 115–129.

Fenton-Smith, B., Humphreys, P., & Walkinshaw, I. (Eds.). (2017). *English medium instruction in higher education in Asia-Pacific: From policy to pedagogy*. Springer.

Foundation for International Cooperation in Higher Education of Taiwan (FICHET). (2020). Study in Taiwan survey report. https://www.fichet.org.tw/en/2020-study-in-taiwan-survey-report/.

Galloway, N., & Numajiri, T. (2020). Global Englishes language teaching: Bottom-up curriculum implementation. *TESOL Quarterly, 54*(1), 118–145.

García, O. (2009). *Bilingual education in the 21st century*. Wiley-Blackwell.

García, O., & Lin, A. M. Y. (2018). English and multilingualism: A contested history. In P. Seargent (Ed.), *Routledge handbook of english language studies* (pp. 77–92). Routledge.

Halliday, M. (2013). *Languages, and language, in today's changing world*. Seminar presented at the University of Hong Kong, Hong Kong.

Hashimoto, K. (2013). 'English-only', but not a medium-of-instruction policy: The Japanese way of internationalising education for both domestic and overseas students. *Current Issues in Language Planning, 14*(1), 16–33.

Hou, A. Y. C., Morse, R., Chiang, C. L., & Chen, H. J. (2013). Challenges to quality of English medium instruction degree programs in Taiwanese universities and the role of local accreditors: A perspective of non-english-speaking Asian country. *Asian Pacific Educational Review, 14*(3), 359–370.

Hu, G. (2019). English-medium instruction in higher education: Lessons from China. *The Journal of Asia TEFL, 16*(1), 1–11.

Hülmbauer, C., Böhringer, H., & Seidlhofer, B. (2008). Introducing English as a lingua franca (ELF): Precursor and partner in intercultural communication. *Synergies Europe, 3*, 25–36.

Ishikawa, T. (2017). Japanese university students' attitudes towards their English and the possibility of ELF awareness. *Journal of English as a Lingua Franca, 6*, 237–263.

Jenkins, J. (2009). *World Englishes* (2nd ed.). Routledge.

Jenkins, J. (2015). Repositioning English and multilingualism in English as a lingua franca. *Englishes in Practice, 2*(3), 49–85.

Jenkins, J. (2018). English medium instruction in higher education: The role of ELF. In Gao, A., Davison, C. & Leung, C. (Eds.), *Second handbook of english language teaching*. Springer, Berlin.

Jenkins, J., & Mauranen, A. (Eds.). (2019). *Linguistic diversity on the EMI campus: Insider accounts of the use of English and other languages in universities within Asia, Australasia and Europe*. Routledge.

Li Wei (2011). Moment analysis and translanguaging space: Discursive construction of identities by multilingual Chinese youth in Britain. *Journal of Pragmatics, 43*, 1222–1235.

Li Wei (2018). Translanguaging as a Practical Theory of Language. *Applied Linguistics, 39*(1), 9–30.

Lin, A. M. Y. (2015). Conceptualizing the potential role of L1 in content and language integrated learning (CLIL). *Language, Culture and Curriculum, 28*(1), 74–89.

Lin, A. M. Y., & Lo, Y. Y. (2018). The spread of English medium instruction programmes: Educational and research implications. In R. Barnard & Z. Hawim (Eds.), *English medium instruction programmes: Perspectives from South East Asian universities* (pp. 87–103). Routledge.

Lin, A. M. Y. (2020). Cutting through the monolingual grip of TESOL traditions—The transformative power of the translanguaging lens. In Z. Tian, L. Aghai, P. Sayer, & J. L. Schissel (Eds.), *Envisioning TESOL through a translanguaging lens*. Switzerland: Springer.

Marsh, D. (2002). *CLIL/EMILE: The European dimension—Actions, trends and foresight potential*. University of Jyväskylä: Finland.

MEXT. (2017). Project for establishing university network for Internationalization: Global 30. https://www.mext.go.jp/component/a_menu/education/detail/__icsFiles/afieldfile/2017/03/30/1383779_06.pdf.

Ministry of Education (MOE), China. (2001). Guanyu jiaqiang gaodeng xuexiao benke jiaoxue gongzuo tigao jiaoxue zhiliang de ruogan yijian [Guidelines for strengthening undergraduate teaching and improving its quality]. Beijing: Author.

Ministry of Education (MOE), Republic of China (Taiwan) (December 17, 2018). Implement in full scale bilingualization of Taiwan's educational system; cultivate bilingual talents to bring Taiwan to the world. Retrieved July 20, 2019, from https://english.moe.gov.tw/cp-13-17790-80201-1.html.

Murata, K. (Ed.). (2018). *English-medium instruction from English as a lingua franca perspective: Exploring the higher education context*. Routledge.

Precht, R. E. (2017). Engagement versus endorsement: Western universities in China. *Open Global Rights*. https://www.openglobalrights.org/engagement-versus-endorsement-western-universities-in-china/.

Robertson, R. (1995). Glocalization: Time-space and homogeneity-heterogeneity. In M. Featherstone, S. Lash, & R. Robertson (Eds.), *Global modernities* (pp. 25–44). Sage Publications.

Rose, H., & Galloway, N. (2019). *Global Englishes for language teaching*. Cambridge University Press.

Seidlhofer, B. (2011). *Understanding English as a lingua franca*. Oxford University Press.

Smit, U., & Dafouz, E. (2012). Integrating content and language in higher education: An introduction to English-medium policies, conceptual issues and research practices across Europe. *AILA Review, 25*, 1–12.

Tsai, M. L. (2014). Collaboration between ESP and EMI teachers. In W. Tsou & S. M. Kao (Eds.), *Resources for teaching English for specific purposes* (pp. 47–68). Taipei, Taiwan: Bookman.

Tsou, W., & Kao, S. M. (2017). Introduction. In W. Tsou & S. M. Kao (Eds.), *English as a medium of instruction in higher education: Implementations and classroom practices in Taiwan* (pp. 3–18). Springer.

Tsou, W. & Kao, S. M. (2014). Introduction. In W. Tsou & S. M. Kao (Eds.), *Resources for teaching English for specific purposes* (pp. 1–12). Taipei: Bookman.

Walkinshaw, I., Fenton-Smith, B., & Humphreys, P. (2017). EMI issues and challenges in Asia-Pacific higher education: An introduction. In B. Fenton-Smith, P. Humphreys, & I. Walkinshaw (Eds.), *English medium instruction in higher education in Asia-Pacific: From policy to pedagogy* (pp. 1–18). Springer.

Wei, R. (2013). Chinese-english bilingual education in China: Model, momentum, and driving forces. *Asian EFL Journal, 15*, 184–200.

Widdowson, H. G. (2013). ELF and EFL: What's the difference? Comments on Michael Swan. *Journal of English as a Lingua Franca, 2*(1), 187–193.

Williams, C. (1994). Arfarniad o Ddulliau Dysgu ac Addysgu yng Nghyd-destun Addysg Uwchradd Ddwyieithog, [An evaluation of teaching and learning methods in the context of bilingual secondary education]. Unpublished Doctoral Thesis (University of Wales, Bangor).

Williams, C. (2002). *A language gained: A study of language immersion at 11–16 years of age.* Bangor: School of Education. http://www.bangor.ac.uk/addysg/publications/Language_Gai ned%20.pdf

Wu, Y. A., & Lin, A. (2019). Translanguaging and trans-semiotising in a CLIL biology class in Hong Kong: Whole-body sense-making in the flow of knowledge co-making. *Classroom Discourse, 10*(3–4), 252–273.

Wu, P., Wang, S., Jiang, X., Zeng, D., Guan, Y., & Li, X. (2010). *Gaodeng xuexiao shuangyu jiaoxue de xianzhuang yanjiu he shijian tansuo [An exploratory study of English-medium instruction in Chinese higher education].* Higher Education Press.

Yang, W.-H. (2017). From similarity to diversity: The changing use of language learning strategies in CLIL (Content and language integrated learning) Education at the Tertiary Level in Taiwan. *English Teaching & Learning, 41*(1), 1–32.

Wenli Tsou is a Full Professor in the Department of Foreign Languages & Literature, and currently Director of the Foreign Language Center at National Cheng Kung University, Taiwan. She received her Ph.D. in Foreign and Second Language Education from the State University of New York at Buffalo, US. She is the project leader of the National Cheng Kung University ESP and EMI programs. She is also the leading figure of bilingual education in Taiwan, helping with its teacher training and curriculum design. Her research interests include teacher training, ESP, English as a Lingua Franca, Content and Language Integrated Learning and English as a Medium of Instruction. Her current research projects have focused on the links between transdiciplinary teaching and translanguaging of bilingual education and EMI. She chairs the 13th International Conference of English as a Lingua Franca and has co-edited the following books: *English as a Medium of Instruction in Higher Education: Implementations & classroom practices in Taiwan* (2017, Springer), *Exploring CLIL: A Resource Book* (2018, Bookman) and *Resources for Teaching English for Specific Purposes* (2014, Bookman).

Part II
Theory, Research and Policy

Chapter 2
English as a Lingua Franca, Translanguaging, and EMI in Asian Higher Education: Implications for Pedagogy

Will Baker

Abstract This chapter explores the links between ELF (English as a lingua franca), translanguaging, and EMI (English medium instruction) research in HE (higher education). The "E" in EMI is conceptualized as ELF, rather than any single variety of English, and furthermore, this is embedded in multilingual contexts with other languages also present. Due to the multilingual nature of EMI, translanguaging and the related ideas of transmodality and transcultural communication are highly relevant. A number of current approaches to EMI that are commensurable with ELF and translanguaging are discussed including the more holistic term EME (English medium education). There is also a focus on how language is conceptualized in EMI research in Asia. The implications for classroom practices in EMI programs in HE are then considered. Pedagogic proposals from ELF, translanguaging and EMI/EME perspectives are presented which center on greater awareness of the multilingual and multicultural nature of EMI/EME and accompanying classroom practices which value students' and teachers' full linguistic and sociocultural repertoires.

Keywords English as a lingua franca (ELF) · English medium instruction (EMI) · English medium education (EME) · Higher education (HE) · Asia · Translanguaging · Transcultural communication

1 Introduction

In this chapter I explore the links between ELF (English as a lingua franca), translanguaging and EMI (English medium instruction) research, with a particular focus on the implications for classroom practices in EMI programs in HE (higher education) in Asia. The first part of the chapter begins from the position that, as noted by a number of scholars, the "E" in EMI is English as a lingua franca, not any single variety of English. Furthermore, in Asian settings the use of ELF is likely to be in multilingual contexts with other languages also present. The chapter then turns to explore current

W. Baker (✉)
Centre for Global Englishes, University of Southampton, Southampton, UK
e-mail: w.baker@soton.ac.uk

© The Author(s), under exclusive license to Springer Nature Singapore Pte Ltd. 2021
W. Tsou and W. Baker (eds.), *English-Medium Instruction Translanguaging Practices in Asia*, https://doi.org/10.1007/978-981-16-3001-9_2

thinking on translanguaging and the related ideas of transmodality and transcultural communication. The links between translanguaging and ELF perspectives are also considered. Next, a number of perspectives on EMI are outlined, including the more holistic term EME (English medium education). There is a focus on how language is conceptualized in EMI and current research in Asia. The first half of the chapter concludes with a discussion of the relevance of ELF and translanguaging to EMI.

In the second part of the chapter, I go on to specifically address pedagogy, outlining the major proposals from ELF, translanguaging and EMI/EME perspectives to classroom teaching and learning. A number of core themes are identified that are shared between all three perspectives in relation to pedagogic practices in EMI/EME settings. In particular, I suggest that a greater awareness of the multilingual and multicultural nature of international HE and the accompanying translanguaging and transcultural practices is needed at all levels within EMI/EME programs. Equally importantly, this awareness should be translated into pedagogic practices in which the classroom becomes a "translanguaging space" (Li, 2018) where students' and teachers' full linguistic and sociocultural repertories are valued and utilized.

2   ELF, Translanguaging and EMI

2.1   ELF in Asia

It is now well-established that English has an extensive presence in Asia in a variety of domains such as tourism, business, education and, specifically the focus of this chapter, HE. English is an official second language in a number of post-colonial "outer circle" settings, such as Singapore, Malaysia and the Philippines (Kachru, 2005), it is the official working language of ASEAN (the Association of South East Asian Nations) and it has also taken on increasing prominence as an additional language in those countries traditionally regards as part of the "expanding circle," such as Taiwan, Japan and China (Kirkpatrick, 2010; Kirkpatrick, Lixun, Patkin, & Subhan, 2019). However, the far-reaching spread of English throughout the "expanding" circle countries in Asia has problematized the boundaries between the Kachruvian three circles. For instance, China now has more English speakers than any other country in Asia and the general population (as opposed to linguists) is becoming increasingly interested in, and invested in, English use (Wang, 2020). Furthermore, English is frequently used for intercultural communication across the region and globally regardless of whether a country is categorized as the outer or expanding circle. Additionally, as the chapters in this book illustrate, English now has an official role in education in many "expanding circle" settings. This has resulted in a blurring of the boundaries and distinctions between the outer and expanding circle and also a questioning of the "norm providing" role of both the inner and outer circle.

A more appropriate perspective is to view English as a lingua franca (ELF) in Asia that transcends geographical boundaries and nation states. This is especially relevant to EMI given the international outlook and rationale behind its introduction in many settings. ELF can be defined as "any use of English among speakers of different first languages for whom English is the communicative medium of choice, and often only option" (Seidlhofer, 2011, p. 7). This well-cited definition underscores that ELF refers to a *use* or function of English rather than any particular type of English. It is important to emphasize that ELF is not about describing the specific features (phonological, syntactical, or lexical) of a variety of English and this distinguishes ELF from descriptions of World Englishes in the outer circle (e.g., Kachru, 2005). Secondly, we can also define ELF as "a field that enquires into various aspects of the use of English among speakers who do not share a first language" (Baird, Baker, & Kitazawa, 2014). This definition draws attention to ELF as a research subject and highlights the wide approach taken through investigations of "various aspects" such as communication strategies and pragmatics, identity, community and culture. Seidlhofer (2011) and Baird et al.'s (2014) definitions are complementary in that the former emphasizes the description of a linguistic phenomenon and the latter a field of research. Most recently Jenkin's has re-defined ELF as "English as a Multilingua Franca, … Multilingual communication in which English is available as a contact language of choice, but is not necessarily chosen." (2015, p. 73). This is an important extension of both the description of the linguistic phenomenon and the research field, drawing attention to the multilingual nature of ELF. While ELF has always been recognized as multilingual (it involves speakers of different L1s), Jenkins definition moves multilingualism from the background to a more prominent place where multilingualism is as important as English. By adding that English "is not necessarily chosen" it also recognizes that speakers may switch in and out of English and other languages during interactions. Jenkins definition is especially relevant to the discussion of EMI in Asia given the multilingual contexts of English use in Asia and the similarly multilingual settings of EMI.

Although ELF is a reasonably new field of research and early studies typically focused on Europe, it did not take long for ELF studies in Asia to emerge (e.g., Deterding & Kirkpatrick, 2006) and there has been a huge increase over the last decade. One of the most notable is the Asian Corpus of English (Kirkpatrick et al., 2019) which comprises a 1 million word corpus of data collected from naturally occurring spoken interactions between proficient 'English-knowing' multilinguals from ASEAN + 3 (the addition of China, Korea, Japan). While earlier research identified a number of potentially shared features among Asian users of ELF (e.g., Deterding & Kirkpatrick, 2006), recent research has moved away from documenting features. Instead, similar to ELF research in other regions, the focus has shifted to the variable processes of communication and sociocultural issues related to ideology, identity, community and culture, as well as, the implications of ELF research language education policies and practices. For instance, there has been extensive research into attitudes and ideologies around English and other languages in various Asian settings including Japan (Ishikawa, 2017), China (Wang, 2020), Taiwan (Tsou & Chen, 2014) and Thailand (Snodin & Young, 2015) among others. Communication and pragmatic strategies have also been of interest such as Deterding's (2013) study of the role of repair and accommodation and Walkinshaw and Kirkpatrick's (2014) exploration of the construction and maintenance of "face" in ELF interactions. My own research has explored the role of ELF in the construction of identity and culture in intercultural and transcultural communication among Thai L1 speakers (Baker, 2009, 2015; Baker & Sangiamchit, 2019). As ELF findings have grown there has been an increasing number of investigations into the relevance and implications of ELF to ELT practices in the region (e.g., Kirkpatrick, 2011; Suzuki, Liu, & Yu, 2018).

2.2   ELF and Translanguaging, Transmodality, and Transcultural Communication

A recent approach to understanding language and communication in which its multilingual, multimodal and multicultural nature is foregrounded is translanguaging. Although there are currently various terms that attempt to capture this multilingual and multimodal nature of communication, such as polylanguaging (Jørgensen, Karrebæk, Madsen, & Møller, 2011), metrolingualism (Pennycook & Otsuji, 2015) and translingual practice (Canagarajah, 2013), here I will follow Li Wei's characterization of translanguaging as "the fluid and dynamic practices that transcend the boundaries between named languages, language varieties, and language and other semiotic systems" (2018, p. 9). Li further states that "Translanguaging offers a practical theory of language that sees the latter as a multilingual, multisemiotic, multisensory, and multimodal resource that human beings use for thinking and for communicating thought" (2018, p. 26). As with the earlier discussion of ELF, the emphasis in translanguaging is on language practices, rather than abstract descriptions of particular structural features of language; although, unlike characterizations of ELF, translanguaging offers a theory of language too. Furthermore, the multimodality of communication is underscored, with linguistic resources just one of the range of resources people use in interactions and meaning-making. The use of multimodal resources in translanguaging has also been termed transmodality with a focus on the processes that result in "the transmodal moment" (Newfield, 2017, p. 103) and blurring of boundaries between different modes to holistically create meaning and effect (e.g., Baker & Sangiamchit, 2019). Another important concept of relevance to the discussion in this chapter is translanguaging space, "a space that is created by and for Translanguaging practices, and a space where language users break down the ideologically laden dichotomies between the macro and the micro, the societal and the individual, and the social and the psychological through interaction" (Li, 2018, p. 23). Significantly, in translanguaging spaces language users are not viewed as *between* different languages but rather as breaking down and *transcending* the borders between languages and other meaning-making resources. Linked to translanguaging space is the notion of transcultural communication which following the trans metaphor is defined as "communication where interactants move through and across, rather than in-between, cultural and linguistic boundaries, thus, "named" languages and cultures can no longer be taken for granted and in the process borders become blurred, transgressed and transcended" (Baker & Sangiamchit, 2019, p. 472). Transcultural communication seeks to understand the construction and nego- tiation of fluid and complex identities, communities and practices in multilingual and multicultural settings, or "translanguaging spaces," which is of particular relevance to many international EMI programs.

As should be clear from the discussion above, there are many parallels and similar- ities between translanguaging, transmodality, transcultural communication, and ELF perspectives on communication. While the newness of trans approaches in applied linguistics means that ELF researchers have only just begun to think about the links, there are a number of conceptual (e.g., Baker, 2018; Jenkins, 2015, 2018; Kimura & Canagarajah, 2018; Li, 2016; Pitzl, 2018), and empirical studies (e.g., Baker & Sangiamchit, 2019; Cogo, 2016) which have incorporated trans-perspectives on ELF. Kimura and Canagarajah (2018) provide a detailed discussion of the similari- ties (and differences) between translingual practices and ELF research. They identify three core shared features involving: a focus on communication between speakers of different linguacultural backgrounds, regardless of nativeness; an emphasis on communicative practices, rather than a description of linguistic forms; and a multi- lingual orientation that "considers ELF as variable manifestations of multilingualism, rather than a superordinate code" (Kimura & Canagarajah, 2018, p. 300). However, they also suggest some differences, including that ELF research still typically seeks to use notions of shared community identity to explain communicative success, especially through the notion of community of practice (Kimura & Canagarajah, 2018, p. 301). In contrast, Kimura and Canagarajah propose that under a translingual practice approach "shared understanding is seen as an interactional accomplish- ment" rather than based on shared community identities (Ibid.). While it may be true that initial attempts in ELF research to replace the traditional concept of speech communities with a more fluid notion of community, such as community of prac- tice, were somewhat simplistic, these were proposals for further investigation. Where researchers have made use of communities of practices, these have typically been in very specific settings such as business professionals or international student groups and ELF has been viewed as a resource in the community's shared multilingual repertoire, rather than a defining feature of the community (e.g., Ehrenreich, 2009; Kalocsai, 2014). At the same time it has been recognized that communities of prac- tice when used, need to be employed in a considerably more flexible manner than originally envisaged (Baker, 2015). Furthermore, more recent research in ELF has turned its attention specifically to transient groupings and how understanding and "sharedness" is created in the interactions, as opposed to assuming a priori (Baker & Sangiamchit, 2019; Jenkins, 2015; Pitzl, 2018). Other areas of difference noted by Kimura and Canagarajah (2018) include the need for more ethnographic, longi- tudinal, multimodal, literary studies, and pedagogic research, all areas that, I would argue, have been taken up in recent ELF research (see Jenkins et al., 2018 for an overview) and in the case of ethnographic, longitudinal research, have been there for some time (e.g., Baker, 2009; Ehrenreich, 2009). In sum, there are important similarities in approaches between translanguaging and ELF and, as Jenkins (2018, p. 601) observes, when considering the future of ELF there will most likely be many kinds of Englishes used predominantly in transcultural communication among multilingual English speakers, who will make use of their full linguistic repertoires as appropriate in the context of any specific interaction. This means, in turn, that their language will involve a good deal of translanguaging.

2.3   EMI, ELF and Translanguaging in Asia

Like ELF, EMI is a relatively new phenomenon and, like ELF, it has expanded significantly in the last few decades with the implementation of EMI programs far outpacing research in the area (Dafouz & Smit, 2016; Dearden, 2014) and there are still ongoing debates about how best to define it (Baker & Hüttner, 2019). These have centered around issues such as the level of education to which it refers, especially whether it is only higher education or includes all education; the settings in which it occurs, that is, whether it should include Anglophone settings or only settings where English is an additional language; how best to characterize the "English" in EMI, for example, standard English, ELFA (ELF in academic settings), multilingual English and so on; and what the "instruction" refers to and whether "education" is a more appropriate term (e.g., Dafouz & Smit, 2020; Jenkins & Mauranen, 2019; Macaro, Curle, Pun, An, & Dearden, 2018). Dafouz and Smit (2016, 2020) use the term EMEMUS (English medium education in multilingual university settings) which "focuses on English-medium education because of the particular role that English plays both as an academic language of teaching and learning as well as a means of international communication" (2016, p. 399). Most recently Dafouz and Smit (2020) have shortened this to EME (English medium education) for convenience and EME and EMI will be used interchangeably in the rest of this chapter. Dafouz and Smit's (2020) characterization has the advantage of placing English within a multilingual setting and hence recognizing the multilingual nature of EME. It also adopts the wider term education, "thus embracing both "instruction" and "learning" instead of prioritizing one over the other" (Dafouz & Smit, 2020, p. 3). Additionally, by focusing on tertiary education it distinguishes EME from other related areas such as CLIL (content and language integrated learning) and allows researchers to focus on the specific issues in HE and internationalization. Finally, the broadness of the term lets researchers engage with the diverse realities of EME, which is highly context-dependent with no single approach to policy or pedagogy predominant (Dafouz & Smit, 2020).

   The rapid expansion of EME in Asia is beginning to be reflected in research (e.g., Barnard & Hasim, 2018; Fenton-Smith, Humphreys, & Walkinshaw, 2017; Galloway, Kriukow, & Numajiri, 2017; Macaro et al., 2018; Murata, 2018; Tsou & Kao, 2017) and is discussed in other chapters in this book, so will not be the main concern here. Instead, I will focus on issues related to the "English" in EME and its relationships to ELF, multilingualism and translanguaging research. As Mauranen and Jenkins highlight in summarizing their project investigating EME in nine universities across the world (including Japan, Malaysia and China), given the international orienta-tion of such settings "these universities had become prime sites for intercultural and hence ELF (A) communication" (2019, p. 263). Furthermore, they argue that not only is a diversity of Englishes used, but that other language are used extensively too with translanguaging "inevitable" (Ibid.). However, these multilingual landscapes and translanguaging practices often contrast with top-down policies which specify particular types of standard English based on Anglophone varieties of English, particularly in entrance examinations. This causes difficulties for students who feel inferior in their use of English in comparison with an idealized native speaker variety (e.g., Murata, Iino, & Konakahara, 2019). At the same time though, both teachers and students adopt pragmatic approaches, valuing content and communicative success over adherence to any particular type of English (e.g., Kaur & Zainuddin, 2019).

Similar conclusions are drawn from Baker and Hüttner's (2017, 2019) comparative study which included a Thai EME program. In the Thai setting students and lecturers were again concerned more with content and communication than observance to any variety of English, with lecturers in particular seemingly well aware of the use of EFLA. Yet at the same time, there were Anglophone standard language ideologies present in the top-down policies and orientation to "native English" among students. Furthermore, while multilingualism and translanguaging were present in practices, they were frequently made invisible through a lack of recognition by stakeholders at all levels (students, lecturers, and administrators). Interestingly, the participants in this study also saw English as a clear goal or "target" of their EME programs, alongside content knowledge, blurring the boundaries between EME and CLIL and underscoring the multitude of approaches within EME and the importance of contextualization (Baker & Hüttner, 2017). Likewise, in the context of Japan, Murata and Iino (2018) and Iino (2018) also suggest that multilingualism is not well recognized in EME and that the "E" is equated with an "English only" approach. Furthermore, this English is based on Anglophone linguacultural norms contributing to an imperialistic and hegemonic role for English at the expense of both the local language and culture and diverse international students' languages and cultures (Iino, 2018).

In sum, many of the studies to date of EMI/EME in Asia have concluded that the English used is ELFA and that, moreover, this is typically part of a multilingual setting, including local L1s and diverse L1s of international students, and hence translanguaging is also prevalent. However, these multilingual environments and translingual practices are often in contrast to the monolingual orientations of policies that favor both an "English only" approach and Anglophone linguacultural norms. Among the key stakeholders themselves (students and lecturers) there is a complex range of orientations to language with content and communicative success often prioritized but alongside a frequent preference for an idealized native English speaker standard. Moreover, while translanguaging practices may be widespread, they are often marginalized or unrecognized by students, lecturers and policymakers. It should also be noted, that although multilingualism and translanguaging practices can generally be seen as a resource that aids in both the teaching and learning experiences in EME, the use of diverse languages can also be an exclusionary practice at times, leaving out those students who are not proficient in all the languages used (Baker & Hüttner, 2017; Kuteeva, 2019; Mauranen & Jenkins, 2019). Having outlined current research findings as regards EMI/EME in Asia through ELF, translanguaging and EME perspectives, in the rest of this chapter I will explore the implications these three perspectives have for pedagogy.

3   Implications for Pedagogy in EME Classrooms

3.1   ELF and Pedagogy

One of the major contributions of ELF research has been the "de-centering" of the native English speaker (NES) in understanding global uses of English to reflect the fact that the vast majority of users are not NES (Jenkins, 2018). While ELF research includes NES, they are no longer seen as the reference point for communicative practices and norms (Seidlhofer, 2011). This has some deep and widespread implications for pedagogy. Firstly, ownership of English is no longer solely in the hands of Anglophone NES, but rather all who use English and, thus, all users are given legitimacy to adapt and make changes to the language as needed for their particular settings, needs, and purposes (Seidlhofer, 2011). Secondly, and following directly from the first point, the targets and aims of ELT pedagogy shift from Anglophone NES norms of communication (although of course, this has always been an idealized simplification of NES communities), to any proficient user of English (e.g., Galloway & Rose, 2018). This is most typically multilingual intercultural communicators rather than the monolingual NES represented in current ELT targets. It also means that the communities that form possible targets shift from the Anglophone world to any English using communities and cultures that are of relevance to English language learners (Baker, 2015). So, for example, in South East Asian settings, given the extensive use of ELF, the most appropriate targets and communities for ELT are likely to be other ASEAN countries (Kirkpatrick, 2011). Thirdly, materials and examples of English use should also be drawn from whatever settings are most relevant to learners, as opposed to the current predominance of Anglophone-based examples in ELT (Baker, 2015; Galloway & Rose, 2018). Linked to this point, learner's own first languages and other languages, cultures, and communities, should be viewed as a valuable resource in communication and incorporated into a multilingual ELT pedagogy (Kirkpatrick, 2011). Finally, and perhaps most fundamentally, to prepare learners for the diverse and widespread uses of English they are likely to encounter, ELT needs to move away from a focus on a fixed "code" around a restricted range of features (lexical, grammatical, and phonological) associated with an idealized NES "norm" and instead incorporate varied, flexible, and multiple forms of English (e.g., Dewey, 2012; Galloway & Rose, 2018; Jenkins, 2012). Moreover, successful intercultural communication through ELF involves more than just linguistic forms, and equally important is a knowledge of communicative and pragmatic strategies embedded within a wider linguistic and intercultural awareness and this too needs to be meaningfully incorporated into ELT pedagogy (Baker, 2015).

A key strand of ELF research has been acknowledging the importance of contextual factors in language use. This has meant that ELF researchers have been reluctant to impose specific recommendations for pedagogy on teachers given that local teachers are most likely to understand the particular needs of their learners (Jenkins, 2012). Nonetheless, over the last decade, or so and the number of ELF-sensitive teaching approaches have been put forward. Dewey (2012) proposes a "post-normative" approach to pedagogy, arguing that changes in ELT need to begin with the teacher and teacher education. He suggests that in teacher education programs teachers should be introduced to the notion of post-normativity which "can be articulated to teachers as a framework of choices available when deciding whether/to what extent/which (if any) language norms are relevant to their immediate teaching contexts" (Dewey, 2012, p. 166). Teachers should be encouraged to reflect on the sociocultural environments in which English used, the diversity of English use globally and the corresponding linguistic diversity, critical discussions of globalization and the role of English, focus on communicative strategies and give less time to NES linguistic forms (Dewey, 2012, p. 163). Also focusing on teacher development, Sifakis and Bayyurt offer ELF-aware teaching and learning, which they define as "the process of engaging with ELF research and developing one's own understanding of the ways in which it can be integrated into one's classroom context" (2018, p. 459). Sifakis and Bayyurt divide ELF-aware teacher education into three phases in which teachers are first "exposed" to Global Englishes and debates around it, then, secondly, teachers move to "critical awareness" in which they reflect on their own position toward English and ELF, and in phase three, "action plan," teachers plan, implement and evaluate teaching activities that integrate their own understanding of ELF with the needs of their learners (2018, pp. 460–462).

Galloway and Rose (2018) take a broad approach in their GELT (Global English language teaching) proposal which incorporates aspects from World Englishes, ELF, EIL, and Translanguaging research. They argue for a move from restricted NES norms and targets in traditional ELT to a GELT paradigm which incorporates: all English users as owners of the language and hence legitimate target; fluid target cultures; teachers as both NES and non-NES; diverse, flexible, and multiple forms as norms; proficient or "expert" English users as role models; material from any relevant English speaking community or context; and first languages and cultures as a valuable resource in ELT (2018, p. 4). In sum, there is an agreement in all the ELF approaches to ELT pedagogy of the need to move away from NES norms and Anglophone settings as the target and model and the importance of incorporating the diversity and fluidity of ELF use. Alongside this, the importance of contextualization is underscored and an acknowledgment that there will be no one approach that is relevant to all settings, but rather that teachers need to incorporate ELF-awareness into pedagogy in a locally appropriate manner. Such a perspective clearly resonates with the previous discussion on diverse linguistic practices and the importance of contextualization in EMI/EME.

3.2   Translanguaging and Pedagogy

It should be remembered that translanguaging began as a theory of pedagogy and its pedagogic principles are still at the forefront of the paradigm (e.g., García & Li, 2014; García & Kleyn, 2016). Garcia and Li (2014, p. 121) outline what they see as the seven principles of teaching to learn content and language through translanguaging.

1. *To differentiate among students' levels* and adapt instruction to different types of students in multilingual classrooms; for example, those who are bilingual, those who are monolingual and those who are emergent bilinguals.
2. *To build background knowledge* so that students can make meaning of the content being taught and of the ways of languaging in the lesson.
3. *To deepen understandings and socio-political engagement*, develop and extend new knowledge, and develop critical thinking and critical consciousness.
4. *For cross-linguistic metalinguistic awareness* so as to strengthen the students' ability to meet the communicative exigencies of the socio-educational situation.
5. *For cross-linguistic flexibility* so as to use language practices competently.
6. *For identity investment and positionality*; that is, to engage learners.
7. *To interrogate linguistic inequality and disrupt linguistic hierarchies and social structures.*

To these, they add a range of strategies that teachers may employ to fulfill the principles such as translation, reading multilingual texts, multilingual listening/visual resources, multilingual writing, multilingual vocabulary inquiry, multilingual syntax/morphology inquiry, and translanguaging in writing, speaking and inner speech (Garcia & Li, 2014, p. 120). Like the earlier discussion of pedagogy in ELF, Garcia and Li also underscore the importance of incorporating translanguaging pedagogy and principles into teacher education so that it is not just an "illicit pedagogical strategy" (2014, p. 124), but an integral and recognized part of teaching and learning.

García and Kleyn (2016) offer recommendations in specific relation to English and EMI classrooms (although they take EMI to refer to school classrooms unlike the focus on HE here). They suggest that a translanguaging pedagogy can be used to "leverage" students' L1s to aid in comprehension but also to raise critical multilingual awareness (2016, p. 26). Translanguaging, they argue, disrupts the borders between languages and the hegemony of English in EMI, transforming the classroom into a multilingual one. Cenoz (2019), in her discussion of translanguaging pedagogies and ELF, also recommends making use of learners' full linguistic repertoires in language classes and giving learners the opportunity to develop metalinguistic awareness of translanguaging through reflection on their own multilingual practices. Canagarajah (2013) also deals with Global Englishes in his discussion of translingual practices and pedagogy. He too recommends making use of the resources (linguistic and otherwise) that students bring with them to classrooms and fostering translingual practices and socialization. Furthermore, Canagarajah proposes that successful translinguals have a range of dispositions related to "language awareness," "social values," and "learning strategies" that make up, what he terms, "performative competence" (2013, p. 180). While Canagarajah cautions that the details of what these features entail will be contextually dependent, he, nonetheless, suggests making students aware of performative competence and exploring it in classroom practices (2013, p. 186). Similar to ELF recommendations for pedagogy, rather than conforming to NES norms in classrooms, Canagarajah argues that forms should be treated as negotiable, and that negotiation itself is key in preparing students for translingual communication.

Expanding on the idea of translingual dispositions, as well as transcultural dispositions, Lee and Canagarajah (2019) report on a study of the translanguaging writing practices of a multilingual student in an English academic writing class in a US HE setting. They show how the student's writing practices resisted the dominant monolingual and monocultural NES ideology of traditional US academic writing. Instead, the student made use of his translingual and transcultural resources, experiences, and dispositions to create a "translanguaging space" (Li, 2018), which was more relevant to him and others in his class. As Lee and Canagarajah conclude in relation to pedagogy, "The [trans] approaches allow us to attend to how individuals negotiate multiple, and at times, conflicting expectations and norms in language and cultural practices for their own voice and identity beyond the limiting cultural categories and boundaries. In turn, the trans-approaches enable us to appreciate how such negotiation leads to new practices" (2019, p. 25).

Linking a transcultural and ELFA approach in my own research I have explored the role of English, transcultural communication, and intercultural education in preparing and supporting students for EMI programs (e.g., Baker, 2016). Due to the multiple scales at which international universities operate including the local, national and international, they should be viewed as transcultural in which the borders between each of these scales are blurred and transcended. This includes settings that are highly multilingual and multicultural, such as Anglophone international universities, and also less linguistically and culturally diverse environments, such as "internationalization at home" approaches which involve local rather than international students (although they may still be linguistically and culturally diverse without being international), since they too frequently aspire to foster international and intercultural connections for students and staff. By approaching EMI programs and settings as transcultural, students and staff are made aware of the complex links between languages and cultures, and especially English, emphasizing the problematic nature of essentialist correlations between a language, culture, and national context. Instead, students and staff should be prepared for intercultural and transcultural communication through ELF and translanguaging. In particular, intercultural citizenship education provides a relevant approach that incorporates the multiple levels of engagement, from local to global, expected by students and staff in internationally orientated EMI programs (e.g., Fang & Baker, 2018).

3.3 EMI/EME and Pedagogy

Given the wide range of settings in which EMI takes place and the highly contextualized nature of EMI practices, like ELF and translanguaging research, there has not been one set of recommendations for pedagogy in EMI which would be applicable in all settings. Furthermore, due to the newness of the field of research most effort has been on descriptions of current practices, rather than recommendations for possible good practice. In research to date, linguistic issues have, unsurprisingly, been central in understanding pedagogic practices. One obvious area of concern relates to linguistic proficiency in English and the extent to which it influences students' ability to access the content of EMI programs and also lecturers' ability to deliver that content (Macaro et al., 2018). Findings have been mixed with some studies in Europe showing English viewed as a useful addition to the program with little influence on content knowledge (e.g., Aguilar & Rodriguez, 2012), while other studies in Asia have reported more negative perceptions, where a lack of English proficiency results in a perceived lack of access to content knowledge (e.g., Hu & Lei, 2014). In a comparative study of EMI programs in Europe and Asia, Baker and Hüttner (2017, 2019) found differences in English proficiency leading to very different approaches to pedagogic practices. In a low proficiency setting in Thailand, students were offered extensive English language support integrated with content instruction, whereas in a high proficiency setting in Austria English language support was viewed as neither relevant nor necessary for the program.

Linked to issues of language proficiency is the type of language support that should be provided for students. This can vary from no support, to general academic English (EAP), subject-specific English for special purposes (ESP), to tailor-made support programs. However, language support is provided it should be well-integrated into the content delivery to be of most benefit to learners (e.g., Galloway et al., 2017). To do this content teachers and language teachers need knowledge of each other's fields or, as Doiz and Lasagabaster propose, "EMI teachers should ideally have expertise in content and language instruction" (2020, p. 2). Dafouz and Smit (2020), among others, suggest that to achieve this EAP and disciplinary language support should be incorporated into teacher education for those going into or already on EMI programs. However, there is often reluctance on the part of content teachers to address linguistic issues which they do not feel are part of their role as a subject teacher or within their area of expertise (e.g., Block & Moncada-Comas, 2019). Moreover, the integration of language teaching with content teaching blurs the boundaries between CLIL and EMI, which may not always be seen as desirable by students, teachers, or policymakers (Baker & Hüttner, 2017; Walkinshaw, Fenton-Smith, & Humphreys, 2017).

An area that links the issues of language, content, and pedagogy is that of disciplinary language. As Baker and Hüttner observe as regards the findings from their comparative study, "English as discipline-specific language use emerged as a key concept, straddling language and content learning and teaching, as well as problematizing simplistic divides between language and content" (2017, p. 501). While lecturers may feel that the focus of teaching is only content and that this carries over into assessment, with only content knowledge graded, students may have different perspectives believing that linguistic proficiency is also assessed. Indeed one participant (a Chinese international student) in Baker and Hüttner's study went as far as claiming that most of the content on his Anglophone EMI program was already known to him and it was just the English that was new "some are new but most of them are same concept but in in English" (2017, p. 510). Moreover, although subject-specific terminology is usually seen as part of content teaching, discourse and genre-related aspects of disciplinary language are not widely recognized by teachers and so not usually explicitly taught (Baker & Hüttner, 2019). Similarly, Airey (2020) claims that disciplinary language or "literacy" is key to successful pedagogy. He argues that it is an issue for all lecturers, whether on EMI programs or teaching in their L1, but that EMI research has brought the importance of disciplinary language to the fore. Airey proposes teacher education to make lecturers more reflective on how they use English, other languages, and other modes to communicate in different settings.

Connected to the need for lecturers to be more reflective about their communicative practices, and again directly linked to ELF and translanguaging research, has been the need for more awareness of other language use, multilingualism and translanguaging in EMI. Many studies have underscored the importance of lecturers adopting a critical understanding of English in their teaching, moving away from monolingual "English only" Anglophone ideologies (e.g., Jenkins & Mauranen, 2019; Murata & Iino, 2018). Equally important has been calls for teacher education to incorporate multilingual and translanguaging pedagogic practices (e.g., Doiz & Lasagabaster, 2020; Galloway et al., 2017; Jenkins & Mauranen, 2019). Even when lecturers may be confident in their use of English, they may still be unaware of the multilingual practices that take place in their classrooms and the possible benefits they bring to pedagogy (Baker & Hüttner, 2019). At the same time though, as already noted, it is important that lectures ensure that translanguaging does not become exclusionary for students who do not share the same range of linguistic resources (Kuteeva, 2019).

As should now be clear from the above overview of ELF, translanguaging, and EMI/EME research into pedagogy there is much overlap and a great deal shared in perspectives between the three approaches. Emerging from this discussion are a number of core features as regards pedagogic practices for EME.

- **The importance of context and recognition of diversity in EME settings and practices**—no one approach is appropriate in all contexts, diverse roles of English and other languages, and different relationships between content and language in program delivery.
- **A critical approach to English in EME**—a move away from an ideology of monolingual Anglophone English use toward a recognition of English used as a multi-lingua franca in academia with variability in use and adaptation to local needs.
- **EME as taking place in multilingual settings with translanguaging practices prevalent**—a greater recognition of the range of linguistic and other multimodal

resources lecturers and students bring with them and the beneficial role these play in education.

- **EME as taking place in transcultural settings with intercultural and transcultural communication prevalent**—both internally in multicultural HE settings and externally in the international and intercultural connections and identities EME programs aspire too.
- **The key role of teacher education in EME**—making lecturers aware of the central place of language in pedagogy and the importance of teaching disciplinary language, as well as, awareness of critical approaches to English and ELF(A), multilingualism, translanguaging, and intercultural/transcultural communication.
- **Appropriate language preparation and support for students which is well-integrated with content teaching**—including language support that is tailored to the proficiency level of students and the program they are undertaking, as well as, making students aware of critical approaches to English and ELF(A), multilingualism, translanguaging, and intercultural/transcultural communication.

4 Conclusion

In this chapter I have explored the links between ELF research, translanguaging and EMI/EME, suggesting that they share important similarities in perspectives toward the internationalization of HE and the associated linguistic practices and pedagogy. However, due to the limitations of what can be adequately covered in a single chapter some significant areas of EMI/EME have not been discussed here including how policy might better reflect ELF and translanguaging, as well as, the crucial gatekeeping role of assessment. Nonetheless, a number of core themes emerge for EME pedagogy which is the importance of context and acknowledgment of diversity in settings and practices; the necessity of a critical approach toward English; recognition of multilingual and multicultural settings and the prevalence of translanguaging and transcultural practices; the importance of teacher education in raising awareness and fostering appropriate practices for lecturers; and the need for appropriate language preparation and support for students which is delivered in a disciplinary relevant manner and incorporates, ELF, translanguaging and transculturality. It is hoped that these broad principles will allow key stakeholders to develop locally relevant pedagogic practices in Asia, that enable teachers and learners to engage in EME in an equitable manner that eschews a dominance of Anglophone linguistic and educational norms, and that values their full range of linguistic and other sociocultural resources and experiences.

References

Aguilar, M., & Rodríguez, R. (2012). Lecturer and student perceptions on CLIL at a Spanish university. *The International Journal of Bilingual Education and Bilingualism, 15*(2), 183–197.

Airey, J. (2020). The content lecturer and English-medium instruction (EMI): Epilogue to the special issue on EMI in higher education. *International Journal of Bilingual Education and Bilingualism*, 1–7. https://doi.org/10.1080/13670050.2020.1732290.

Baird, R., Baker, W., & Kitazawa, M. (2014). The complexity of English as a Lingua Franca. *Journal of English as a Lingua Franca, 3*(1), 171–196.

Baker, W. (2009). The cultures of English as a lingua franca. *TESOL Quarterly, 43*(4), 567–592. https://doi.org/10.1002/j.1545-7249.2009.tb00187.x.

Baker, W. (2015). *Culture and identity through English as a lingua franca: Rethinking concepts and goals in intercultural communication.* Berlin: De Gruyter Mouton.

Baker, W. (2016). English as an academic lingua franca and intercultural awareness: Student mobility in the transcultural university. *Language and Intercultural Communication, 16*(3), 437–451. http://www.tandfonline.com/doi/full/10.1080/14708477.2016.1168053.

Baker, W. (2018). English as a lingua franca and intercultural communication In J. Jenkins, W. Baker & M. Dewey (Eds.), *The Routledge handbook of English as a lingua franca* (pp. 25–36). Abingdon: Routledge.

Baker, W., & Hüttner, J. (2017). English and more: A multisite study of roles and conceptualisations of language in English medium multilingual universities from Europe to Asia. *Journal of Multilingual and Multicultural Development, 38*(6), 501–516. https://doi.org/10.1080/01434632.2016.1207183.

Baker, W., & Hüttner, J. (2019). "We are not the language police": Comparing multilingual EMI 441 programmes in Europe and Asia. International Journal of Applied Linguistics, 29(1), 78–94.https://doi.org/10.1111/ijal.12246

Baker, W., & Sangiamchit, C. (2019). Transcultural communication: Language, communication and culture through English as a lingua franca in a social network community. *Language and Intercultural Communication, 19*(6), 471–487. https://doi.org/10.1080/14708477.2019.1606230.

Barnard, R., & Hasim, Z. (Eds.). (2018). *English medium instruction programmes: Perspectives from South East Asian Universities.* Abingdon: Routledge.

Block, D., & Moncada-Comas, B. (2019). English-medium instruction in higher education and the ELT gaze: STEM lecturers' self-positioning as NOT English language teachers. *International Journal of Bilingual Education and Bilingualism*, 1–17. https://doi.org/10.1080/13670050.2019.1689917.

Canagarajah, S. (2013). *Translingual practice: Global Englishes and cosmopolitan relations.* London: Routledge.

Cenoz, J. (2019). Translanguaging pedagogies and English as a lingua franca. *Language Teaching, 52*(1), 71–85. https://doi.org/10.1017/s0261444817000246.

Cogo, A. (2016). Conceptualizing ELF as a translanguaging phenomenon: Covert and overt resources in a transnational workplace. *Waseda Working Papers in ELF, 5*, 1–17.

Dafouz, E., & Smit, U. (2016). Towards a dynamic conceptual framework for english-medium education in multilingual university settings. *Applied Linguistics, 37*(3), 397–415. https://doi.org/10.1093/applin/amu034.

Dafouz, E., & Smit, U. (2020). *ROAD-MAPPING English medium education in the internationalised university.* Cham, SWITZERLAND: Palgrave Macmillan UK.

Dearden, J. (2014). English as a medium of instruction—A growing global phenomenon: British Council.

Deterding, D. (2013). *Misunderstandings in English as a lingua franca.* Berlin: De Gruyter Mouton.

Deterding, D., & Kirkpatrick, A. (2006). Emerging South-East Asian Englishes and intelligibility. *World Englishes, 25*(3), 391–409.

Dewey, M. (2012). Towards a post-normative approach: Learning the pedagogy of ELF. *Journal of English as a Lingua Franca, 1*(1), 141–170. https://doi.org/10.1515/jelf-2012-0007.

Doiz, A., & Lasagabaster, D. (2020). Dealing with language issues in English-medium instruction at university: A comprehensive approach. *International Journal of Bilingual Education and Bilingualism*, 1–6. https://doi.org/10.1080/13670050.2020.1727409.

Ehrenreich, S. (2009). English as a lingua franca in multinational corporations: Exploring business communities of practice. In A. Mauranen & E. Ranta (Eds.), *English as a lingua franca: Studies and findings* (pp. 126–151). Newcastle: Cambridge Scholars.

Fang, F., & Baker, W. (2018). 'A more inclusive mind towards the world': English language teaching and study abroad in China from intercultural citizenship and English as a lingua franca perspectives. *Language Teaching Research, 22*(5), 608–624. https://doi.org/10.1177/136216881 7718574.

Fenton-Smith, B., Humphreys, P., & Walkinshaw, I. (Eds.). (2017). *English medium instruction in higher education in Asia-Pacific: From policy to pedagogy*. Berlin: Springer.

Galloway, N., Kriukow, J., & Numajiri, T. (2017). Internationalisation, higher education and the growing demand for English: An investigation into the English medium of instruction (EMI) movement in China and Japan. *British Council ELT Research Papers, 17*(2).

Galloway, N., & Rose, H. (2018). Incorporating global Englishes into the ELT classroom. *ELT Journal, 72*(1), 3–14. https://doi.org/10.1093/elt/ccx010.

García, O., & Kleyn, T. (Eds.). (2016). *Translanguaging with multilingual students*. Abingdon: Routledge.

García, O., & Li, W. (2014). *Translanguaging: Language, bilingualism and education*. Basingstoke: Palgrave Macmillan.

Hu, G., & Lei, J. (2014). English-medium instruction in Chinese higher education: A case study. *Higher Education, 67*(5), 551–567. https://doi.org/10.1007/s10734-013-9661-5.

Iino, M. (2018). EMI (English-medium instruction) in Japanese higher education: A paradoxical space for global and local sociolinguistic habitats. In K. Murata (Ed.), *English-medium instruction from English as a lingua franca perspective: Exploring the higher education context* (pp. 78–95). Abingdon: Routledge.

Ishikawa, T. (2017). Japanese university students' attitudes towards their English and the possibility of ELF awareness *Journal of English as a Lingua Franca, 6*, 237.

Jenkins, J. (2012). English as a lingua franca from the classroom to the classroom. *ELT Journal, 66*(4), 486–494.

Jenkins, J. (2015). Repositioning English and multilingualism in English as a lingua franca. *Englishes in Practice, 2*(3), 49–85. https://doi.org/10.1515/eip-2015-0003.

Jenkins, J. (2018). The future of English as a lingua franca? In J. Jenkins, W. Baker, & M. Dewey (Eds.), *The Routledge handbook of English as a lingua franca* (pp. 594–605). Abingdon: Routledge.

Jenkins, J., Baker, W., & Dewey, M. (Eds.). (2018). *The Routledge handbook of English as a lingua franca*. Abingdon: Routledge.

Jenkins, J., & Mauranen, A. (Eds.). (2019). *Linguistic diversity on the EMI campus: Insider accounts of the use of English and other languages in universities within Asia, Australasia and Europe*. Abingdon: Routledge.

Jørgensen, N., Karrebæk, M. S., Madsen, L. M., & Møller, J. S. (2011). Polylanguaging in superdiversity. *Diversities, 13*(2), 23–38.

Kachru, B. (2005). *Asian Englishes: Beyond the canon*. New Delhi: Oxford University Press.

Kalocsai, K. (2014). *Communities of practice and English as a lingua franca: A study of Erasmus students in a Central-European context*. Berlin: DeGruyter Mouton.

Kaur, J., & Zainuddin, S. Z. (2019). Going global: EMI policies and practices at a Malaysian public university. In J. Jenkins & A. Mauranen (Eds.), *Linguistic diversity on the EMI campus* (pp. 172–194). Routledge.

Kimura, D., & Canagarajah, S. (2018). Translingual practice and ELF. In J. Jenkins, W. Baker, & M. Dewey (Eds.), *The Routledge handbook of English as a lingua franca* (pp. 295–308). Abingdon: Routledge.

Kirkpatrick, A. (2010). *English as a lingua franca in ASEAN*. Hong Kong: Hong Kong University Press.

Kirkpatrick, A. (2011). English as an Asian lingua franca and the multilingual model of ELT. *Language Teaching, 44*(2), 212–224.

Kirkpatrick, A., Lixun, W., Patkin, J., & Subhan, S. (2019). The Asian Corpus of English. Retrieved February 26, 2020 from http://corpus.ied.edu.hk/ace/.

Kuteeva, M. (2019). Revisiting the 'E' in EMI: Students' perceptions of standard English, lingua franca and translingual practices. *International Journal of Bilingual Education and Bilingualism*, 1–14. https://doi.org/10.1080/13670050.2019.1637395.

Lee, E., & Canagarajah, S. (2019). The connection between transcultural dispositions and translingual practices in academic writing. *Journal of Multicultural Discourses, 14*(1), 14–28. https://doi.org/10.1080/17447143.2018.1501375.

Li, W. (2016). New Chinglish and the Post-Multilingualism challenge: Translanguaging ELF in China. *Journal of English as a Lingua Franca, 5*(1), 1–25.

Li, W. (2018). Translanguaging as a practical theory of language. *Applied Linguistics, 39*(1), 9–30. https://doi.org/10.1093/applin/amx039.

Macaro, E., Curle, S., Pun, J., An, J., & Dearden, J. (2018). A systematic review of English medium instruction in higher education. *Language Teaching, 51*(1), 36–76. https://doi.org/10.1017/s0261444817000350.

Mauranen, A., & Jenkins, J. (2019). Where are we with lingusitic diversity on a UK university campus?. In J. Jenkins & A. Mauranen (Eds.), *Linguistic diversity on the EMI campus* (pp. 263–273). Routledge.

Murata, K. (Ed.). (2018). *English-medium instruction from English as a lingua franca perspective: Exploring the higher education context*. Abingdon: Routledge.

Murata, K., & Iino, M. (2018). EMI in higher education. In J. Jenkins, W. Baker, & M. Dewey (Eds.), *The Routledge handbook of English as a lingua franca* (pp. 400–412). Abingdon: Routledge.

Murata, K., Iino, M., & Konakahara, M. (2019). Realities of EMI practices among multilingual students in a Japanese university In J. Jenkins & A. Mauranen (Eds.), *Linguistic diversity on the EMI campus* (pp. 149–171). Routledge.

Newfield, D. (2017). Transformation, transduction and the transmodal moment. In C. Jewitt (Ed.), *The Routledge handbook of multimodal analysis* (2nd ed., pp. 100–114). Abingdon: Routledge.

Pennycook, A., & Otsuji, E. (2015). *Metrolingualism: Language in the city*. Abingdon: Routledge.

Pitzl, M.-L. (2018). Transient international groups (TIGs): Exploring the group and development dimension of ELF. *Journal of English as a Lingua Franca, 7*(1), 25–58. https://doi.org/10.1515/jelf-2018-0002.

Seidlhofer, B. (2011). *Understanding English as a lingua franca*. Oxford: Oxford University Press.

Sifakis Nicos, C., & Bayyurt, Y. (2018). ELF-aware teaching, learning and teacher development. In J. Jenkins, W. Baker, & M. Dewey (Eds.), *The Routledge handbook of English as a lingua franca* (pp. 456–467). Abingdon: Routledge.

Snodin, N. S., & Young, T. J. (2015). 'Native-speaker' varieties of English: Thai perceptions and attitudes. *Asian Englishes, 17*(3), 248–260. https://doi.org/10.1080/13488678.2015.1083354.

Suzuki, A., Liu, H., & Yu, M. (2018). ELF and ELT in East Asian contexts. In J. Jenkins, W. Baker, & M. Dewey (Eds.), *The Routledge handbook of English as a lingua franca* (pp. 494–505). Abingdon: Routledge.

Tsou, W., & Chen, F. (2014). EFL and ELF college students' perceptions toward Englishes. *Journal of English as a Lingua Franca, 3*(2), 363–386. https://doi.org/10.1515/jelf-2014-0021.

Tsou, W., & Kao, S.-M. (Eds.). (2017). *English as a medium of instruction in higher education*. Singapore: Springer.

Walkinshaw, I., Fenton-Smith, B., & Humphreys, P. (2017). EMI issues and challenges in Asia-Pacific higher education: An introduction. In B. Fenton-Smith, P. Humphreys, & I. Walkinshaw (Eds.), *English medium instruction in higher education in Asia-Pacific: From policy to pedagogy* (pp. 1–18). Berlin: Springer.

Walkinshaw, I., & Kirkpatrick, A. (2014). Mutual face preservation among Asian speakers of English as a Lingua Franca. *Journal of English as a Lingua Franca, 3*(2), 269–291.

Wang, Y. (2020). *Language ideologies in the Chinese context: Orientations to English as a Lingua Franca*. Berlin: DeGruyter Mouton.

Will Baker is an Associate Professor of Applied Linguistics and Director of the Centre for Global Englishes at the University of Southampton, UK. His research interests are English as a Lingua Franca, Intercultural and Transcultural Communication, English medium instruction, Intercultural education, Intercultural Citizenship and ELT, and he has published and presented internationally in all these areas. His current research projects have focused on the links between Intercultural Citizenship, Internationalisation of HE and EMI including the recently completed "From English language learners to intercultural citizen" https://www.teachingenglish.org.uk/article/english-lan guage-learners-intercultural-citizens. Recent publications include: Baker, W., & Ishikawa, T. *Transcultural Communication through Global Englishes.* (2021, Routledge), co-editor of the 'Routledge Handbook of English as a Lingua Franca' (2018), author of the monograph 'Culture and Identity through English as a Lingua Franca' (2015, DGM), and co-editor of the book series 'Developments in English as Lingua Franca' (DGM).

Chapter 3
Translanguaging and English-Within-Multilingualism in the Japanese EMI Context

Tomokazu Ishikawa

Abstract This chapter aims to bridge theory and practice with a focus on the Japanese higher education context. It first reconceptualizes the "E" and "M" in EMI according to a currently prominent notion in the ELF field, English as a multi-lingua franca (EMF) (Jenkins in Engl Pract 2:49–85, 2015). EMF views English as embedded in wider multilingual, multicultural, and multimodal resources as well as effectuated through translanguaging, transcultural, and transmodal processes (Ishikawa in Engl Pract 4:31–49, 2017a; Baker in The Routledge handbook of English as a lingua franca, Routledge, pp 25–36, 2018). This chapter then proposes to revitalize the "I" in EMI by incorporating EMF awareness (Ishikawa in ELTJ 74:408–417, 2020a) as a pedagogic intervention to subvert ideological monolingualism. EMF awareness integrates the conceptual understanding of EMF and relevant notions with motivational attitudes and effective communication practices. Empirical data suggest that EMF awareness should find its place in EMI, and international higher education more broadly, within Japan and potentially beyond.

Keywords Translanguaging · English as a multilingua franca (EMF) · Multilingualism · English as a lingua franca (ELF) · English medium instruction (EMI) · Higher education · Japan

1 Introduction

The ever-growing visibility of English medium instruction (EMI) in higher education is somewhat like our elephant in the classroom. This concept appears to be difficult to decipher since it requires understanding the nature of "English" and "medium" as well as the application of this understanding for "instruction". One key research field for EMI is English as a lingua franca (ELF), and a leading ELF handbook (Jenkins, Baker, & Dewey, 2018) devotes one section to the heightened complexity of English and literacy in international academia. ELF research in EMI and beyond

T. Ishikawa (✉)
Center for English as a Lingua Franca, Tamagawa University, Tokyo, Japan
e-mail: t.ishikawa@lab.tamagawa.ac.jp

© The Author(s), under exclusive license to Springer Nature Singapore Pte Ltd. 2021
W. Tsou and W. Baker (eds.), *English-Medium Instruction Translanguaging Practices in Asia*, https://doi.org/10.1007/978-981-16-3001-9_3

has documented how English and multilingual resources are used dynamically and contextually when English functions as a global lingua franca (Seidlhofer, 2011). Along this line, a currently prominent notion in the field, English as a multilingua franca (EMF), coincides with translanguaging (e.g., Li, 2018) and foregrounds the inherent multilingualism of global encounters through English (Jenkins, 2015).

The present chapter aims to further the discussion of EMI in the Japanese higher education context both theoretically and empirically. It seeks to reconceptualize the "E" and "M" in EMI according to EMF and translanguaging. Also, it proposes to revitalize the "I" in EMI by incorporating EMF awareness (Ishikawa, 2020a) as a pedagogic intervention.

2   Reconceptualizing the "E" and "M" in EMI

To find a way to unveil the intricacies of EMI, the current section examines each of the "E" and "M" in EMI theoretically while drawing on the notion of EMF in the ELF field. ELF enquiry is essentially an academic quest to comprehend global communication among English users. Therefore, it has a direct relevance to EMI, a phenomenon coinciding with the widespread use of English and the internationalization of higher education (e.g., Murata, 2019). In accord with the tenor of this book, EMF is considered in the light of translanguaging toward the end of this section.

2.1   EMF and the "E" in EMI

EMI has become a common phenomenon for international universities in Asia and elsewhere. Not surprisingly, many students and instructors use English as their additional language. Put differently, the "E" in EMI, or English in higher education generally, serves as an academic lingua franca in this age of globalization.

As evidenced by a rising tide of international students and a wide variety of distance learning opportunities across the world, globalization is fundamentally about our increased spatial connections or "supraterritorial relations" along with territorial ones (Scholte, 2008, p. 1496). In other words, in collaboration with the shrinking of territorial space, simultaneous and instant mobility at a global scale furthers the complexity of our social relations. For example, graduate students in different parts of the world may be reading this book at the present moment and later discuss some of its content via email exchange. As a corollary of such everyday mobility, we are experiencing complex web-like linguistic flows across spatial borders through ubiquitous contact between English users.

Against this backdrop, ELF research has explored the first two linguistic domains out of the three or "the two 'natural' loci of language" (Risager, 2006, p. 74) in consideration of the third one. These three loci are (1) linguistic resources and repertoires (i.e., totalities of individually available linguistic resources) at the psychological or cognitive level; (2) linguistic practices at the interactional level; and (3) linguistic constructs at the ideological level (Harris, 1997; Mauranen, 2012; Risager, 2006, 2007). This final locus takes a "macrosocial" (Harris, 1997; Mauranen, 2012) or "system-oriented" (Risager, 2006, 2007) view toward observable linguistic phenomena (e.g., Vetchinnikova, 2015), usually in the form of "politically named languages" (Li, 2016, p. 6) such as English and Japanese. In contrast, our real-world "mobile resources" (Blommaert, 2010) are specific parts of language deployed in and for each different interaction which may have different indexical and referential functions (i.e., representing who speakers are and delivering what they have to say).

Regarding the two real-world domains of language, multilingual influences and practices have always been a crucial part of descriptive work in ELF research (e.g., Hülmbauer & Seidlhofer, 2013; Seidlhofer, 2017). After all, it is natural that mobile linguistic resources in a multilingual world are multilingual. The notion of EMF foregrounds this multilingualism as the theoretical raison d'être of the target linguistic phenomenon, namely, "[m]ultilingual communication in which English is available as a contact language of choice, but is not necessarily chosen" (Jenkins, 2015, p. 73). EMF addresses the empirical evidence that "the best solutions [for mutual understanding] need not be the most standardized-like or native-like … [or] even English" (Mauranen, 2018, p. 114), and that global communication brings out multilingualism with varying degrees of overtness (Cogo, 2018). Mobile multilingual resources are relevant to all global encounters even when interactions appear to take place entirely in English, as well as potentially relevant to all English users irrespective of their ability in other languages. While multilingual practices are sometimes overt (e.g., Cogo, 2010), covert multilingual resources in Cogo's term take notice of individuals' "knowledge and experience that shapes their language" (2016, p. 63) and "concern the influence of the user's multilingual resources on their communication, which nonetheless remains in English … on the surface" (2018, p. 358). She stresses the permeability and malleability of named languages across linguistic levels (e.g., phonology, lexicogrammar, pragmatics, and discourse structure), and that multilingualism in EMF is not just about overt code-switching or translanguaging (see Sect. 2.3).

Meanwhile, first language (L1) English speakers may have opportunities to expose themselves to mobile multilingual resources. English speakers with monolingual repertoires may also learn "to engage in the dynamic exploitation of previously unfamiliar linguistic resources by adapting to a multilingual environment" (Ishikawa, 2017a, p. 38). Jenkins (2015) would call this capability *multilanguaging*, and this term itself derives from Nguyen (2012), who argues that it "helps elucidate the dynamic mechanisms of language use and reduce any possible association of multilingualism with an accomplished and perfectionist state" (p. 68, cited in Jenkins, 2015, p. 78). Hereinafter in the present chapter, the term *multilingual* includes multilanguaging as defined above.

EMF highlights the tension between observable, fluid, flexible mobile linguistic resources and enumerable, objectified languages in an ideological sense. The linguistic resources we use and encounter become increasingly associable with multiple languages, rendering many individuals' repertoires variably multilingual. Put differently, it is more common that mobile linguistic resources are multilingual, and that individuals' linguistic repertoires are dynamically multilingual too (Blommaert, 2010; May, 2014). Despite this reality, however, at the ideological level, languages are neatly separated into named categories, usually at the national level, and very often in association with national cultures and speech communities. Here languages are assumed to be bounded systems, but as ideological entities, we cannot describe and delineate any of them to a full extent. The constructed ideology of languages as fixed "objects" remains powerful whenever we learn a language and communicate. Even so, individual language development and use through global networks encounter linguistic resources in a dynamic process as with cultural resources. To borrow Pennycook's (2007) words: "Caught between fluidity and fixity, then, cultural and linguistic forms are always in a state of flux, always changing, always part of a process of the refashioning of identity" (p. 8).

EMF invites us to look at inherent multilingualism in the "E" in EMI. More precisely, this "E" entails multilingual influences and practices which are emergent since the actualization of linguistic resources depends on each interactional environment and each constellation of the individuals involved, all of whom have their own social, linguistic, and cultural backgrounds. As such, "contextual embodiment is crucial" (Baird, Baker, & Kitazawa, 2014, p. 181) in understanding the "E"(-within-multilingualism) in each EMI setting.

2.2   EMF and the "M" in EMI

The term *English medium* obviously designates "English" as a way of communicating information, and in the case of EMI, communicating academic content. As communication is a social act, the word *medium* may better be treated as a verb whose meaning is something like "to effectuate as a means". In this regard, ever since the landmark publication of Jenkins (2000), the research field of ELF has identified the pragmatic strategy of linguistic accommodation as crucial for securing mutual understanding. Linguistic accommodation refers to adjusting and adapting language use in accordance with the situation (Jenkins, 2000, 2014), including pre-empting misunderstanding or non-understanding (Cogo & Pitzl, 2016; Kaur, 2009). Given that the "E" in EMI is English-within-multilingualism (Sect. 2.1), this accommodation is inevitably *multilingual* accommodation. It has been reported that the accommodative employment of multilingual resources facilitates comprehending abstract notions in and outside academia (Mauranen, 2014; Vettorel, 2014). Multilingual accommodation may feature the effective use of "English" as a communication means or the "M" in EMI. Even if "what is distinctive about ELF lies in the communicative strategies that its speakers use" (Seidlhofer, 2009, p. 211), the other strategies documented in ELF research, mostly pragmatic strategies, are more likely to be found in any communication. Pietikäinen (2018), for example, cites clarification questions (e.g., who?); incomprehension tokens (e.g., hmm?); repeating (e.g., this is our second try — second try?) and self-repeating; paraphrasing (e.g., you mean …?) and self-paraphrasing; discourse reflexivity or organization (e.g., what I want to say now is …); and confirmation checks (e.g., sure?).

As anyone at international universities may have experienced, effective communication is not just about language. EMF scenarios are fundamentally concerned with intercultural communication. At the same time, the growing pervasiveness of digital communication "has woken human beings' sense of multimodal communication once again and begun to shift the attention to other modalities of human communication" than language (Li, 2020, p. 245). Having questioned "the 'lingua bias' of communication" (Li, 2018, p. 15), some ELF researchers argue that accommodation should not only be multilingual but also be transcultural and transmodal (Baker & Ishikawa, 2021; Ishikawa & Jenkins, 2019). In other words, effective communication in EMI requires adjusting and adapting the use of meaning-making resources in accordance with the situation without an exclusive focus on linguistic forms. To begin with, as an updated notion in the field of intercultural communication, transcultural communication problematizes the fixed scope of named cultures typically at the national level, coupled with the essential in-betweenness of different cultures (e.g., Baker, 2018). Such a simplistic assumption of cultural "us" and "others" would hinder, rather than facilitate, communication (Holliday, 2011; Piller, 2017). In reality, interactants' cultural understandings and orientations are not only various within and across different scales (e.g., local, national, global) but also variable over the course of each interaction (Baker, 2015). In the first place, it depends on an interactional context how far culture affects or influences meaning-making and whether other relevant social differences (e.g., age, gender, geographical origin, professional occupation) play a part in cultural interpretation (Risager, 2015). Multilingual accommodation should thus accompany transcultural accommodation or "a conscious understanding of the role culturally based forms, practices, and frames of reference can have in intercultural communication, and an ability to put these conceptions into practice in a flexible and context-specific manner in communication" (Baker, 2015, p. 163).[1]

In addition, the notion of transmodal communication gathers increasing attention in applied linguistics (Murphy, 2012; Newfield, 2017), since "the separation of language from the complexity of signs with which its use is associated has limited our understanding of a broader semiotics" (Pennycook, 2007, p. 49). Put differently, linguistic expressions coexist with other signs and symbols, such as facial expression, fragrance, gesture and posture, image, light, place and position, and sound. While the term *multimodality* takes notice of the significance and multiplicity of non-verbal modes, real-world interactional practices blur the boundaries of meaning-making modes by the simultaneous and collaborative activation of them, that is, transmodal (Hawkins, 2018). This is especially palpable in digital communication where individuals see these multiple modes generating meaning synergetically whenever they video chat, text, share materials, and find friends online (Baker & Sangiamchit, 2019).

---

[1]Baker (2015) calls this capability intercultural awareness or ICA, and uses "intercultural" as a generic term derived from the research field of intercultural communication.

Given that communication contains non-linguistic cues, multilingual accommodation should accompany transmodal accommodation or the conscious understanding and appropriation of meaning-making affordances.

EMF accords with both transcultural and transmodal communication and thereby invites us to look at what mediation act should be enacted to communicate through "English". More specifically, the "M" in EMI entails accommodating the way of using language appropriately from situation to situation while consciously aware of the effect of cultural interpretations and available meaning-making modes. Again, "contextual embodiment is crucial" (Baird et al., 2014, p. 181) in understanding the "M" as a verb or action in any given interaction in each EMI setting.

2.3   EMF and Translanguaging

Arguably, translanguaging embraces code-switching (García, 2009; Auer, forth-coming; cf. Otheguy, García, & Reid, 2015; Goodman & Tastanbek, 2021), whose research has a longer tradition (e.g., Gumperz, 1964). Certainly, it may be posited that "code-switching preserves named language categories intact", and that translan-guaging "takes up an internal perspective to describe the languaging of speakers who are said to be bilingual or multilingual" (Vogel & García, 2017, p. 5). However, available publications with a discussion of code-switching in the ELF field (e.g., Cogo, 2010; Klimpfinger, 2009; Pietikäinen, 2014) suggest that individuals perceive language categories as subjective and variable rather than as intact, and that their internal perspectives are not detached from "external" named categories, linguistic or otherwise, but linked to them "through their interpretive filters" (Kitazawa, 2013, p. 264). In short, translanguaging may be seen as carrying on code-switching research while deemphasizing the involvement of perceived different codes and emphasizing the artificial, ideological nature of linguistic boundaries.

Translanguaging research has observed bilinguals' and multilinguals' exploitation of available meaning-making resources to understand, interact with, and challenge their society (e.g., Li & Lin, 2019). Currently, the translanguaging lens aims to develop three strands: transcendent or transgressive, transformative, and transdis-ciplinary. To be specific, in line with García and Li (2014), Li (2018) summarizes the three as referring to:

- the fluid practices that go beyond, that is, *transcend*, socially constructed language systems and structures to engage diverse multiple meaning-making systems and subjectivities;
- the *transformative* capacity of the Translanguaging process not only for language systems but also for individuals' cognition and social structures; and
- the *transdisciplinary* consequences of reconceptualizing language, language learning, and language use, and working across the divides between linguistics, psychology, sociology, and education (p. 27).

Translanguaging concurs with EMF since it observes our fluid, flexible interactional practices and associated cognitive and social development (Li, 2016; Kimura & Canagarajah, 2018). In the past, ELF research has challenged the existing power structures that place Anglophones as a core part of applied linguistics, and English language teaching (ELT) in particular (Jenkins, 2000, 2007). Along this line, EMF now argues for multilingualism as the norm whether English is an individual's L1 or not. At the same time, while power relationships (e.g., Guido, 2012; Jenks, 2018) and pedagogic issues (e.g., Bayyurt & Akcan, 2015; Dewey, 2012) have been part of ELF enquiry, social and educational engagement may be wider and more salient in translanguaging enquiry. García and Li (2014) expect that "orders of discourses shift and the voices of Others come to the forefront, relating then translanguaging to criticality, critical pedagogy, social justice and the linguistic human rights agenda" (p. 3). At the same time, as a major research field in applied linguistics, ELF is by definition as transdisciplinary as translanguaging in order to engage in "[t]he theoretical and empirical investigation of real-world problems in which language is a central issue" (Brumfit, 1995, p. 27).

Similarities between EMF and translanguaging are striking, especially when it comes to the first strand (i.e., to transcend). Within it, EMF "may be regarded as broadly conceptualized translanguaging … which emerges across individuals, time and space" (Ishikawa, 2017a, p. 38). Nonetheless, there are a number of modest differences between EMF and translanguaging. First of all, EMF takes the malleability and permeability of named languages at the cognitive and interactional levels as its starting point because it is immanent in *all* global communication (Jenkins, 2015). Accordingly, while translanguaging tends to observe overt multilingual practices, EMF targets any global communication to enquire into situational multilingual influences and practices (see covert multilingual resources in Sect. 2.1). In addition, as implied by the term "repertoires in flux" (Jenkins, 2015, p. 76), multilingualism in EMF is the gross property of the individuals involved, along with local surroundings (Ishikawa, 2017a). With a focus on effective interaction, ELF enquiry has evidenced how crucial linguistic accommodation is among English users, irrespective of an individual's ability in other languages (Sweeney & Zhu, 2010; Baird et al., 2014; see multilanguaging in Sect. 2.1). More drastically, and with a focus on cognition, translanguaging "challenges the idea that different named languages, which exist as historical, political, and ideological entities, exist as cognitive entities in the human mind" (Li & Ho, 2018, p. 37). Finally, the availability of English is different from multilingualism and translanguaging, both of which can dispense with English (e.g., Fei & Weekly, 2020; Pennycook, 2020). In this regard, targeted scenarios in the ELF field may be narrower. Even so, global communication can be difficult without this currently most prominent lingua franca.

While recognizing the dynamic communicative process foregrounded by the term *translanguaging*, EMF retains the *multi-* in its appellation (i.e., English as a *multi*lingua franca) to underscore the interplay between the ideological being of multiple, enumerable languages and real-world fluid, flexible linguistic resources and practices (see the three loci of language in Sect. 2.1). Globalization does not diminish the relevance of named language categories but rather accentuates their existence as ideological constructs, frequently those of "standard" languages, and in the case of EMI, that of Standard English. Against the backdrop of ideological language policy, the next section turns to consider how to implement the notion of EMF in the Japanese higher education context.

3   Revitalizing the "I" in EMI at Japanese Universities

The previous section identifies the "E" in EMI as English-within-multilingualism and the "M" as situationally appropriate meaning-making. The current section considers the application of the reconceptualized "E" and "M" to the "I" or instruction at Japanese universities. For this purpose, this section first overviews a pervasive language ideology in Japan which embraces monolingualism and decontextualized correctness, and then introduces the empirically researched pedagogic intervention of EMF awareness (Ishikawa, 2020a) to subvert this ideology for the sake of effective communication. The subsequent discussion examines the efficacy of EMF awareness while citing my EMI modules as examples.

3.1   Ideological Language Policy

Unlike in multilingual communication scenarios today, in the Japanese higher education context, instructors and all students often share their L1 (i.e., Japanese). Within this context, there exists no national guideline for language education or language use in education (MEXT, 2014). In reality, what may be called the monolingual Standard English ideology circulates in Japanese society so pervasively that it almost saturates citizens' consciousness of language (Houghton & Rivers, 2013; Ishikawa, 2017b) and serves as "a de facto language policy" (Shohamy, 2003, p. 283). Ideologically, the best English is presumed to be spoken monolingually or "genuinely" without any interference from other languages, as well as "correctly" based on a national standard of the traditional English-speaking world. It should be noted, however, that any standard or standardized language variety continues to change over generations, unlike Standard English in ELT.

The nature and mechanism of the monolingual Standard English ideology are beyond the scope of this chapter (see, e.g., Ishikawa, 2020b). It will suffice to indicate here that a number of fallacies inhere in this ideology:

- to compartmentalize individual multilingual development as if it were plural acquisitions of one language after another,
- to equate a nationally institutionalized Anglophone variety at a certain period with the internationally used lingua franca of a multilingual world,
- to assume Anglophones from particular geographical territories to be monolingual experts in this "standard" variety, and

- to misrecognize prestige as residing in linguistic features themselves while the socio-political, historical reasons behind are consigned into oblivion in society (Baker & Ishikawa, 2021).

Without regard to diverse communicative contexts, none of these essentialist ideas is compatible with either the reconceptualized "E" in EMI as emergent multilingual influences and practices with English (Sect. 2.1) or the "M" as the communicative action of multilingual, transcultural, and transmodal accommodation (Sect. 2.2). Hence, in a society circumscribed by the monolingual Standard English ideology like Japan, the "I" in EMI needs to be featured or undergirded by EMF awareness (Ishikawa, 2020a).

3.2   EMF Awareness as the "I" in EMI

EMF awareness integrates conceptual understanding, motivational attitudes, and communicative practices. More precisely, it does not only refer to raising students' linguistic and cultural awareness and nurturing confidence as English users. It also refers to enabling students to connect this conscious understanding to their own transcultural and transmodal communication by appropriating English and multilingual resources. It is hoped that they will continue developing the ability to communicate through actual experiences and reflections.

EMF-aware sociolinguistics modules in Ishikawa (2020a) are designed according to two principles: (1) providing students with experiences of EMF scenarios, and (2) encouraging their critical thinking about language and culture in reference to their experiences and in reference to published research. It is not easy to provide multilingual experiences when students share their L1. However, an instructor can work with international students on campus or run a module in collaboration with a classroom abroad through his or her research network. Alternatively, a module can be scheduled in association with students' study-abroad programs in which they will meet other students from different parts of the world. They can prepare and reflect on their communication experiences during sojourns in their local classrooms.

To encourage critical thinking about language and culture, an instructor can give mini-lectures on the advancement of ELF research, including accommodative processes attested by corpora (see, e.g., Jenkins, 2022). Meanwhile, he or she can encourage proactive discussion, debate, or presentation about language and culture, based on either students' individual experiences or communication extracts from publications, such as the example below. In this adapted extract from Sangiam-chit (2018), three international friends, Diego (Columbian), Ken (Thai), and Nikhil (Indian), are exchanging messages on Facebook about a cartoon that has been posted by Ken.

Example 3.1

01 Diego:	Sometimes…	
02 Ken:	Always.	
03 Diego:	Jajajaja. Unfortunately, you may be right.	
04 Nikhil:	Yayyy… Look the speaker on the stage is a goat, just like us.	
05 Ken:	No… We are more cute. 5555	

(Adapted from Sangiamchit, 2018, p. 352)

The Facebook cartoon is a satire on democracy in which the sneaky wolf (a politician) manipulates a puppet sheep to obtain support from a flock of sheep (the general public) for his own benefit. Students in small groups may be asked to explain this situation before sharing their ideas with the class. They may easily recognize that participants are all amused by this depiction of democracy, and that their meanings are created through the integration of the cartoon and text messages. Some of the students may notice that laughter is expressed as "Jajajaja" (Line 03) and "5555" (Line 05), both of which are pronounced as hahahaha in Spanish and Thai respectively. Perhaps, Ken and Nikhil read "Jajajaja" as such with no problem, owing to their experience of cyber communication. Others may suggest that the participants consider either sheep or goats (Line 04) to be symbols of the weak and dependent as per their cultural backgrounds, and that this different interpretation does not cause any communication problems.

An EMI instructor needs to decide how far and in what way to implement EMF awareness, considering each setting and academic program. What follows are examples from my sociolinguistics modules for Japanese students and that of an English medium faculty, in which EMF awareness was featured for the purpose of assisting students' future academic and professional lives. While the former cases cite Ishikawa's (2020a) published study, the latter case is unpublished at the time of writing but will be included in Baker and Ishikawa (2021).

3.3   EMF Awareness: L1-Shared EMI Cases

My open-ended questionnaire study in L1-shared EMI classrooms (Ishikawa, 2020a) is among the first few studies to investigate EMF in relation to pedagogy, and more specifically, whether and how exposure to EMF scenarios affects students' views of their communication outside the classroom. The study targeted undergraduates who had selected my semester-long sociolinguistics module on global communication, which was given at both a humanities faculty of a top comprehensive institution in Tokyo (University A) and a university of foreign studies in the suburbs of Tokyo (University B). Everyone's strongest language was Japanese in both classes. In total,

91 students (out of 108, from Years 1 to 4) and 15 students (out of 15, from Years 3 and 4) were willing to fill in the questionnaire.

All 106 participants were English majors. Unlike University B, which attracted exchange students from Asia, Australasia, Americas, and Europe on its small campus throughout the academic year, University A's faculty in question consisted almost exclusively of Japanese students. Even so, the class at University A was run in collaboration with that of an international university in Taiwan found through an ELF research network. According to the first principle of EMF-aware modules (Sect. 3.2), students at University A studied a similar syllabus to a class at the Taiwanese university and exchanged ideas via Skype during three in-class video conferences followed by individual discussions at home. However, I did not make any similar efforts at University B because all the 15 students had regular contact, mainly in English, with exchange students. Meanwhile, according to the second principle (Sect. 3.2), at both universities, I gave an occasional mini-lecture on ELF research and a regular classroom activity about language and culture to facilitate sharing students' individual experiences during the semester and discussing them reflexively. I also used published extracts as sample EMF scenarios (see Baker & Ishikawa, 2021) to encourage extra small group exchanges of views, followed by the class discussion.

I administered the following questionnaire in each classroom at Universities A and B toward the end of the semester.

Reflect on one or a few recent intercultural communication[2] opportunities you had.

Q1. Is there anything you would learn from your own experience?

Q2. What does English mean for you as (future) English users?

Q3. What do you think a capable user of English is like in the 21st century?

The three open-ended questions (Q1–Q3) were intended to encourage participants to reflect on their own most memorable communicative experiences, which they had shared already with peers in class. With the help of NVivo software, the collected data were subjected to qualitative content analysis (e.g., Schreier, 2012), which proceeds by coding what is in the data, grouping the codes under overarching categories, and interpreting the relationships between the categories.

While detailed findings are available elsewhere in Ishikawa (2020a), participants unequivocally recalled in Q1 that they learned the act of multilingual and transmodal accommodation as key for perceived success in communication, and that this action led not only to mutual understanding but also to more active engagement in communication. Also, it was evident from Q2 that participants expected English to connect them with a globalized world in a positive way, prospectively serving career purposes. Furthermore, all participants agreed in Q3 that capable English users were experienced in multilingual and transmodal accommodation while embodying an interest and respect for what interactants had to say and not being judgmental of who interactants were.

Conversely, accommodation would not always be practical "if we stick to English only" (Q3, Participant 1, University B). Indeed, participants at University A would

---

[2]"Intercultural communication" was used as a generic term for my modules.

text in Chinese characters as a "quick method" (Q1, Participant 2). In one participant's words:

> I feel that today's societies focus on boundaries. To give an example, we tend to distinguish English [from other languages] and then we often prefer American or British English to other English. [But] we should produce new communities, ideas and customs by using English in multilingual environment. (Q3, Participant 3, University A)

Participant 3 seemed to associate flexible use of English and multilingual resources with achieving a new, broader understanding of language and the world. More drastically, participants at University B said that they often slipped into Indonesian, Spanish, or Korean whether consciously or subconsciously. One of them remarked that even when Korean was suspended, "I can get her English because I know her English is influenced by Korean" (Q1, Participant 4).

At the same time, participants at both universities would use image or voice translation on smartphones "to support communication" (Q1, Participant 5, University B) as necessary, or find facial and bodily expressions so indispensable as to say, for instance:

> I learned what [my Skype partner] thought about intercultural communication ... and how difficult to communicate without using *full body language*. (Q1, Participant 6, University A; emphasis added)

As such, it appears that what participants had to say was embedded in multiple modes blended for communication either via Skype or face to face. It is important to note that what participants did not mention was any cultural misunderstanding. This adds empirical support to the argument that cultural differences as obstacles to achieving meaning are not always clear in transcultural communication (Ishikawa, 2017a), and that eschewing essentialist accounts of cultural "differences" and "problems" in pedagogy is crucial (Baker, 2015).

Inside the classroom, a discussion of multilingual experiences among English-knowing students appeared to create another EMF scenario by itself when they disassociated English from monolingualism via their multilingual repertoires. To this effect, an L1-shared classroom can be an authentic site for emergent multilingual influences and practices in present-day communication, thereby resonating with the transcendent and possibly also transformative strands of translanguaging (see Sect. 2.3).

3.4 EMF Awareness: An International EMI Case

After the completion of the previous study (Ishikawa, 2020a), not in the form of pedagogic intervention research, I taught a similar but more intensive sociolinguistics module at the EMI faculty of University A. My students were 57 undergraduates (from Years 2 to 5) with diverse social, linguistic, and cultural backgrounds, originally from Asia, Americas, and Europe. Pedagogic efforts were directed at encouraging students' critical thinking about their everyday multilingual practices both inside and outside the campus. A typical three-hour class consisted of my lecture to facilitate the reflection of their own and peers' communication experiences, students' group presentation on one chapter from the *Routledge handbook of ELF* (Jenkins et al., 2018), and my follow-up lecture on the same chapter. My lectures were interspersed with group and class discussions, and students' presentations often involved one or more discussion opportunities.

Toward the end of the semester, each student gave a final presentation on a topic of his or her choice, and many presentations cited personal experiences on their mobile phones as below with my translation in brackets. In the following example, a Taiwanese student texted with a Japanese student from the same faculty. They were meeting up on a street.

Example 3.2

01 Student A: セブンの隣ね [so it's next to the 7(-Eleven)]
02 Student B: 我在インフォ
03　　　　　的前面 [I'm in front of the info(mation board)]

(Baker & Ishikawa, 2021, p. 149)

The Japanese language combines three different scripts: *kanji* (i.e., Chinese characters), *hiragana* (literally "ordinary") phonograms, and *katakana* (literally "fragmentary" but in effect "foreign") phonograms, and both セブン [7] and インフォ [info] were written in katakana. Line 01 made sense as Japanese, and lines 02 and 03 were largely Chinese. During the presentation, many students thought of Student A as Japanese and Student B as Taiwanese. However, the opposite was true, and Student A was the Taiwanese presenter. Similar to Cogo's (2016) data, English-speaking interactants may use available resources from their communication partners' L1s.

In the next example, a Japanese presenter (Student D below) showed her instant messenger. Two Japanese exchange students in southeast Spain were talking about their trip.

Example 3.3

01 Student C: あとギリシャについてはギリシャ人から返信なんもこないので無
　　　　　視 [Re Greece there's no reply at all from the Greecian and so ignore it]!
02 Student D: Valeee [okk]
03　　　　　I bought a dome case for the gopro dakara [therefore] creo que Podemos
　　　　　sacar buenas fotos [I think we can take good photos]!!
04 Student C: っしゃあああ [Woooooo]! あざすあざす [Thx thx]!

(Baker & Ishikawa, 2021, p. 151)

At first glance, it may appear that the students did not adjust or adapt their language use to one another. However, they actually accommodated it in their different ways. Student C's pragmatic use of highly informal Japanese set a friendly tone since both students shared so much of its colloquialism as peer students. At the same time, student D's flexible use of multilingual resources represented everyday situations they faced and coped with together.

In this final example, students born and raised in Japan and the United States respectively were discussing breakfast, and the latter (Student F) was a presenter.

Example 3.4

01 Student E: i recommend はなまるうどんのサラダうどん [Hanamaru Udon's salad udon noodles]
02 Student F: It's not breakfast food…
03 Student E: its good tho
04 Student F: What about Platform Café?
05 Student E: 行ったことない [I've never been there]
06 Student F: I'll go then
07   They have yummy breakfast food~
08 Student E: pictures
09   i think サラダうどん [salad udon] is perfect breakfast tho lol
10 Student F: 忘れた [I forgot]… just I got boiled egg and toast
11   それおかしいよ [I think that's strange]
12 Student E: おかしくないよ [I don't think it's strange]
13 Student F: おかしい [It's strange]
14 Student E: healthy healthy
15 Student F: I usually just eat a みかん [satsuma orange] at breakfast, so I'm very happy to have breakfast food~~~

(Baker & Ishikawa, 2021, pp. 146–147)

Student E named a chain udon restaurant and "salad udon noodles" (Line 01). For her, the salad and udon noodles dish was a "perfect breakfast" (Line 09) and "healthy healthy" (Line 14). However, Student F regarded it as "not breakfast food" (Line 02) and thus strange (Lines 11, 13). They were on parallel tracks throughout this extract but in a friendly manner, thanks to their shared multilingual identities. Their linguistic resources were not always identifiable with a particular language as shown in the name of the restaurant "Platform Café" (Line 04) and the global cyber slang "lol" (Line 09). Disagreement was further mitigated by colloquial language, including "tho" (Lines 03, 09) and "よ" (Lines 11, 12), as well as by cyber symbols, namely "…" (Line 02), " ~ " (Line 07), and " ~~~ " (Line 15).

Importantly, both Students E's and F's breakfast practices represented the complex nature of food culture which enabled them to have equally flexible orientations. While udon noodles are of East Asian origin, "salad udon" is not very popular for breakfast in Japan, at least, where boiled eggs and toasts may be more commonly eaten as with abroad. Similarly, while satsuma orange is originally from southern Japan, it is not unusual to have orange or orange juice in the morning at a global scale.

As seen in the above three examples, students shared and reflected on their own everyday experiences to substantiate their understanding of EMF. Like translanguaging, EMF has shifted away from decontextualizing and delineating language, culture, and meaning-making modes. As global communication is not reducible to any particular languages, cultures, or modes, its effectiveness relies on the dynamic, adaptive, and reflexive use of communicative resources in context from moment to moment. Arguably, the ability to continue learning from such actual interaction experience is indispensable for students and instructors alike in globalized EMI. It may be claimed that my modules in both L1-shared (Sect. 3.3) and international (Sect. 3.4) classes helped students develop this very ability by bringing to the fore the value of learning from out-of-class communication experiences.

4 Discussion and Conclusion

The present chapter has argued for the shift from ideological monolingualism to multilingual reality and from a linguistic to a more holistic approach to meaning-making resources. Admittedly, it is easy to feature EMF awareness in sociolinguistics modules, particularly on global communication, as was the case in the courses presented here. However, this is not likely to be the case in other content subjects. Future research could be conducted to explore how far and in what way EMF awareness finds its place in EMI settings across disciplines.

More straightforwardly, higher education institutions would be able to make similar EMF-aware sociolinguistics modules (see Sects. 3.3–3.4) widely available to students across faculties and departments, preferably at an earlier stage of academic curricula. These modules would lend support to future EMI in many different fields, or effective "English" communication in international academia more broadly. Alternatively, similar interventions might be arranged in the later stages of ELT at school or as general education English subjects at university. In fact, it is common for Japanese universities to offer English as required liberal arts courses. There is a potential for developing these courses toward EMF awareness, and my colleagues and I are working in this direction at Tamagawa University's Center for English as a Lingua Franca (Ishikawa & McBride, 2019; Oda, 2019; Suzuki, 2019).

Equally important as students' EMF awareness is pre- and in-service teacher training to prepare EMI and ELT instructors themselves for today's mobility and English-within-multilingualism. Unfortunately, there is no formal EMI teacher training in Japan (MEXT, 2014). Instead, many Japanese universities provide faculty development workshops to support teaching in English and teaching English (see, e.g., UTokyo English Academia, 2019). EMF awareness might well be essential for teacher training and faculty development in Japanese and other similar contexts.

Citing García (2009) and Creese and Blackledge (2015), Li (2018) foresees that "Translanguaging empowers both the learner and the teacher, transforms the power relations, and focuses the process of teaching and learning on making meaning, enhancing experience, and developing identity" (p. 15). This is exactly true of EMI if accompanied by EMF awareness on the part of both the instructor and the instructed.

References

Auer, P. (forthcoming). 'Translanguaging' or 'doing languages'? Multilingual practices and the notion of 'codes'. In J. MacSwann (Ed.), *Language(s): Multilingualism and its consequences*. Multilingual Matters.

Baird, R., Baker, W., & Kitazawa, M. (2014). The complexity of ELF. *Journal of English as a Lingua Franca, 3*, 171–196.

Baker, W. (2015). *Culture and identity through English as a lingua franca: Rethinking concepts and goals in intercultural communication*. De Gruyter Mouton.

Baker, W. (2018). English as a lingua franca and intercultural communication. In J. Jenkins, W. Baker, & M. Dewey (Eds.), *The Routledge handbook of English as a lingua franca* (pp. 25–36). Routledge.

Baker, W., & Ishikawa, T. (2021). *Transcultural communication through Global Englishes: An advanced textbook for students*. Routledge.

Baker, W., & Sangiamchit, C. (2019). Transcultural communication: Language, communication and culture through English as a lingua franca in a social network community. *Language and Intercultural Communication, 19*, 471–487.

Bayyurt, Y., & Akcan, S. (Eds.). (2015). *Current perspectives on pedagogy for English as a lingua franca*. De Gruyter Mouton.

Blommaert, J. (2010). *The sociolinguistics of globalization*. Cambridge University Press.

Brumfit, C. (1995). Teacher professionalism and research. In G. Cook & B. Seidlhofer (Eds.), *Principle & practice in applied linguistics* (pp. 27–41). Oxford University Press.

Cogo, A. (2010). Strategic use and perceptions of English as a Lingua Franca. *Poznań Studies in Contemporary Linguistics, 46*, 295–312.

Cogo, A. (2016). Conceptualizing ELF as a translanguaging phenomenon: Covert and overt resources in a transnational workplace. *Waseda Working Papers in ELF, 5*, 61–77.

Cogo, A. (2018). ELF and multilingualism. In J. Jenkins, W. Baker, & M. Dewey (Eds.), *The Routledge handbook of English as a Lingua Franca* (pp. 357–368). Routledge.

Cogo, A., & Pitzl, M.-L. (2016). Pre-empting and signalling non-understanding in ELF. *ELT Journal, 70*, 339–345.

Creese, A., & Blackledge, A. (2015). Translanguaging and identity in educational settings. *Annual Review of Applied Linguistics, 35*, 20–35.

Dewey, M. (2012). Towards a post-normative approach: Learning the pedagogy of ELF. *Journal of English as a Lingua Franca, 1*, 141–170.

Fei, Y., & Weekly, R. (2020). Examining the parameters of translanguaging in the context of Chinese bilinguals' discourse practices. *International Journal of Multilingualism*, Latest Articles.

Garcia, O. (2009). *Bilingual education in the 21st century: A global perspective*. Wiley-Blackwell.

García, O., & Li, W. (2014). *Translanguaging: Language, bilingualism and education*. Palgrave Macmillan.

Goodman, B., & Tastanbek, S. (2021). Making the shift from a codeswitching to a translanguaging lens in English language teacher education. *TESOL Quarterly, 55*, 29–53.

Guido, M. G. (2012). ELF authentication and accommodation strategies in crosscultural immigration encounters. *Journal of English as a Lingua Franca, 1*, 219–240.

Gumperz, J. J. (1964). Hindi-Punjabi code-switching in Delhi. In H. Lunt (Ed.), *Proceedings of the Ninth International Congress of Linguists* (pp. 1115–1124). Mouton.

Harris, R. (1997). From an integrational point of view. In G. Wolf & N. Love (Eds.), *Linguistics inside out: Roy Harris and his critics* (pp. 229–310). John Benjamins.

Hawkins, M. R. (2018). Transmodalities and transnational encounters: Fostering critical cosmopolitan relations. *Applied Linguistics, 39*, 55–77.

Holliday, A. (2011). *Intercultural communication and ideology*. Sage.

Houghton, S. A., & Rivers, D. J. (Eds.). (2013). *Native-speakerism in Japan: Intergroup dynamics in foreign language education*. Multilingual Matters.

Hülmbauer, C., & Seidlhofer, B. (2013). English as a lingua franca in European multilingualism. In A.-C. Berthed, F. Grin, & G. Lüdi (Eds.), *Exploring the dynamics of multilingualism* (pp. 387–406). John Benjamins.

Ishikawa, T. (2017a). Conceptualising English as a global contact language. *Englishes in Practice, 4*, 31–49.

Ishikawa, T. (2017b). Japanese university students' attitudes towards their English and the possibility of ELF awareness. *Journal of English as a Lingua Franca, 6*, 237–263.

Ishikawa, T. (2020a). EMF awareness in the Japanese EFL/EMI context. *ELT Journal, 74*, 408–417.

Ishikawa, T. (2020b). Complexity of English as a Multilingua Franca: Place of monolingual Standard English. In M. Konakahara & K. Tsuchiya (Eds.), *English as a lingua franca in Japan: Towards multilingual practices* (pp. 91–109). Palgrave Macmillan.

Ishikawa, T., & Jenkins, J. (2019). What is ELF? Introductory questions and answers for ELT professionals. *Center for English as a Lingua Franca Journal, 5*, 1–10.

Ishikawa, T., & McBride, P. (2019). Doing justice to ELF in ELT: Comments on Toh (2016). *Journal of English as a Lingua Franca, 8*, 333–345.

Jenkins, J. (2000). *The phonology of English as an international language.* Oxford University Press.

Jenkins, J. (2007). *English as a Lingua Franca: Attitude and identity.* Oxford University Press.

Jenkins, J. (2014). *English as a Lingua Franca in the international university: The politics of academic English language policy.* Routledge.

Jenkins, J. (2015). Repositioning English and multilingualism in English as a Lingua Franca. *Englishes in Practice, 2*, 49–85.

Jenkins, J. (2022). *Global Englishes: A resource book for students* (4th ed.). Routledge.

Jenkins, J., Baker, W., & Dewey, M. (Eds.). (2018). *The Routledge handbook of English as a lingua franca.* Routledge.

Jenks, C. (2018). Uncooperative lingua franca encounters. In J. Jenkins, W. Baker, & M. Dewey (Eds.), *The Routledge handbook of English as a lingua franca* (pp. 279–291). Routledge.

Kaur, J. (2009). Pre-empting problems of understanding in English as a lingua franca. In A. Mauranen & E. Ranta (Eds.), *English as a lingua franca: Studies and findings* (pp. 107–123). Cambridge Scholars Publishing.

Kimura, D., & Canagarajah, S. (2018). Translingual practice and ELF. In J. Jenkins, W. Baker, & M. Dewey (Eds.), *The Routledge handbook of English as a lingua franca* (pp. 295–308). Routledge.

Kitazawa, M. (2013). *Approaching conceptualisations of English in East Asian contexts: Ideas, ideology, and identification.* Southampton (UK) PhD thesis, University of Southampton.

Klimpfinger, T. (2009). She's mixing the two languages together — Forms and functions of code-switching in English as a lingua franca. In A. Mauranen & E. Ranta (Eds.), *English as a lingua franca: Studies and findings* (pp. 348–371). Cambridge Scholars Publishing.

Li, W. (2016). New Chinglish and the post-multilingualism challenge: Translanguaging ELF in China. *Journal of English as a Lingua Franca, 5*, 1–25.

Li, W. (2018). Translanguaging as a practical theory of language. *Applied Linguistics, 39*, 9–30.

Li, W. (2020). Multilingual English users' linguistic innovation. *World Englishes, 39*, 236–248.

Li, W., & Ho, W. Y. J. (2018). Language learning sans frontiers: A translanguaging view. *Annual Review of Applied Linguistics, 38*, 33–59.

Li, W., & Lin, A. M. Y. (2019). Translanguaging classroom discourse: Pushing limits, breaking boundaries. *Classroom Discourse, 10*, 209–215.

Mauranen, A. (2012). *Exploring ELF: Academic English shaped by non-native speakers.* Cambridge University Press.

Mauranen, A. (2014). Lingua franca discourse in academic contexts: Shaped by complexity. In J. Flowerdew (Ed.), *Discourse in context* (pp. 225–245). Bloomsbury.

Mauranen, A. (2018). Second language acquisition, world Englishes, and English as a Lingua Franca (ELF). *World Englishes, 37*, 106–119.

May, S. (2014). Contesting metronormativity: Exploring indigenous language dynamism across the urban-rural divide. *Journal of Language, Identity, and Education, 13*, 229–235.

MEXT. (2014). 大学における教育内容・方法の改善等について *Concerning the improvement etc. of educational content and teaching methods in universities and colleges* (Trans.). Retrieved July 31, 2020, from https://www.mext.go.jp/a_menu/koutou/daigaku/index.htm.

Murata, K. (2019). *English-medium instruction from an English as a lingua franca perspective: Exploring the higher education context*. Routledge.

Murphy, K. M. (2012). Transmodality and temporality in design interactions. *Journal of Pragmatics, 44*, 1966–1981.

Newfield, D. (2017). Transformation, transduction and the transmodal moment. In C. Jewitt (Ed.), *The Routledge handbook of multimodal analysis* (2nd ed., pp. 100–113). Routledge.

Nguyen, H. H. (2012). The multilanguaging of a Vietnamese American in South Philadelphia. *Working Papers in Educational Linguistics, 27*(1), 65–85.

Oda, M. (2019). Beyond global English(es): University English program in transition. In K. Murata (Ed.), *English-medium instruction from an English as a lingua franca perspective: Exploring the higher education context* (pp. 259–270). Routledge.

Otheguy, R., García, O., & Reid, W. (2015). Clarifying translanguaging and deconstructing named languages: A perspective from linguistics. *Applied Linguistics Review, 6*, 281–307.

Pennycook, A. (2007). *Global Englishes and transcultural flows*. Routledge.

Pennycook, A. (2020). *Translingual Entanglements of English. World Englishes, 39*, 222–235.

Pietikäinen, K. S. (2014). ELF couples and automatic code-switching. *Journal of English as a Lingua Franca, 3*, 1–26.

Pietikäinen, K. S. (2018). Misunderstandings and ensuring understanding in private ELF talk. *Applied Linguistics, 39*, 188–212.

Piller, I. (2017). *Intercultural communication: A critical introduction* (2nd ed.). Edinburgh University Press.

Risager, K. (2006). *Language and culture: Global flows and local complexity*. Multilingual Matters.

Risager, K. (2007). *Language and culture pedagogy: From a national to a transnational paradigm*. Multilingual Matters.

Risager, K. (2015). Linguaculture: The language–culture nexus in transnational perspective. In F. Sharifian (Ed.), *The Routledge handbook of language and culture* (pp. 87–99). Routledge.

Sangiamchit, C. (2018). ELF in electronically mediated intercultural communication. In J. Jenkins, W. Baker, & M. Dewey (Eds.), *The Routledge handbook of English as a lingua franca* (pp. 345–356). Routledge.

Scholte, J. A. (2008). Defining globalisation. *The World Economy, 31*, 1471–1502.

Schreier, M. (2012). *Qualitative content analysis in practice*. Sage.

Seidlhofer, B. (2009). Accommodation and the idiom principle in English as a lingua franca. *Intercultural Pragmatics, 6*, 195–215.

Seidlhofer, B. (2011). *Understanding English as a lingua franca*. Oxford University Press.

Seidlhofer, B. (2017). English as a lingua franca and multilingualism. In J. Cenoz, D. Gorter, & S. May (Eds.), *Language awareness and multilingualism: Encyclopedia of language and education* (pp. 391–404). Springer.

Shohamy, E. (2003). Implications of language education policies for language study in schools and universities. *The Modern Language Journal, 87*, 278–286.

Suzuki, A. (2019). What does "teaching English as a lingua franca" mean? Insights from university ELF instructors. In H. Reinders, S. Ryan, & S. Nakamura (Eds.), *Innovation in language teaching and learning: The case of Japan* (pp. 141–160). Palgrave Macmillan.

Sweeney, E., & Zhu, H. (2010). Accommodating toward your audience: Do native speakers of English know how to accommodate their communication strategies toward nonnative speakers of English? *Journal of Business Communication, 47*, 477–504.

UTokyo English Academia (2019) *English Academia 3*. Retrieved July 31, 2020, from https://uto kyo-ea.com/courses/course-v1:UTokyo-PAGE+EA003+2019/about/en.

Vetchinnikova, S. (2015). Usage-based recycling or creative exploitation of the shared code?: The case of phraseological patterning. *Journal of English as a Lingua Franca, 4*, 223–252.

Vettorel, P. (2014). *English as a lingua franca in wider networking: Blogging practices*. De Gruyter Mouton.

Vogel, S., & García, O. (2017). Translanguaging (19 pp.). *Oxford research encyclopedia of education*. Retrieved from https://oxfordre.com/education/view/10.1093/acrefore/978019026 4093.001.0001/acrefore-9780190264093-e-181.

Tomokazu Ishikawa is an Assistant Professor at the Center for English as a Lingua Franca, Tamagawa University, Tokyo, Japan and a postdoctoral member at the Centre for Global Englishes, the University of Southampton, UK. Prior to that, he taught English at Japanese institutions for university entrance exam preparation. He has published on ELF mainly in relation to multilingualism, language attitudes and ideologies, and ELT. He is a co-author of *Transcultural communication through Global Englishes: An advanced textbook for students* (with Will Baker, Routledge, 2021) and a guest co-editor of the 2021 special issue of *Asian Englishes* on English in Japan and Japanese English (with Ariane M. Borlongan, Taylor & Francis, 2021).

Chapter 4
Translanguaging and Language Policy in Thai Higher Education EMI Programs

Jaewon Jane Ra and Will Baker

Abstract Thai higher education (HE) and the Thai government have implemented internationalization strategies since the 1990s and this has led to an increase in the number of EMI (English Medium Instruction) courses (Lavankura in J Stud Int Educ 17:663–676, 2013). Furthermore, as English has been officially adopted as the ASEAN lingua franca since 1967 (Kirkpatrick in English as a lingua franca in ASEAN. Hong Kong University Press, Hong Kong, 2010), relevant authorities of English education in Thailand have been faced with tasks to equip citizens with English language skills required in this globalized world. As a result, English has become a significant part of various Thai language education policies over the last 30 years. However, in spite of tremendous efforts made by the government to improve Thai citizens' English skills, the effectiveness of English education policies has been viewed as very mixed (Kaur et al. in English language education policy in Asia. Springer International Publishing, Cham, 2016). In this chapter, we propose that two of the causes of this perceived lack of success are an unrealistic focus on Anglophone "native speaker" English and a lack of recognition of the multilingual landscape and translanguaging practices in Thailand in general and in Thai education in particular. Until now, very little investigation has been done in terms of translanguaging in EMI in the Thai context. This chapter aims to explore to what extent multilingualism is recognized by the Thai government and three major Thai universities by looking into English language policies on websites and documents publicly displayed. We sought to understand underlying language ideologies within the policies and consider how these might be informed by translanguaging and ELF theory. Findings suggest that bilingual, Thai, English, policies and the recognition of English as an ASEAN lingua franca have become more conspicuous in both the Thai government's general and HE policies. They also commonly put emphasis on harmonizing diversity and building networking relations with ASEAN. However, this seems to be only superficial and has not been reflected in actual language policies.

J. J. Ra (✉)
Research Institute for Languages and Cultures of Asia, Mahidol University, Nakhon, Thailand

W. Baker
Centre for Global Englishes, University of Southampton, Southampton, UK

W. Tsou and W. Baker (eds.), *English-Medium Instruction Translanguaging Practices in Asia*, https://doi.org/10.1007/978-981-16-3001-9_4

1   Introduction

Since the 1990s, Thai HE has embarked on internationalization processes and the Thai government has initiated an increase in the number of EMI (English Medium Instruction) courses (Lavankura, 2013). Furthermore, English has been officially adopted as the ASEAN lingua franca since 1967 (Kirkpatrick, 2010) and it has been particularly important for relevant authorities of English education in Thailand to equip citizens with the English language proficiency needed to partake in ASEAN. This has resulted in English forming a significant part of various incarnations of Thai language education policy over the last 30 years. However, in spite of tremendous efforts made by the government to improve Thai citizens' English skills, the effectiveness of English education policies has been viewed as very mixed (Kaur, Young, & Kirkpatrick, 2016). The reasons behind this perceived lack of success in English education policy are multiple but in this chapter, we argue that two of the causes are an unrealistic focus on Anglophone "native speaker" English and a lack of recognition of the multilingual landscape of Thailand in general and of Thai education in particular.

To support this argument, we draw on recent work on translanguaging pedagogy (García & Li, 2014) which emphasizes the importance of incorporating multilingual resources into pedagogic practice and policy. We also situate the chapter within English as a lingua franca (ELF) research as ELF scholars have argued for a shift from native speaker models to more localized and flexible forms of English as part of a repertoire of multilingual resources (Jenkins, 2015). Recent ELF research has also explored the relevance of ELF to EMI in an increasing variety of settings and stressed the need for more recognition of local uses of English and multilingualism in both policy and practice (Jenkins, 2014; Jenkins & Mauranen, 2019). For example, ELF scholars have suggested incorporating multilingual approaches (e.g. translanguaging) into language policies in EMI programs where there tend to be students of diverse L1s who use English as an additional language (e.g. Baker & Hüttner, 2019; Jenkins & Mauranen, 2019; Murata, 2018). Despite the fact that language education policies, in general, draw strict lines between separate languages, it is often the opposite case in actual classroom settings where multilingual practices are frequent (García & Li, 2014). Accordingly, recognizing translanguaging in language policies would legitimize classroom practices that have already take place.

Until now, very little investigation has been done in terms of translanguaging in EMI in the Thai context. Therefore, this chapter aims to explore to what extent multilingualism is recognized by major Thai universities and the government by examining English language policies through websites and documents publicly displayed. We focus on the formal policy level as it through official policy that underlying language ideologies, such as monolingualism or multilingualism, are manifested and put into practice (Shohamy, 2006). We also consider how this might be informed by translanguaging and ELF theory and provide implications for future EMI policies and practices in Thailand.

2 Translanguaging, Pedagogy, and Policy

A discussion of translanguaging theory is not the focus of this chapter (and is discussed in detail elsewhere in this book), however, it will be helpful to make clear the perspective adopted in this chapter. Here we follow Li Wei's definition of translanguaging as "the fluid and dynamic practices that transcend the boundaries between named languages, language varieties, and language and other semiotic systems" (2018, p. 9). For García and Kleyn (2016) translanguaging entails a shift in perspective from external socially constructed categories of named languages, e.g. English, Chinese, Arabic, to an internal linguistic perspective for individuals. In the case of bilinguals this may consist of features from many different externally "named" languages, which are part of one unified linguistic system for the bilingual user. For instance, the second author of this chapter lives in a bilingual household in which words such as " ข้าว," "chicken," " น้ำส้ม," and "toast" are commonly used in the kitchen. From an external perspective, these words would be associated with "Thai" and "English" but from the internal perspective, they are just the words used to discuss various foods in the kitchen in this house.

A translanguaging perspective has fundamental implications for education. Most significantly, it begins from the perspective outlined above, that bilingual students have a range of linguistic resources which are not distinguished according to named languages. As García and Kleyn (2016, p. 15) explain,

> we start to teach bilingual children from a different place. It means that we start from a place that leverages all the features of the children's repertoire, while also showing them when, with whom, where, and why to use some features of their repertoire and not others, enabling them to perform according to the social norms of named languages as used in schools.

Although García and Kleyn are referring to school education here, we believe that such a perspective is equally relevant to HE in which bilingual students are present, as is the case with EMI programs. Translanguaging approaches to education are, therefore, different from bilingual approaches which typically have separated language systems taught at separate times, in separate subjects and/or by separate teachers. In contrast, in translanguaging education the full linguistic repertoire of students should be used through pedagogic strategies including translation, reading multilingual texts, multilingual listening/visual resources, multilingual writing, multilingual vocabulary inquiry, multilingual syntax/morphology inquiry, and translanguaging in writing and speaking (García & Li, 2014, p. 120). However, this does not ignore the importance of external classifications of named languages and, as the previous quote made clear, students should be made aware of "when, with whom, where, and why" particular aspects of their linguistic repertoire can be appropriately used or not. For instance, students may research and read information for a task in a range of languages but be asked to write an essay in only one named language.

Translanguaging perspectives and pedagogic practices also entail a change in language education policies. While many education policies strictly separate languages, following a bilingual education model, García and Li argue that "students and teachers constantly violate this principle" (2014, p. 52). More appropriate then is a language education policy that recognizes translanguaging and gives it a legitimate place in education so as to validate practices that are already part of teaching and learning. As with pedagogic strategies, this does not rule out policies that allow spaces for named languages, which is especially important with minority language education. Neither does a translanguaging education policy deny the necessity of focusing on a single named language for particular tasks or purposes (e.g. assessment). Nonetheless, it does suggest that language education policies need to adopt more "porous" borders between the named languages they address (García & Kleyn, 2016, p. 28). In an empirical study of ESL education in New York schools, Menken and Sánchez (2019) show how the introduction of translanguaging pedagogic practices leads to a disruption of the monolingual language ideologies in the schools. This resulted in a significant shift to multilingual language education policies in a number of the schools, through formalizing the use of translanguaging strategies in classes and/or the introduction of new bilingual programs to make the most of students' L1s.[1]

We believe that such findings in relation to translanguaging from the school level are likely to be applicable to HE and EMI were given a number of similarities between them. Firstly, like bilingual and multilingual schools, in EMI programs English is typically an additional language for the students and there may also be diverse L1s in international programs. Secondly, in EMI and bilingual schooling, there is a focus on content rather than language in terms of outcomes. Thirdly, in both EMI and bilingual schooling, there are internal and external monolingual pressures such as examinations and ideologies in wider society. From a HE perspective, there is an increasing amount of research, particularly in the field of ELF/EFLA (English as a lingua franca in academia), highlighting the multilingual nature of EMI, including translanguaging, and the need to incorporate this in a substantial manner into university policies (e.g., Baker & Hüttner, 2019; Jenkins & Mauranen, 2019; Murata, 2018). However, at present, there is still little research explicitly exploring the links between translanguaging and language education policies in EMI.

3   English in Language Education Policy, Higher Education, and EMI in Thailand

Although Thailand is often portrayed as monolingual and monocultural (National Identity Board, 2000), it is linguistically and culturally diverse with an estimated 70 minority languages and associated varieties including, various Chinese dialects, Malay, Lao, Khmer, Burmese, and Mon (Premsrirat, 2014). Standard Thai is the language of education, government, and the media; however, Thai can be divided into three distinct varieties with Northern' Thai (e.g., Kham Muang), "Southern"

---

[1] Menken and Sánchez (2019, p. 760) recognise the problems of bilingual programmes maintaining separations between named languages, but claim that a bilingual approach was the most suitable under state regulations and the teachers employed translanguaging teaching strategies.

Thai (e.g. Pak Tai), and "Central" Thai (which forms the standard variety). Therefore, it is estimated that for between one in ten and one in fifteen of the population, "standard" Thai is an L2 (Warotamasikkhadit & Person, 2011). Within this multilingual landscape, English has been positioned as the predominant "foreign" language for over a century as a means of connecting politically, economically, academically, and culturally with the rest of the world (Baker & Jarunthawatchai, 2017). The place of English in Thai society has increased further in recent decades with the use of English as the official language of ASEAN (Association of southeast Asian Nations) and ASEAN +3 (China, Japan, S. Korea) (Kirkpatrick, 2010). Furthermore, English is also used extensively in Thailand's large tourism industry (Tourism Authority of Thailand, 2016). However, it is important to note that English is positioned as a lingua franca in Thailand. English is viewed as an "outside" language and there has been strong resistance to giving it any official status in policy (Baker & Jarunthawatchai, 2017). Moreover, English is predominantly used with other L2 users of English (rather than native English speakers), most obviously through ASEAN but also in regards to the large number of tourists from East Asia. At the same time though, the "outside" role of English is complicated by its "internal" use among urban, middle classes in bilingual and EMI education programs, in the media and advertising, electronic communication, and social media, and its extensive presences in urban linguistic landscapes (Baker & Jarunthawatchai, 2017; Huebner, 2006; Seargeant, Tagg, & Ngampramuan, 2012). Nonetheless, it should also be noted that the spread of English is quite uneven and it has much less prominence both in general and in education in rural settings (Draper, 2012).

Unsurprisingly this extensive role for English in Thai society has been reflected in education and educational language policy. English is a compulsory "prescribed" foreign language in primary and secondary education with other foreign languages optional (OBEC, 2008). The importance of English language education was further increased in response to greater ASEAN integration. This was most prominent through the MOE (Ministry of Education) "Thailand English Teaching Project" with the objective to have Thai students prepare for "ASEAN community 2015." This project aimed to improve Thai school students' English proficiency by having British undergraduates teach English at Thai schools for three months. Currently, English is still listed as one of the four foci of the policies of the Ministry of Education (MOE Thailand, 2017). There has also been a rapid expansion over the last decade in bilingual English-Thai programs, in part, supported by government policies to increase English proficiency (Kaur et al., 2016). In specific relation to higher education, again English has had a significant role for some time, particularly as regards its function as a "core" subject in entrance exams and also as a required subject to be passed before graduation in many institutions (Baker & Jarunthawatchai, 2017). Further discussion of recent government policies as regards HE is provided in the analysis section below. In sum, English has been given an important place in language education policies at all levels from primary to HE resulting in an education environment that is predominantly bilingual with Thai as the national L1 and English as the main "foreign" language. Furthermore, while there is increasing recognition of English used in ASEAN as a lingua franca, there is still an orientation to Anglophone Englishes as shown by the recruitment of British English teachers in the "Thailand English Teaching Project."

Similar to many other settings both in Asia and worldwide alongside the expansion of English in Thai higher education, has been an increase in international programs with the two treated as synonymous and the majority of international programs in Thailand being EMI (MOE, 2017). It has been reported that by 2014, Thai HE institutions offered 769 international programs (EMI courses) at both undergraduate and postgraduate levels (MOE, 2017). The internationalization of HE has been part of the government agenda since the 1990s underpinned by a variety of rationales. Lavankura (2013) divides this internationalization into three phases firstly, during the economic boom of the late 1980s and 1990s internationalization was underpinned by a predominantly economic rationale and global competitiveness; secondly, following the economic crisis of the late 1990s internationalization was re-interpreted to focus inwardly on how it might benefit localization and Thai identity in a globalized world; thirdly, current policy has oriented to a more global outlook again but more specifically focused on ASEAN and Asia with the aim of making Thailand a regional educational hub. Nonetheless, the majority of students enrolled in this "international" EMI programs remain Thai students (Lavankura, 2013). Despite the increasingly important role of internationalization and EMI programs there are currently very few studies looking at either policies or practices in EMI in Thailand (see Hengsadeekul, Koul, & Kaewkuekool, 2014; Baker & Hüttner, 2017, 2019; Sameephet, 2020 for exceptions).

4   Investigating Current Policies

To investigate the role of English, multilingualism and translanguaging in HE further and to explore the degree to which the macro-level linguistic landscape described previously influences particular contexts and programs, we now turn to the study of language policies as regards current government HE policies and the policies of a select number of prominent Thai HE institutes with extensive international programs. The policies are drawn from publically accessible websites since they are a particularly fruitful source of overt information on language policies (Baker & Hüttner, 2019; Jenkins, 2014; Jenkins, Baker, Doubleday, & Wang, 2019; Saarinen & Nakula, 2013). At both government and HE institutional levels, they provide an important source of information for key stakeholders. Furthermore, through being publically accessible they also offer a window for an "outside" audience providing both information and marketing. As such the content is likely to be carefully controlled by government and university management to ensure it reflects current approaches and perspectives on language policy (Jenkins, 2014).

The study is theoretically grounded in Spolsky's (2009) tripartite extended language policy model comprised of language practices, beliefs, and management. We will examine language management defined as "the explicit and observable effort by someone or some group that has or claims authority over the participants in the domain to modify their practices or beliefs" (Spolsky, 2009, p. 4). Language management includes formal policy documents such as government and institutional (i.e., universities) language and education policies. Management is an especially worthwhile level to focus on as it is through the overt mechanisms of formal education and language policy that explicit attempts to turn language ideologies into language practices are manifested (Shohamy, 2006). However, as a caveat and limitation, it is important to note, as Spolsky (2009) does, that language management is not always successful and does not translate "automatically" into beliefs and practices, particularly when it is in conflict with existing language beliefs and practices. Qualitative content and discourse analysis were implemented for analyzing language policies and keywords/phrases related to internationalization and language found on government and university websites. Discourse analysis was conducted to identify to what extent multilingualism is accepted in language policies if there is any adherence to NSEs regarding English references and to draw out underlying language ideologies based on texts which include international and English references (Jenkins, 2014; Jenkins et al., 2019).

In order to analyze the Thai government's language policies, the websites of the Thai Ministry of Education (MOE) and its branches: the Office of Higher Education Commission (OHEC), the Ministry of Higher Education, Science, Research and Innovation (MHESI) and the Office of the Basic Education Commission (OBEC) have been investigated. Any parts that were only displayed in the Thai language were translated by a native Thai academic. Sections on language policies on the websites and downloadable documents were examined. Taking into account the criteria of Times Higher Education and QS World University Rankings, three of the most prestigious universities in Thailand were chosen for analysis: Mahidol, Chulalongkorn, and Chiang Mai. The overall university rankings, which included international impact, and the number of international students were two important factors considered for selection. For analyzing university websites, initial data were recorded on a word document and this was reorganized and classified into four themes: (1) main university websites, (2) general information on international programs, (3) specific international program outlines, and (4) admission requirements. The selected universities have their main website and each program has its own website separately. The university and international program websites generally do not display specific language policies on teaching or assessment. Therefore, the majority of information collected is based on aims, missions, history, and marketing of the universities, outlines of selected programs, and their admissions policies from the English version of the websites. An overview of the websites and sources of data collection is in Table 1.

Table 1 Data collection sites and sources

Organization	Number of international students/programs (2019/2020)	Data collection faculties/programs	Data collection areas/sections
Mahidol University	Number of international students: 1358 (Total: 29,209) Number of international programs: 49	Undergraduate level: – Biomedical Engineering – Chemical Engineering – Actuarial Science – Industrial Mathematics – International college (Humanities & Language, Business Administration, Tourism & Hospitality Management)	– University's main website: main webpage, *News and Events. About, Current students, General admissions* sections – International program websites: *About, Admissions, Courses* sections
Chulalongkorn University	Number of international students: 731 (Total: 37,880) Number of international programs: 101	Undergraduate level: – Business Administration – Nano Engineering – Language and Culture Postgraduate level: – Southeast Asian Studies	– University's main website: main webpage, *About. Admissions, News & Knowledge, Academics (Life at CU)* sections – International program websites: *About. Admissions, Prospective students, Courses, Curriculum, News* sections
Chiang Mai University	Number of international students: 1037 (Total: 32,992) Number of international programs: 40	Undergraduate level: – Business Administration – College of Art – Media and Technology Postgraduate level: – Graduate School Faculty	– University's main website: *About, News, Studying at CMU (Application of International Program)* – International program websites: *About, Admissions, News*
Ministry of Education, Thailand (MOE)	NA	NA	– Office of Higher Education Commission (OHEC) – Ministry of Higher Education, Science, Research and Innovation (MHESI) – Office of the Basic Education Commission (OBEC)

5 Findings from Current Policies

5.1 Recent Government Language Policy Documents on Higher Education

In 2013, the Ministry of Education (MOE), Thailand introduced its aims and strategies for improving English language proficiency among staff and students in Thai HE. The MOE laid out reasons for improving English proficiency at Thai universities. Some relevant ones are: "[m]obility and exchanges for students/staff/researchers, [i]nternational and intercultural understanding and [d]iversity source of faculty and students." Many of the strategies were for preparing Thai HE for ASEAN, such as to: "[p]roduce graduates of international quality, [r]eform language education (English and neighboring country's languages), [e]xtend role of Thai HE in ASEAN and [w]ork closely with AUN, SEMEAO, RIHED etc." Furthermore, one of MOE's (OHEC branch) projects to enhance English proficiency in Thai HE is the "Teaching and learning in English and neighboring country's languages." This project aims to "[i]mprove English teaching class[es] to meet the demand of ASEAN, [p]romote neighboring country's languages teaching; Bahasa, Burmese, Laos and Vietnamese, [d]evelop English skills among students, teachers and education staff." The role of English was further enhanced in 2016 when the Commission of Higher Education announced a policy to upgrade English language standards in HE through new and more extensive university English language policies, ELT practices and assessment of students' English language proficiency (Baker & Jarunthawatchai, 2017).

. The Office of the Education Council, MOE has also presented a national report on education development in 2017 and they have a particular section on international education. They have strong intentions to develop international education in both secondary and higher education in the country and to promote this area globally. While English is the only medium of instruction at most international schools and international programs at universities, a few international schools include the Chinese language as well. The number of international programs and colleges at universities has been continuously on the rise. It has been reported that by 2014, Thai HE institutions offered 769 international programs (EMI courses) at both undergraduate and postgraduate levels.

Most recently, MOE has adopted an adapted version of the Common European Framework of Reference for Languages (CEFR) as a means of conceptualizing and gauging English proficiency at all levels of education (Hiranburana et al., 2017). An examination of several other recent government language policy documents including the "Draft National Language Strategy Plan 2560–2564" and "Policy and Strategy of Thailand HESI," is similar to the earlier policies in placing Thai as the first language but also recognizing some minority languages, as well as regional languages. There is a reference to "foreign languages" to help the Thai economy but the policies contained no specific mentions of English or other languages at the HE level and so policy appears to remain unchanged.

5.2   University Websites

5.2.1   Mahidol University

Main website

The main page predominantly focuses on advertising university facilities and world rankings. The university's world ranking from several reputable sources is displayed on sliders. Although the investigated website is the English version, the Thai language is extensively present especially on *News* and *Events* headlines. Overall, not much diversity is seen on the main website compared to how multilingual and multicultural the university is (see below). The majority of images on the website are of Southeast Asian ethnicity but international student-related pages only show Caucasians. Furthermore, the university's website supports only the Thai and English language and these are represented by the Thai and British flag respectively. There are various international references on the *About* page. For example, the university is "determined to be a world class university" and the *strategies* section include keywords such as "[i]nternationalization," "[h]armony in diversity" and "[l]isting of global problems and local solutions." The university also emphasizes both its regional and global connections but particularly specifies its networks with ASEAN such as the ASEAN University Network (AUN) and Asia-Pacific Association for International Education (APAIE). The *current students* page has a dedicated section for international students. On this page, students can download a handbook that includes various information about Thailand and it encourages international students to find a Thai/local buddy to learn more about Thailand and Thai culture.

International programs

On the general admissions for international programs page (on the main website), it lists all international programs but the majority of the information is in Thai. Prospective students who do not speak Thai, need to go into each program's English website for more detailed information on the curriculum and admissions in English. At Mahidol, there are majors that have both Thai and international programs. These are mainly science and engineering majors. The university also has *International College* which is a faculty with several programs in sciences, social sciences, arts and humanities, and the curriculum is dealt in English.

The international programs (which also have Thai programs) that have been examined are *Biomedical Engineering, Chemical Engineering, Actuarial Science* and *Industrial Mathematics*. There are international references in the outlines of programs. For example, one of the objectives of the Biomedical Engineering undergraduate program is to analyze and solve "international problems related to ASEAN based on knowledge from biomedical engineering," and for Actuarial Science, the students are to be equipped with English for "employment in international organizations." The Chemical Engineering undergraduate program website mentions that they have partnerships with "world class" universities and research collaborations with both national and "international" institutions.

In terms of undergraduate admissions, all four programs require English proficiency test results and the minimum scores slightly vary depending on each program. The types of tests that are accepted include IELTS, TOEFL-ITP, TOEFL-IBT, SAT and MU Grad/MU-ELT tests which are run by Mahidol. Prospective students also need to submit a copy of their high school diploma; however, the Chemical Engineering program only lists diplomas from the American, British, and Thai education system. For the Industrial Mathematics program, prospective students in Thailand must pass an entrance examination and interview, and the written examination concerns Mathematics and English.

International College (MUIC)

There is a central website for all *International College* programs. The main page focuses on marketing and recruitment displaying how international MUIC is with a list of "awarded world-class accreditation." The students and lecturers that appear on this website are of either Caucasian or Southeast Asian ethnicities. Despite that there are 28 different nationalities within the faculty, (see "fast facts" below which is mentioned on the main page), the website only supports English and Thai language which again are represented by the British and Thai flag, respectively.

Fast Facts

33	28	3,606	9,569
Years of Operation	Nationalities of Faculty and Students	Students	Alumni

On the admissions requirements page (for both prospective undergraduate and postgraduate students), it states "[n]on-native English speaking applicants must submit official results from either the TOEFL iBT or Copy of IELTS Academic with at least 2 years' validity." This faculty does not accept the university's MU tests.

Three undergraduate programs in this faculty have been investigated which are *Humanities and Language, Business Administration*, and *Tourism and Hospitality Management*. All three program outlines strongly highlight their relevance to international society and global citizenship. Some keywords mentioned on the programs' information pages are "diverse international faculty," "global citizenship," "internationally relevant," "competent global citizens," "excel in the global arena," "international reputation," and "cultural sensitivity."

In conclusion, the university as a whole and individual international programs seem to put importance on harmonizing diversity and particularly emphasize on ASEAN relations. They frequently make international connections in the outlines of the programs. However, language policies outlined on the university's and programs' webpages do not reflect this and are rather bilingual language policies: Thai and English. No other language is mentioned other than these two languages. Moreover, English seems to be perceived by underlying native speaker ideologies. For example, entrance exams are NES-oriented, the English language support tab on the university and *International College* websites use the British flag and certain international programs only list the American and British education systems for high school diplomas that need to be submitted.

5.2.2 Chulalongkorn University

Main website

Chulalongkorn University's main page advertises its world rankings from various sources and it also emphasizes on being a "green" university. On the English version of the website, every part is in English and there is no Thai detected. The ethnicities of students are portrayed as Southeast Asian, East Asian, or Caucasians. The university has an introductory video which is the first content visitors can see on the *About* page. The narrator in the 8-min-long video speaks with an American accent and Thai people's interviews are subtitled in English. In the video, the university includes references such as "the forefront of the international community" and "local transformation, global benchmarking." The university's priority addressed in the video is about developing local communities to be part of the global community. There are several international references found on the *About* page. For example, the university's vision is "[t]o be the world-class university, generating knowledge and innovation for the creative and sustainable transformation of Thai society." Some of the university's *Action Plans* are to "[d]evelop graduates that are valuable citizens of the country and the world," "[e]ncourage the production of academic research, output and creativity that will resolve or are in line with the global issues raised" and "[p]ush for better education, matching international standards." On the university's *News* page, there is a section on "International Partnerships" where it contains news related to international collaborations, international relations or any type of international events happening at the university. Furthermore, there is no particular section for international students but there is a *Life at CU* tab where these students can learn more about Thailand.

International programs

The general admissions page for international programs displays only Caucasian students. There is a list of international programs on this page with accessible links and no other information is found. International programs have their own websites and they also have Facebook pages which makes it easier for prospective/current students to communicate with the administration staff. International programs that have been examined are *Business Administration, Nano Engineering, Language and Culture* and *Southeast Asian Studies* (master's). The outlines of the programs use international references but they also link them to the local context. Some examples are "commitment to Thailand, the Asia-Pacific region and the global community," "to produce world class international engineers," "by offering cutting edge programs that address global and local challenges," and "international engagement and community involvement offered by the program."

The *Language and Culture* program additionally mentions their focus on "English along with foreign language competence" and "diversify[ing] and globaliz[ing] the program" by accepting exchange students from "many universities around the world." Although detailed descriptions cannot be found on the taught courses, the program seems to reflect the diversity of language and cultures in global contexts. The program provides courses such as "Global Cultures," "Language in Socio-cultural Contexts," "Public Speaking in Multicultural Society," "Culture and Economy in Global Contexts," and also eight different foreign language courses other than English. For the *Southeast Asian Studies* program, there is no inclusion of languages other than English on the *About Us* page or course outlines although the program concentrates on ASEAN-related issues. However, the program offers some Southeast Asian language courses (Burmese and Vietnamese) to the general public and university students.

In terms of admissions, the *Nano Engineering* program mentions that "[a]pplicants must have completed high school, passed an equivalent high school standard test, or be currently in their final year of high school (Grade 12 in the US system or year 13 in the British system)." Language requirements slightly differ among the programs and they accept TOEFL, IELTS, SAT and local tests offered by the university. The *Southeast Asian Studies* program also requires a "strong command of English" along with IELTS and TOEFL scores except for students from English speaking countries: "Britain, USA, Canada, Australia and New Zealand." The *Business Administration* and *Language and Culture* programs also mention that applicants need to pass interviews conducted in English.

In sum, several international references are present on the Chulalongkorn University main website and international program information pages. In addition, the university advertises its ongoing contribution to sustainability and local communities. Same as Mahidol, only Thai and English languages are supported on the university and program websites and NES orientations to English are noticed in language policies. Moreover, language policies displayed on program websites, in general, lacks diversity and this goes the same for *Language and Culture* and *Southeast Asian Studies* programs. However, multilingualism and multiculturalism are recognized in the two programs' course contents. For the language admissions requirement, the university includes TOEFL and IELTS as well as their local tests.

5.2.3 Chiang Mai University

Main website

The main website of Chiang Mai University supports the Chinese language alongside Thai and English. Similar to Chulalongkorn's website, there is no dedicated section for international students. On Chiang Mai's main website, international or internationalization references are not as frequently seen as Mahidol or Chulalongkorn

University websites. For example, the main page has only one single international reference "global citizen" and the rest draws its attention to developing sustainability, greenness, and local communities. On the *About CMU* page, the university mentions its vision to become "a world class [u]niversity committed to social responsibility and create a [d]evelopment for sustainable excellence." Key phrases found on the university's *Mission* are "social and economic development of the region and the country," "[p]reserve and nurture our religious and cultural heritage," and "sustainably develop the resources…of Northern Thailand."

International programs

For international programs, the admissions requirements (including language proficiency) are the same for all undergraduate international programs. Applicants who are "[n]on-native English speakers or from a country where English is not an official language" must submit official English test certificates and IELTS, TOEFL, TOEIC, and CMU-English test results are accepted. Furthermore, applicants need to submit their high school certification which is equivalent to Thailand's high school diploma and the web page only lists GED (American) and GCSE (British) results and, the New Zealand national certificate for comparison.

The Graduate School faculty website states that "English language is used as one of the foreign language conditions" but no other language proficiency tests are mentioned.

The websites of faculties with international programs which have been investigated are *Business Administration, College of Art, Media and Technology*, and the *Graduate School* faculty. Unlike Chiang Mai University's main focus to develop local communities especially in the Northern Thailand region, the faculty websites include various international references such as "being equipped with modern and international body of knowledge on business administration that suits well with [the] Thai society," "contributing to…internationalization of business administration," "can apply innovative knowledge into an international environment," and "to achieve global literacy for all students."

Overall, Chiang Mai University and individual faculties, in general, put as much importance on sustainability and contributing to local communities as developing students' global competence. However, English is the only language dealt with in the international program curriculums and language admissions requirements. Yet, the university seems to have considered a large number of Chinese international students in Thailand HE and included a Chinese version of the main university website.

6 Discussion

6.1 Government Policy

The extent to which the language education policies analyzed above align with the multilingual landscape of Thailand, the use of English as a lingua franca and translanguaging practices in HE would appear limited. A previous draft language policy appeared to signal a greater recognition of multilingualism and other important regional languages such as Chinese and Japanese (Warotamasikkhadit & Person, 2011); however, this never made it into the final policy (Srichampa, Burarungrot, & Samoh, 2018), and while a recent draft policy also adopts some of this recognition of multilingualism it has also not become official policy. In contrast, recent trends suggest a strengthening of a bilingual Thai, English policy, as seen in the analysis of many of the general and HE policies described above. There is some shift away from the Anglophone world in terms of the focus of English and much greater recognition of English as a language of ASEAN in current policies and, indeed, this is frequently explicitly cited as one of the core drivers for the expansion of English (Baker & Jarunthawatchai, 2017). Nonetheless, this has not been matched by recognition in policy that English in ASEAN will be ELF, in multilingual settings, alongside other languages, and with different norms to "native" English use. The adoption of the CEFR framework further adds to this native English speaker orientation with its frequent references to native-speaker norms and lack of recognition of ELF (Pitzl 2015). While updated formulations of CEFR incorporate more pluralingualism, these elements have not been taken up in Thai policies (Savski, 2019). Furthermore, there is a perception in Thailand that English proficiency is low which forms part of the drive for increased English language education and frequent policy updates (Hiranburana et al., 2017; Savski, 2019). Yet, these perceptions are based on inappropriate native English speaker-based test scores and a strong monolingual English native speaker ideology which is at odds with the multilingual and multicultural settings in which English functions in Thailand (Baker & Jarunthawatchai, 2017). We argue that ELF and translanguaging perspectives provide a more suitable approach to conceptualizing English use for policy and practices, particularly in international HE in which multilingualism and multicultural settings and outlooks are the norms. At present though, while multilingualism is at least recognized nationally and regionally, the main driver of government policy appears to be a bilingual Thai and English approach underpinned by a monolingual, standard language, native speaker ideology.

6.2 University Websites

Overall, not much flexibility has been detected regarding the three universities' language policies portrayed on their websites. Compared to the universities' emphasis on embracing diversity and strengthening ASEAN relations, rather bilingual language policies (Thai and English) are featured on the websites. All three universities only accept English proficiency test results for their admissions language requirements but they include their own university's English tests (i.e., MU, CU, CMU) other than IELTS and TOEFL. English is the only language mentioned in the outlines and curriculums of the programs while most programs highlight developing students' "global competence" or "global citizenship" so that they become "world-class" graduates. Even in *Language and Culture* and *Southeast Asian Studies* programs where students are expected to enhance cultural awareness in global contexts, English is the only language dealt with for admissions and for the majority of taught courses. However, the contents of the *Language and Culture* program courses appear to reflect the diversity of language and cultures in global contexts.

Furthermore, no actual evidence of orientations to translanguaging has been identified in the universities' language policies. According to the Bureau of International Cooperation Strategy (2018), the majority of international students in Thai HE are from China (nearly 40%) followed by students from Myanmar, Cambodia, Vietnam, and Lao PDR (Nomnian, 2018). This statistic implies that multilingualism and translanguaging are likely to be present in EMI classrooms at Thai universities, although, they are not recognized in language policies found on university and program websites. Indeed, a recent study of an EMI program in Thailand (Baker & Hüttner, 2017, 2019) revealed extensive translanguaging and multilingualism in teaching and learning practices, but as found here, little recognition of this in university policy. It would, thus, appear that the type of bottom-up transformation toward translanguaging language education policies documented by Menken and Sánchez (2019) has not yet occurred in Thai HE. In conclusion, similar to the findings of Thai government policies, multilingualism is perceived on the surface level (e.g., missions and aims of courses) at the three universities; however, when looking deeper into language policies, only Thai and English language are noticed. Moreover, English at the universities has been framed within native speaker ideologies and has been yet to be understood as a global lingua franca (see Jenkins and Mauranen (2019) for similar findings in a range of EMI settings). While Chiang Mai University still made an effort to support a third language (Chinese) on their website, all three universities in general lack commitment to diversity (in terms of language and culture) compared to the amount of international references exhibited on websites. Given that the three chosen universities have the largest number of international students and programs in Thailand and that the number of incoming students especially from China and Southeast Asia is increasing, we suggest that language policies at the HE level reflect this phenomenon and take into account ELF, translanguaging and multilingualism approach, particularly within international programs.

7 Conclusion

This chapter aimed to explore to what extent multilingualism is recognized by the Thai government and three major Thai universities by looking into English language policies on websites and documents publicly displayed. We sought to understand underlying language ideologies within the policies and consider how these might be informed by translanguaging and ELF theory. For the government language policies, websites of MOE Thailand and its branches: OHEC, MHESI and OBEC have been examined, and this was followed by an investigation of Mahidol, Chulalongkorn, Chiang Mai university's main websites and websites of selected international programs.

Findings reveal that bilingual, Thai, English, policies and the recognition of English as an "ASEAN" lingua franca have become more conspicuous in both the Thai government's general and HE policies. Furthermore, the three universities in general aim to cultivate their students to become "global" or "world-class" citizens and the awareness of multilingualism and multiculturalism is also very apparent on their websites. They also commonly put emphasis on harmonizing diversity and building networking relations with ASEAN. However, despite the various references in relation to multilingualism, diversity, and global citizenship exposed on the government and university websites, this seems to be only superficial and has not been reflected on actual language policies.

Overall, there is a lack of language diversity at the government and university policy level despite the fact that English has been adopted as the ASEAN lingua franca for decades and that the number of incoming international students particularly from China and Southeast Asia is steadily increasing. As Garcia and Kleyn (2016) suggest, language education policies ought to view language in a more flexible manner and make efforts to embrace multilingual approaches. This can start from disassociating native speaker ideologies and infusing ELF and translanguaging perspectives within English language policies. There is a need for more studies that look at translanguaging in EMI in the Thai context. Further research which explores language practices and perspectives in EMI classrooms in Thai HE would facilitate the understanding of translanguaging practices that occur among the students and the lecturer regardless of what the language policies outline. We argue that the accumulation of such research that reflects the reality of language diversity in Thai EMI settings could progressively inform updated language policy and EMI practices.

References

Baker, W., & Hüttner, J. (2017). English and more: A multisite study of roles and conceptualisations of language in English medium multilingual universities from Europe to Asia. *Journal of Multilingual and Multicultural Development, 38*(6), 501–516. https://doi.org/10.1080/01434632.2016.1207183

Baker, W., & Hüttner, J. (2019). "We are not the language police": Comparing multilingual EMI programmes in Europe and Asia. *International Journal of Applied Linguistics, 29*(1), 78–94. https://doi.org/10.1111/ijal.12246

Baker, W., & Jarunthawatchai, W. (2017). English language policy in Thailand. *European Journal of Language Policy, 9*(1), 27–44.

Draper, J. (2012). Reconsidering compulsory English in developing countries in Asia: English in a community of Northeast Thailand. *TESOL Quarterly, 46*(4), 777–811.

García, O., & Kleyn, T. (Eds.). (2016). *Translanguaging with multilingual students.* Abingdon: Routledge.

García, O., & Li, W. (2014). *Translanguaging: Language, bilingualism and education.* Basingstoke: Palgrave Macmillan.

Hengsadeekul, C., Koul, R., & Kaewkuekool, S. (2014). Motivational orientation and preference for English-medium programs in Thailand. *International Journal of Educational Research, 66*, 35–44. https://doi.org/10.1016/j.ijer.2014.02.001

Hiranburana, K., Subphadoongchone, P., Tangkiengsirisin, S., Phoochaeoensil, S., Gainey, J., Thogsngsri, J., … Taylor, P. (2017). A framework of reference for English language education in Thailand (FRELE-TH)—based on the CEFR, The Thai experience. *LEARN Journal: Language Education and Acquisition Research Network Journal, 10*(2), 90–119.

Huebner, T. (2006). Bangkok's linguistic landscapes: Environmental print, codemixing and language change. *International Journal of Multilingualism, 3*(1), 31–51.

Jenkins, J. (2014). *English as a Lingua Franca in the international university. The politics of academic English language policy.* London: Routledge.

Jenkins, J. (2015). Repositioning English and multilingualism in English as a Lingua Franca. *Englishes in Practice, 2*(3), 49–85. https://doi.org/10.1515/eip-2015-0003

Jenkins, J., Baker, W., Doubleday, J., & Wang, Y. (2019). How much linguistic diversity in an English dominant UK university? In J. Jenkins & A. Mauranen (Eds.), *Linguistic diversity on the EMI campus* (pp. 226–260). Routledge.

Jenkins, J., & Mauranen, A. (Eds.). (2019). *Linguistic diversity on the EMI campus: Insider accounts of the use of English and other languages in universities within Asia, Australasia and Europe.* Abingdon: Routledge.

Kaur, A., Young, D., & Kirkpatrick, R. (2016). English education policy in Thailand: Why the poor results? In R. Kirkpatrick (Ed.), *English language education policy in Asia* (pp. 345–361). Cham: Springer International Publishing.

Kirkpatrick, A. (2010). *English as a lingua franca in ASEAN.* Hong Kong: Hong Kong University Press.

Lavankura, P. (2013). Internationalizing higher education in Thailand: Government and university responses. *Journal of Studies in International Education, 17*(5), 663–676. https://doi.org/10.1177/1028315313478193

Li, W. (2018). Translanguaging as a practical theory of language. *Applied Linguistics, 39*(1), 9–30. https://doi.org/10.1093/applin/amx039

Murata, K. (Ed.). (2018). *English-medium instruction from English as a Lingua Franca perspective: Exploring the higher education context.* Abingdon: Routledge.

Menken, K., & Sánchez, M. T. (2019). Translanguaging in English-only schools: From pedagogy to stance in the disruption of monolingual policies and practices. *TESOL Quarterly, 53*(3), 741–767. https://doi.org/10.1002/tesq.513

Ministry of Education, Thailand. (2017). Policy's focus point of Ministry of Education Thailand. Retrieved March, 2020, from http://www.en.moe.go.th/enMoe2017/index.php/policy-and-plan/policies-of-ministry-of-education.

National Identity Board. (2000). *Thailand into the 2000s.* Bangkok: Office of the Prime Minister.

Nomnian, S. (2018). *Synergizing transcultural learning of global Englishes: Voices of Chinese exchange students in a Thai university.* Bangkok: ELT education (Thailand).

Office of the Basic Education Commission, (OBEC). (2008). *Basic education core curriculum.* Bangkok: Bureau of Academic Affairs and Educational Standards.

Premsrirat, S. (2014, July). *Endangered languages in Thailand and SEA.* Paper presented at the Collaboration for language preservation and revitalisation in Asia, Mahidol University, Thailand.

Saarinen, T., & Nikula, T. (2013). Implicit policy, invisible language: Policies and practices of international degree programmes in Finnish higher education. In A. Doiz, D. Lasagabaster, & J. M. Sierra (Eds.), *English-medium instruction at universities: Global challenges* (pp. 131–150). Bristol: Multilingual Matters.

Sameephet, B. (2020). *On the fluidity of languages: A way out of the dilemma in English medium instruction classrooms in Thailand.* Doctor of Philosophy (Ph.D. thesis) Doctoral, The University of Waikato, Hamilton, New Zealand. Retrieved from https://hdl.handle.net/10289/13498.

Savski, K. (2019). Putting the Plurilingual/Pluricultural back into CEFR: Reflecting on policy reform in Thailand and Malaysia. *The Journal of Asia TEFL, 16*(2), 644–652.

Seargeant, P., Tagg, C., & Ngampramuan, W. (2012). Language choice and addressivity strategies in Thai–English social network interactions. *Journal of Sociolinguistics, 16*(4), 510–531.

Shohamy, E. G. (2006). *Language policy: Hidden agendas and new approaches.* Abingdon: Routledge.

Spolsky, B. (2009). *Language management.* Cambridge: Cambridge University Press.

Srichampa, S., Burarungrot, M., & Samoh, U. (2018). Language planning through policy in Thailand, Malaysia and Singapore for Unskilled migrant workers. *Journal of Language and Linguistics, 36*(2), 89–121.

Tourism Authority of Thailand (TOT). (2016). International tourist arrivals to Thailand in 2016 (by nationality and by country of residence). Retrieved March 20, 2017, from http://www.tatnews.org/images/press_kit/TTM%202013%20%20FINAL.pdf.

Warotamasikkhadit, U., & Person, K. (2011). Development of the national language policy (2006–2010): Committee to draft the national language policy. *The Journal of the Royal Institute of Thailand, III*, 29–44.

Jaewon Jane Ra is a lecturer at the Research Institute for Languages and Cultures of Asia (RILCA), Mahidol University, Thailand. Before Thailand, she has taught EAP courses at higher education level in the UK. At Mahidol, she currently teaches English as an international language, Qualitative research methods, ESP for teachers and EAP to students of different disciplines. She obtained her Ph.D. degree in Applied Linguistics from the University of Southampton, UK. Her research interests include Global Englishes, English as a lingua franca (ELF), English language teaching (ELT), intercultural communication, internationalization of higher education, intercultural citizenship, interculturality and translanguaging.

Will Baker is an Associate Professor of Applied Linguistics and Director of the Centre for Global Englishes at the University of Southampton, UK. His research interests are English as a Lingua Franca, Intercultural and Transcultural Communication, English medium instruction, Intercultural education, Intercultural Citizenship and ELT, and he has published and presented internationally in all these areas. His current research projects have focused on the links between Intercultural Citizenship, Internationalisation of HE and EMI including the recently completed "From English language learners to intercultural citizen" https://www.teachingenglish.org.uk/article/english-language-learners-intercultural-citizens. Recent publications include: Baker, W., & Ishikawa, T. *Transcultural Communication and Global Englishes: Exploring intercultural communication through English in a multilingual world.* (2021, Routledge), co-editor of the '*Routledge Handbook of English as a Lingua Franca*' (2018), author of the monograph '*Culture and Identity through English as a Lingua Franca*' (2015, DGM), and co-editor of the book series '*Developments in English as Lingua Franca*' (DGM).

Part III
Classrooms and Lectures' Practices and Perspectives

Chapter 5
Translanguaging Strategies for EMI Instruction in Taiwanese Higher Education

Shin-Mei Kao, Wenli Tsou, and Fay Chen

Abstract Using English as the medium of instruction (EMI) in content areas has become popular in Asian universities to attract international students. EMI teachers in Taiwanese universities, typically with little EMI pedagogical training, need to cope with students speaking different native languages with mixed English proficiency levels. Using multiple languaging resources with other modalities, or known as translanguaging, seems a promising approach to deal with the current challenges. This study investigated how eight EMI university teachers in Taiwan used different language resources to assist content delivery, student comprehension, and teacher–student interaction. Two strategies were identified from the discourse data: instructional and interactional. The former was used to enhance student comprehension of the content materials through translation and paraphrasing. The latter was used to engage students' participation and enhance communication fluency, but it may be less advantageous to students who are not competent in all the applied languaging resources. More instructional than interactional strategies were found in the data, though the difference between the two types was small. The study suggests that organizing in-service workshops for content teachers about the natures and effects of different translanguaging strategies may enhance EMI curriculum efficiency in higher education.

Keywords English as the medium of instruction (EMI) · Higher education · Translanguaging · Instructional strategies · Interactional strategies · Teacher training

1 Introduction: EMI in Asia and the Motivation of the Study

Higher education (HE) institutions around the world are adapting to pressures arising from internationalization. Responding to the call for changes, European universities

S.-M. Kao · W. Tsou (✉) · F. Chen
National Cheng Kung University, Taiwan, ROC
e-mail: wtsou@ncku.edu.tw

began to offer English Medium Instruction (EMI) courses in 1990s to accommodate the academic needs of increasing international students, to prepare domestic students for the global job market, and to raise the institutional profiles (Doiz, Lasagabaster, & Sierra, 2011). Asian universities caught up with the trend quickly, especially in the regions where English is traditionally taught as a foreign language (EFL). With strong government support, the quantities and varieties of EMI programs in Asian universities have greatly increased and become an important factor for international students when choosing their destinations of studies (Tsou & Kao, 2017).

Take Japan as an example. Japan's "Top Global University Project" (TGUP) launched in 2014, was sponsored by its Ministry of Education, Culture, Sports, Science and Technology (MEXT, 2020). One of the TGUP's goals is to offer quality EMI undergraduate- and graduate-level degree programs to attract excellent international students. In the past, international students must possess a Japanese language proficiency certificate of N1 (around B2 + on CEFR) for graduate studies, or N2 (around B2 on CEFR) for undergraduate studies in Japan (Rose & McKinley, 2018). With TGUP's new policy that no Japanese proficiency is required at the time of admission, the number of international students to Japanese HE institutes quickly increased from 138,075 in 2011, to 208,901 in 2018 (Japan Student Services Organization, 2019). Note that Japanese EMI programs primarily target at foreign students, so there are comparatively fewer local students studying together with international students.

Korea is taking a more aggressive approach to promote EMI in the HE system. Instead of offering special EMI programs for foreign students, some leading Korean universities, such as Korea Advanced Institute of Science and Technology (KAIST, #39 on the QS World University Rankings in 2021) and Pohang University of Science and Technology (POSTECH, #77 on the QS World University Rankings in 2021), decided to transfer a large part of their programs into EMI for all their students. Cho (2012) reported in a survey study that all academic courses in KAIST, including Korean history and Korean literature, were taught in English in 2006, and about 88% of undergraduate courses and 95% of graduate courses in POSTECH were taught in English in 2010. Positive and negative effects had been discussed among concerned stakeholders. On the one hand, the "English Only" policy was criticized for not taking local students' readiness and English proficiency into consideration (Byun et al., 2011); on the other hand, a more friendly environment for mobile students was quickly established in Korea (Bae, 2015). The government statistics reported a surge of international students from 91,332 in 2015 to 160,165 in 2019 (Koh & Kim, 2019).

Taiwanese universities took a more progressive approach in implementing EMI than the Japanese and Korean counterparts. In 2005, the Ministry of Education (MOE) of Taiwan launched the national-level "*Top University Program*" to promote internationalization in HE (Lawson, 2008). This program encouraged HE institutes to offer EMI courses extensively and to screen international students to Taiwan by their English, instead of Chinese proficiency. This policy brought a sharp surge in the total number of international degree-seeking students from 21,356 in 2010 to 56,788 in

2019 (Department of Statistics, MOE, 2019). The increasing enrollment of international students on campus brought new phases to the academic contexts in Taiwanese universities.

EMI courses in Taiwanese universities are generally open to both international and local students. This arrangement allows international students of various language and cultural backgrounds to quickly adapt to local academic environments and simultaneously provides local students the opportunities to communicate and learn content knowledge in English. EMI courses in Taiwanese universities are typically taught by local teachers with experience of studying abroad or with fluent command in English. In other words, English is used as a lingua franca (ELF) by teachers with local and international students in the classroom. Meanwhile, new challenges have emerged due to students' varied English proficiency levels, and the lack of pedagogical training for content specialists in delivering lectures (Kao & Tsou, 2017).

The study discussed in this chapter was originally motivated by observing EMI classes for developing teacher training workshops requested by some departments offering EMI programs extensively in the university where the researchers were based. The research team was invited to provide pedagogical suggestions to the content teachers from the viewpoints of language teachers after the observation. Therefore, the research team first recorded several class periods of each course while observing the instructional processes, and then transcribed and analyzed the classroom data. The phenomenon of using multiple languages with the support of other modalities for enhancing their instruction was found as one of the prominent strategies across all the EMI classes of different fields taught by different teachers. This chapter will discuss how these teachers used both English and Chinese Mandarin to carry out their instruction to a diverse student body with a large percentage of local Taiwanese students and a small percentage of international students from many different regions of the world. English was the lingua franca among all the participants in these classes, while Chinese Mandarin, was the common language used outside the classroom, as well as the shared first language (L1) of all the instructors and the local students.

The approach of using available linguistic, cognitive, and semiotic resources for teaching and learning, or translanguaging strategies (García & Li, 2014), has been widely discussed in bilingual education research at the primary or secondary level. However, research set in HE contexts, especially in ELF environments, only began in the past few years, with surveys and interviews as the primary research methods. This study chose discourse analysis to investigate the instructional strategies in terms of language choices in Taiwanese EMI content classes in engineering and creative industries. This chapter explores how translanguaging was realized naturally in teacher talks as pedagogical strategies to assist content delivery, student comprehension, and teacher-student interaction. The findings can extend our understanding of the pedagogical functions of translanguaging strategies for adult students to provide suggestions to EMI teachers for enhancing teaching efficiency in the classroom.

2   Literature Review

2.1   *Ideology Shift of Translanguaging*

Translanguaging has emerged as a new term in bilingual education and research. It values the use of multiple languages as facilitating resources of learning and communication (García & Li, 2014). Translanguaging implies a meaning-making process of multilingual users to cross not only linguistic boundaries, but also interactional, disciplinary, and cultural borders (Otheguy, García, & Reid, 2015). The concept of translanguaging was first proposed as "*trawsieithu*" in Welsh in Williams' study (1994). Williams described the pedagogy of providing bilingual children inputs in one language, i.e., English, and encouraging them to express their understanding in another language, i.e., Welsh, their heritage language in the classroom. The concept was later defined by Baker (2011) as "the planned and systematic use of two languages inside the same lesson" (p. 288). The original idea was inspired by the behavior of multilingual speakers who naturally use all their available languages as resources to access information, express themselves, and communicate with others (Baker, 2011).

Introducing translanguaging as a pedagogy in the school setting has challenged the traditional ideology of bilingual education set from a post-colonial perspective that views bilingual students' heritage languages as additional entities to the mainstream language in terms of standard and usage (García & Lin, 2016). Classroom translanguaging practices can be "integrated in talk, written text, and diagrams—in other words, as dynamic practices that crisscrossed through the modes of classroom communication" (Mazak & Herbas-Donoso, 2015, p. 700). García and Sylvan (2011) argue that translanguaging is realized in different forms.

> Translanguaging includes code-switching—defined as the shift between two languages in context–and it also includes translation, but it differs from both of these simple practices in that it refers to the process in which bilingual students make sense and perform bilingually in the myriad ways of the classroom—reading, writing, taking notes, discussing, signing, and so on (García & Sylvan, 2011, p. 389).

This definition suggests that code-switching and translation are possible forms of translanguaging, when the process of meaning-making occurs to the participants. This concept opens new perspectives for exploring classroom discourses produced by multilingual teachers and students in the classroom.

In contrast to recent translanguaging studies, the ideology in previous studies has been strongly influenced by the traditional structuralism as the linguistic norm which "postulates languages maintaining their separate structures and identities even in contact" (Canagarajah, 2018, p. 31). Research conducted with a structuralist perspective takes monolingual education as the norm, which sees switching between codes as unfavorable behaviors of bilinguals when they do not know how to express something in one of their languages (Martínez, 2010).

MacSwan (2017) argues that a repertoire is not a grammar but "a catalog of the ways we each can talk in different social contexts" (p. 188). Canagarajah (2018) calls for a shift in understanding translingual practices, especially in educational contexts, "according to a spatial orientation that embeds communication in space and time, considering all resources as working together as an assemblage in shaping meaning" (p. 31). Both MacSwan (2017) and Canagarajah (2018) suggest that classroom translanguaging is a meaningful process deliberately constructed by the participants, which combines multiple languaging modes and symbols in spoken, written, or semiotic representations.

2.2 Educational Functions of Translanguaging

In the past decade, comprehensive studies of translanguaging indicate that both learners and teachers have been empowered by using translanguaging in the classroom to make meaning, enhance experiences and develop identity (Li & Lin, 2019). A large number of studies took place in primary and secondary school settings. By reviewing previous literature, Ferguson (2003) suggests that code-switching (CS) is frequently practiced by both teachers and students in post-colonial African schools to assist content delivery, interpersonal communication, and task management. Fennema-Bloom (2010) in a case study reports three high-school science teachers who were Chinese–English bilinguals used code-switching as the scaffold for delivering content knowledge to their newly arrived Chinese immigrant students. It was found that CS was also used to reformulate language elements and as a habitual discourse style in their content classroom. Creese & Blackledge (2010) report teachers' and administrators' extensive uses of multiple languages in four complementary English–Gujarati and English–Chinese bilingual schools in the UK. They found both teachers, administrators, and students applied flexible bilingual label quests, repetition, and translation to facilitate the simultaneous development of bi-literacies, engage the audience, provide greater access to the curriculum, and establish identity positions in the content discussed. More importantly, they found both languages were needed for conveying and negotiating meanings, and the participants were fully aware of their choices and functions of their translanguaging strategies in the classrooms. Mokgwathi & Webb (2013) found CS was used as an instructional strategy in four senior secondary schools, even though English was designated as the sole official language of learning and teaching in all Botswana schools. It was found that CS was beneficial for increasing learner participation and lesson comprehension; however, it might not contribute to learners' proficiency development and confidence in speaking English.

Though translanguaging research in HE is at its infant stage, there is a fast-growing interest in exploring issues related to using multiple languaging repertoires for various purposes. Recent studies have examined issues on delivering and managing language and content-specific classes, self-learning, conducting lab or project discussion, and even composing professional papers with international partners (Mazak, 2017). Tertiary language teachers seem to possess diverse attitudes toward taking translanguaging as a pedagogical strategy in the classroom.

The factors include the teachers' language learning experiences, classroom policies, and institutional opportunities and constraints. The teachers who had received their language learning and teacher training education set in post-colonial contexts held a more conservative attitude toward the practice of translanguaging in the classroom (MacSwan, 2017; Tsou & Kao, 2017). Burton and Rajendram (2019) point out that there is a gap between accepting translanguaging as a concept and putting it into practice among college-level English-as-a-second-language (ESL) teachers in Canadian universities. Their survey findings reveal that though the use of translanguaging of students was accommodated in the classroom, the instruction was carried with rather "monolingual and standardized language ideologies" (p. 40). In a large-scale survey study, Turnbull (2018) asked the opinions of both Japanese EFL students ($n = 373$) and teachers ($n = 261$) about the use of Japanese in the L2 (English) learning process. The results indicate that although the respondents acknowledged that Japanese was used with various degrees across all classrooms, both teachers and students were uncertain about the potential effects of translanguaging for language learning. However, Bartlett (2018) provided counter-evidence in embedding translanguaging strategies in Japan's college-level language classrooms. By comparing the outcomes in the classes with English as the only medium vs. with active translanguaging strategies, Bartlett (2018) found that Japanese students achieved higher motivation levels, higher exam scores, and better presentation performances when additional languaging resources were promoted in the language classroom.

The role and practice of translanguaging appear quite differently in tertiary content-area teaching and learning. In his pioneer study, Canagarajah (2011) reports how one graduate student used code meshing to make meaning with Arabic, English, French, and symbols in her academic writing. Canagarajah (2018) further illustrates the multilingual and polysemiotic practices of international scholars and graduate students in science fields for learning, teaching, and professional communication. Mazak and Herbas-Donoso (2015) analyze how translanguaging practices were applied for academic presentation in science classes by a bilingual professor in an officially bilingual university in Puerto Rico. Their results indicate that the teachers permeably used translanguaging as an instructional strategy to interact with the students, present content materials, assign academic reading, and even give exams. Mazak and Herbas-Donoso (2015) point out that code-switching was mainly used to assist student comprehension in professional terms and concepts. Kagwesage (2013) found that in a Swedish university where content courses were offered in English to both local and Erasmus exchange students, responsible code-switching and other types of translanguaging strategies were used to mediate cognitively demanding academic tasks. Caruso (2018) also reported a successful case of a content-area professor promoting all available languaging resources, including group discussion and exams, to a mixed group of local and international students in Portugal.

The above review shows interesting research findings of translanguaging as a theoretical framework in curriculum planning and classroom practices. However, some discrepancies were found between teachers' and students' perceptions toward translanguaging, and between its possible impacts on language and on content instruction and learning. Therefore, there is a call for a more careful analysis of the complexity of translanguaging as an instructional tool and how exactly it is used by teachers and students, respectively. Most studies of translanguaging in HE used surveys, interviews, and class observations as the research methods. More qualitative studies based on classroom discourse are needed to describe its multiple phases in the application so that instructional suggestions can be formed for teacher training purposes.

3 Methodology

3.1 Setting and Participants

The study collected classroom discourse data from eight EMI courses taught by eight different Taiwanese instructors in a major research-based comprehensive university in Taiwan. The 18-week-long 3-credit courses were offered in three graduate institutes: Creative Industry, Environmental Engineering, and Mechanical Engineering. The research team observed and recorded the classes arranged by the three institutes to provide pedagogical suggestions to the teachers and administrators of their EMI programs targeting international students. Eight instructors received our interviews after the data collection stage and agreed to participate in this study for research purposes.

All eight instructors shared similar profiles: they spoke Chinese as their L1 and English as a second language. They all had the experience of studying or even teaching/working in English-speaking countries. They accepted our interviews to discuss some of the translanguaging patterns observed in their classes. All the classes consisted of local and international students, but the ratios varied from class to class. The international students came from regions worldwide, with Czech, English, French, German, Indonesian, Malay, Mongolian, Russian, Spanish, and Vietnamese as their major L1s. International students from non-English speaking countries were required to have at least a B2 level of English proficiency upon admission to the target university. However, local students were not particularly screened for EMI content classes, so their English levels ranged widely, from A2 to C1. The university required all international students to take at least two 2-credit conversational Chinese courses, focusing on speaking and listening for everyday communication. From our observation, all the international students in the study appeared to be able to communicate in simple Chinese with their classmates, but might lack adequate Chinese proficiency for academic purposes. The primary medium of these classes was English.

3.2   Data and Analytical Procedures

The primary data were the audio recording of the lectures collected in the eight EMI courses. Each course was observed and recorded two times during the semester. The instructors received interviews at their offices at a separate time. Since the research focused on EMI lectures, data on student presentation, and class/group discussion sessions were excluded from the analysis. However, during the lecture sessions, the student talks, such as their questions and replies, were used to assist in analyzing the communication functions and purposes of the teacher talks. A total of 23.5 hours of lecturing, containing 119,906 words in the transcription, was used as the base data for this study. The field notes and interviews were used to support the interpretation of the analytical results.

The first step in analyzing the data was to identify all the discourse occasions involving uses of multiple languages. In this study, only English and Chinese were found in the data. The utterances around each multiple language usage were extracted, and then were segmented into speech units according to the syntactic structure proposed by Foster, Tonkyn, and Wigglesworth (2000). Chinese expressions quoted in this paper were denoted by Hanyu pinyin system with their English translation provided in square brackets behind each occasion.

Though previous literature had provided many translanguaging examples from real data, there was no discussion on quantifying the data. Thus, this study needed to set up a quantification procedure to transform the qualitative data into quantifiable values for further analysis. In this study, one translanguaging practice is realized by a language shift within one speech unit or across two speech units. Excerpt 2 is an example of one practice within one unit (see the Results section). In Excerpt 2, two Chinese terms, *Liufucun* (the name of a local amusement park) and *Jianhushan* (the name of another local amusement park) were embedded in one unit spoken in English. It counts for only one practice. Excerpt 3 shows an example of one practice that is across several speech units. In Excerpt 3 (see the Results section), the speech starts in English and shifts to Chinese after "*ok?*", and then it shifts back to English after "*nage shi zui jiben de*" (literary meaning, that is the most fundamental). Though it is a long segment, only one practice is counted. After all the translingual practices were identified, they were analyzed and grouped into types, according to the discourse functions carried, but not the linguistic forms realized This approach was used by Mazak and Herbas-Donoso (2015) on how science professors used different forms of translanguaging to help students make sense of their lectures.

4   Results and Discussion

The analysis shows that the base language in the eight courses was English. However, all the EMI instructors used Chinese to support content delivery, especially for the local students with lower English proficiency. Two major types of strategies were identified: interactional and instructional. The features and functions of the two types are described with examples taken from the data. The following sections present the results of the analysis of the two strategies with a few examples taken from the data. A brief discussion is presented after each strategy based on the research team's field notes and the interviews with the instructors.

4.1   Interactional Strategies

An interactional translanguaging strategy is realized by a shift between English and Chinese without repeating the information in each language. The primary function of an interactional strategy is to present information at an average conversational pace with an uninterrupted representation of meanings. It was often used for engaging students' attention and for promoting active participation. Sometimes, it appeared to be a habitual style of communicating ideas among the speakers who are fluent in both languages. Take Excerpt 1 as an example. The instructor used two specific English terms, *"Delta X"* and *"Delta Y"* in a Chinese speech unit. Though the two English terms are mixed into the Chinese syntactic structure, the utterance sounds fluent, and information carried by these two English terms is not repeated in Chinese in the unit, nor before or after this unit. This usage is probably due to the difficulty of finding the equivalent terms in Chinese in this situation. Besides, it might be awkward to translate these mathematical terms into Chinese. Though this utterance's base structure is Chinese, it should not cause too much comprehension problem to the international students because the structure was simple, short, and colloquial. This type of practice is often accompanied by other supportive modalities, such as equations written on the board or images projected to the screen.

Excerpt 1
Data from the course, *Chemical Principles for Environmental Engineering*
   yunqi hao [luckily]. *Delta X dengyu* [equals to] *Delta Y*.
   Chinese terms are often embedded in the English syntactic structure as shown in Excerpt 2. The instructor said the names of the two Taiwanese amusement parks in Chinese, *Liufucun* and *Jianhushan*, while comparing the differences of the two parks. Her speech sounded very natural and fluent, with the two inserted Chinese terms. This utterance should not cause any difficulty to the students since the two parks were the primary targets of comparison in this class period. When the names of the two amusement parks were said in Chinese for the first time earlier in the class, a PowerPoint slide of the place images was presented. These two places were always said in Chinese, but not in Anglophone pronunciation.

Excerpt 2
Data from the course, *Creative Industry Investigation*
   maybe Liufucun [name of an amusement park] *is more famous and technology is better than* Jianhushan [name of an amusement park].

Another representation of interactional strategy is to mix two languages across several speech units, as shown in Excerpt 3. The instructor told the class that concrete examples must be provided in writing, regardless of what topic it was about. Then she switched to Chinese after "*ok?*" to emphasize that this requirement was essential in writing. Both the English and the Chinese utterances were complete in their meanings and syntactic structures.

Excerpt 3

Data from the course, *Professional English Writing for Creative Industry*
    and I sort of feel. I can easily reject. no matter how good the topic is. the writing is. ok? suoyi yiding yao kan. nage shi zui jiben de. [so (you) must see. that's the most fundamental].

4.2   Discussion on Interactional Strategies

The phenomenon of mixing technical terms or proper nouns in two languages was also reported in the study of Creese and Blackledge (2010), which found that code-mixing was used because each language was insufficient to complete the utterances. Interactional strategies seem to be preferable to those who are competent in both languages. This is especially apparent when the instructors switched from English to Chinese and continued the Chinese speech without any explanation or repetition in English. International students who were not competent in both languages might be lost easily. The research team raised this question to all the instructors in the interviews. The instructors were aware of this issue, and it seemed to be their habit of mixing two languages in speech. However, all the instructors said they tried to avoid delivering content knowledge in this manner. Some said they usually switched to Chinese to remind local students of important course management issues, which had been announced to the class in English because some students with lower English proficiency might miss the English information. Furthermore, one instructor said he switched to Chinese when telling jokes to bring a lively atmosphere to the lectures, in his answer to the question, "How do you motivate your students in the class?" as shown in Excerpt 4.

Extract 4

Interview data from Teacher L of *Applied Mechanics.*
    Giving examples, telling jokes, and having exams are the best ways to motivate them. When you told them, you will find this in the exam. Students would suddenly wake up and take notes.

Interestingly, several teachers indicated that telling jokes in English was not an easy task. "How would international students follow the jokes?" asked the research team. One teacher said when the international students with limited Chinese heard laughter from the class, they would ask for a translation from the local students and get the punch lines a bit later. "In this way, Chinese students would also interact more with the foreign students," said this teacher.

Overall, switching between languages for interactional purposes was a common phenomenon in these EMI classrooms. The primary function of this strategy is to maintain fluent communication, as found by Baker (2011) among bilingual speakers. In addition, it was also used for managing the class and creating lively interaction with the students. Interestingly, the EMI teachers appeared to perform language shifts with purposes and were cautious about the effects. However, they all claimed to have no official training in handling classes in a foreign language.

4.3 Instructional Strategies

Instructional translanguaging strategies were used to help students comprehend content knowledge. Two types of instructional strategies were identified in this study: translating and paraphrasing. Translating between languages refers to saying the exact meaning of a word, phrase, or sentence in another language; paraphrasing, on the other hand, refers to restating, explaining, or expanding the definition of a word, phrase, or sentence in another language. In the present study, translating was found from both English to Chinese and Chinese to English. However, paraphrasing was mostly made in Chinese to elaborate on the information presented in English and occasionally in English for Chinese concepts.

Excerpt 5 shows an example of translating, in which the instructor first asked the question in English, and then immediately translated the entire question word-by-word into Chinese.

Excerpt 5
Data from the course, *Principles of Chemistry*.
　how big is bacteria? xijun duo da [How big is bacteria]?

The analysis shows that the EMI teachers usually translated terms, phrases, or short speech units, rather than long speech segments. Excerpt 6 shows a rare example of translating a long chunk of information from English to Chinese. In this segment, the instructor first explained the equation in English while writing up the equation on the board, and then he translated the entire segment into Chinese by pointing at the board again. Interestingly, before he translated, he explicitly told the class, "*so let me say it in Chinese*". This strategy was helpful to the international students because they would know that the following speech in Chinese repeated the same information presented before.

Excerpt 6
Data from the course, *Heat Transfer*
　you have one easy way to check that. to verify with the coefficient in front of temperature. here you have one and one so you get minus two… so let me say it in Chinese. ruguo ni xiangyao jiancha [if you want to check]. *yi ge hen jiandan de*

fangfa [there is an easy way]. *jiushi shouxian ni jiancha yixia wendu de xishu* [that is you first check the temperature coefficient]...*suoyi yi jia yi yiding yao dengyu fu er* [so one plus one must equal to minus two].

Different from translating, paraphrasing features the speaker's interpretation of the presented concepts in another language. In Excerpt 7, to explain the idea of "toxic," the instructor said in Chinese that it would bring harmful effects to the environment.

Excerpt 7

Data from the course, *Principles of Chemistry*

it's very toxic to the ecosystem. ok. ta dui huanjing shanghai haishi hen da de [It poses rather great harm to the environment.]

Paraphrasing was used more often with long speech segments, rather than within one speech unit. In other words, the teachers would not explain an idea in two languages within one sentence; they usually completed the utterances in one language, and then elaborated the concepts in another language in a more comprehensive manner, as shown in Extract 8. When explaining the concept of temperature changes in English, the instructor wrote the formula on the board. To help the local students, the instructor elaborated the same formula once more in Chinese by referring to the formula on the board. Even though the information presented in the two languages was roughly the same, the Chinese segment was elaborated with more details.

Extract 8

Data from the course, *Heat Transfer*

in this part from the left side. from the right side you have x and t... and since the temperature is a kind of continuous change. then you should be able to find this kind of curve and mark at different location. you have M which is the middle ...you have m-1/2 and the other is m + 1/2... zhege zai zhe limian ne [This, inside here]. *yinwei wendu suizhe kongjian shi lianxu de bianhua* [because temperature going along with space shows a continuous change] *...suoyi ne zai zhebian women yinggai shi keyi zuo* [so at this side we should be able to do]. *ba zhongjian zhe dian women jiao M* [we call the middle point, M]. *youbian jiao M jia yi* [the right side is called M plus 1], *zuobian jiao M jian yi* [the left side is called M minus 1]. *na lianxu liang xianglin dian haiyou zhongdian* [that are two adjacent points and the midpoint]. *zhongjian dian women ye keyi biaohao* [we can also mark the midpoint].

4.4 Discussion on Instructional Strategies

Both translating and paraphrasing were used to enhance teaching in these classrooms. Translating was often used with words/terminologies or phrases to save time, while paraphrasing was used more with an extensive explanation of a concept, procedure, or formula. Interestingly, some particular discourse signals often appeared together with instructional translanguaging strategies, such as "so" in the "so let me say it in Chinese" in Excerpt 6. Similar expressions in Chinese were detected, such as "*zai yong zhongwen jiang yi ci* [(I) will explain that in Chinese once more]", in the data. These signals, called "metalinguistic markers" by Schiffrin (1987), appeared in both English and Chinese to raise the attention of the students about language shifts. Chinese markers, such as "*jiushi* [that is], *jiushishuo* [that is to say], and *suoyi* [so], were used to attract the attention of the Chinese speakers on the concepts to be explained in Chinese again. This strategy indicates that the instructors were aware of their language shifts with instructional functions, because these markers were not found before the appearance of interactional translanguaging practices.

In the interviews, some instructors pointed out that delivering the same message twice in two languages was time-consuming. They preferred paraphrasing than translating in Chinese. Since the instructional medium was English, a new concept was always introduced, explained, and elaborated in English first to the class until a general comprehension was acknowledged by the students. The translanguaging strategy of translating from Chinese into English or paraphrasing Chinese concepts in English was rarely found in these EMI classes. Instructional translanguaging strategies were mostly used when the teachers felt that some students, usually those who could not follow the English lectures, needed further elaboration. Different teachers used Chinese on different occasions or stages of the course. For example, Teacher C in Excerpt 9 indicated that he preferred to use more English for the content familiar to the students but used more Chinese for new concepts.

Excerpt 9

Interview data from Teacher C of Applied Mechanics

[Chinese] might help, but I think it is not good. Students may expect Chinese and ignore English. They would wait for the Chinese part. However, I still use English and Chinese in class. I think the complicated content should be explained clearly so [local students] can understand better.… As a result, I used more English in the beginning of the course, because the content is to review what they had learned in high school. However, I used more Chinese in the latter sessions of the course, which involved new knowledge. In order to make them understand, I, therefore, applied more Chinese to teach [later in the semester].

Similar instructional functions have been discussed in Mazak and Herbas-Donoso (2015), in which the bilingual EMI instructor who shared Spanish with the students as a shared L1 also switched between Spanish and English to facilitate the delivery of science lectures.

It was found from the interviews that all the instructors gave the quizzes and exams in English not only for the EMI courses but also for their Chinese medium instruction courses, as exemplified in Excerpt 10. This language choice shows that English had become a lingua franca in accessing academic knowledge at different degrees in the three content areas in our study.

Excerpt 10
Interview data from Teacher C of Heat Transfer
My exam papers are in English for both Chinese and EMI classes. It is because I used English textbooks for both classes, so I use English for the assessment….The important knowledge is introduced in English. [If I use] Chinese [in the exam papers], the students [still] have to think the term and knowledge in English first, then, translate it into Chinese. It is risky, because the Chinese may not be appropriate for it.

4.5 Distribution of Different Types of Translingual Strategies

Altogether 1148 translingual practices were identified from the data. Among them, 480 were interactional (41.8%), while 668 were instructional (58.2%). In other words, on average, the eight EMI instructors used more instructional than interactional functions of translanguaging in the classrooms. Table 1 presents a summary of the frequency counts with the percentages of each type of translanguaging strategies.

Under the interactional type, two subtypes were identified: mixing within a speech unit (296 times, accounting for 25.8% of the total), as shown in the speech unit, "*Delta X dengyu* [equals to] *Delta Y*" presented in Excerpt 1, and mixing across speech units (184 times, accounting for 16.0% of the total), as shown in Excerpt 3.

Under the instructional types, there are also two subtypes: translating (140 times, accounting for 12.2% of the total) and paraphrasing (528 times, accounting for 46.0% of the total). Since translating content knowledge is time-consuming, the EMI teachers preferred paraphrasing rather than directly translating when they noticed incomprehension from the students.

Table 1 Frequency and percentage of the translanguaging strategies

Type	Subtype	Frequency	Individual percentage (%)	Percentage (%)
Interactional	Within a speech unit	296	25.8	41.8
	Across speech units	184	16.0	
Instructional	Translating	140	12.2	58.2
	Paraphrasing	528	46.0	
	Total	1148	100	100

4.6 Discussion of Teacher Interviews and Field Notes

Though the instructors used more instructional than interactional translanguaging strategies, the percentage of the later type is also high. In the interviews, many instructors expressed their concerns of the diverse English proficiency levels among the students. Screening the students, especially the local ones, by their proficiency levels, might be a solution. However, this solution would only apply to the bigger programs that could offer the same course in both English and Chinese, such as EMI programs in engineering fields. The phenomenon of a high percentage of interactional strategy also indicates that it is critical to engage students more in the language they are familiar with. However, since the instructors did not have the knowledge of all the L1s of students, this strategy was only applied to the local students with Chinese as their L1. Although student discourse was not investigated in this study, our field notes indicated that the EMI teachers did not mind students using their L1s in the classroom for exchanging ideas or asking help from other students sharing the same L1, or taking notes in their preferred modes or languages. The instructors welcomed questions raised in Chinese by the local students and would translate the Chinese questions into English for discussion.

Our observation showed that "mixing-within-a-speech-unit" subtype is probably more accessible than the "across-unit" type for international students when the base structure was in Chinese. Our field notes indicated that the international students did not show a particular sign of incomprehension when Chinese terms were embedded in English. In the interviews, some instructors said that they would pay attention to both local and international students' needs when switching languages and would repeat the information in the other language once they noticed any sign of incomprehension from the students.

Overall, these teachers made use of all available resources to facilitate the delivery of the lectures. Together with the teacher interviews, the distribution of the strategies confirms that the EMI teachers paid attention to their language choices. They were aware of the instructional functions of combining translanguaging strategies with other types of modalities, such as explaining concepts with PowerPoint slides or equations written on the board, to enhance student comprehension. These findings support the claim that the students' L1 can be used as a beneficial learning resource (Creese & Blackledge, 2010; García & Sylvan, 2011; Li, 2011). Finally, the teachers showed their appreciation when the research team shared the preliminary analysis of their classroom discourses. They indicated that EMI teachers would benefit greatly by attending in-service workshops about using translingual practices as EMI pedagogy with efficiency.

5 Conclusion

The current study identified two types of translanguaging strategies used by Taiwanese EMI teachers: interactional and instructional. These two types were used extensively to facilitate their lecturing with students of various L1s and mixed English proficiency levels. The results show that the EMI teachers used more instructional than interactional strategies, though the percentages of the two types were close. The findings imply that the content specialists, though without official training in EMI pedagogy, were aware of using multiple languages with visual and other modalities to enhance engagement, interaction, and comprehension of students of different needs. However, the extensive use of interactional translanguaging strategies may be less favorable to those who were not competent in Chinese and English. The translanguaging strategies and their pedagogical functions identified in the study can be used for designing teacher training materials to help content specialists understand the educational functions of their classroom language so that they can plan classroom tasks and deliver lectures with higher efficiency.

Since the focus of this study was on the patterns of the teachers' translanguaging practices, it did not explore the effects of the teachers' discourses on the students' understanding of the content knowledge, nor did the study examine how the students use translanguaging strategies to enhance their participation and learning in the classroom. Future studies should look into the students' perceptions of these strategies and the connection between the teachers' translanguaging strategies and the students' learning outcomes in EMI classes. It will also be interesting to analyze the translanguaging strategies used by the students in teacher–student interaction, such as raising and answering questions, and student–student interaction, such as group discussion.

This study used given classrooms as the investigation targets, which may restrict the generalization of EMI classes in other academic fields or different countries while their language policies are different. Finally, translanguaging practices include multi-modalities and semiotic resources, so future studies should investigate how verbal practices can be combined with varying types of languaging resources in the meaning-making process for ELF speakers in the EMI classroom.

Acknowledgements This study was financially supported by the Ministry of Science and Technology, Taiwan, Republic of China (Grant number: MOST 107-2410-H-006-069).

References

Bae, S. (2015). An analysis on the international student recruitment and management policies in South Korea. *International Journal of Education and Research, 3*(9), 331–342.

Baker, C. (2011). *Foundations of Bilingual Education and Bilingualism* (5th ed.). Bristol, UK: Multilingual Matters.

Bartlett, K. A. (2018). Applying translanguaging techniques in Japanese EFL settings. In *The Asian conference on language learning 2018: Official conference proceedings*, pp. 239–252.

Burton, J., & Rajendram, S. (2019). Translanguaging-as-resource: University ESL instructors' language orientations and attitudes toward translanguaging. *TESL Canada Journal, 36*(1), 21–47.

Byun, K., Chu, H., Kim, M., Park, I., Kim, S., & Jung, J. (2011). English-medium teaching in Korean higher education: Policy debates and reality. *Higher Education, 62*(4), 431–449.

Canagarajah, S. (2011). Codemeshing in academic writing: Identifying teachable strategies of translanguaging. *The Modern Language Journal, 95*(3), 401–417.

Canagarajah, S. (2018). Translingual practice as spatial repertoires: Expanding the paradigm beyond structuralist orientations. *Applied Linguistics, 39*(1), 31–54.

Cho, D. W. (2012). English-medium instruction in the university context of Korea: Trade off between teaching outcomes and media-initiated university ranking. *The Journal of Asia TEFL, 9*(4), 135–163.

Creese, A., & Blackledge, A. (2010). Translanguaging in the bilingual classroom: A pedagogy for learning and teaching? *The Modern Language Journal, 94*(1), 103–115.

Caruso, E. (2018). Translanguaging in higher education: Using several languages for the analysis of academic content in the teaching and learning process. *Language Learning in Higher Education, 8*(1), 65–90.

Department of Statistics, MOE. (2019). *Annual Educational Statistics*. Retrieved from https://dep art.moe.edu.tw/ED4500/cp.aspx?n=1B58E0B736635285&s=D04C74553DB60CAD.

Doiz, A., Lasagabaster, D., & Sierra, J. (2011). Internationalisation, multilingualism and English-medium instruction. *World Englishes, 30*(3), 345–359.

Fennema-Bloom, J. (2010). Code-scaffolding: A pedagogic code-switching technique for bilingual content instruction. *Journal of Education, 190*(3), 27–35.

Ferguson, G. (2003). Classroom code-switching in post-colonial contexts: Functions, attitudes and policies. *AILA Review, 16*(1), 38–51.

Foster, M., Tonkyn, A., & Wigglesworth, G. (2000). Measuring spoken language: A unit for all reasons. *Applied Linguistics, 21*(3), 354–375.

García, O., & Li, W. (2014). *Translanguaging: Language, bilingualism and education*. New York, NY: Palgrave Macmillan.

García, O., & Lin, A. M. (2016). Translanguaging in bilingual education. In O. García & A. M. Lin (Eds.), *Bilingual and multilingual education* (pp. 117–130). Netherlands: Springer.

García, O., & Sylvan, C. E. (2011). Pedagogies and practices in multilingual classrooms: Singularities in pluralities. *The Modern Language Journal, 95*(3), 385–400.

Japan Student Services Organization. (2019). *International students in Japan*. Retrieved from https://www.jasso.go.jp/en/about/statistics/intl_student/index.html.

Kao, Y.-T., & Tsou, W. (2017). EMI course assessment: A survey study of the issues. In W. Tsou & S.-M. Kao (Eds.), *English as a medium of instruction in higher education: Implementations and classroom practices in Taiwan* (pp. 183–205). Singapore: Springer.

Lawson, C. (2008). *Taiwan's aim for the Top University Program: Innovation, internationalisation and opportunity. Australian Government: Australian Education International*. Retrieved from https://internationaleducation.gov.au/research/Publications/Documents/Taiwans_Aim_Top.pdf.

Li, W. (2011). Moment analysis and translanguaging space: Discursive construction of identities by multilingual Chinese youth in Britain. *Journal of Pragmatics, 43*(5), 1222–1235.

Li, W., & Lin, A. M. (2019). Translanguaging classroom discourse: Pushing limits, breaking boundaries. *Classroom Discourse, 10*(3–4), 209–215.

Kagwesage, A. M. (2013). Coping with English as language of instruction in higher education in Rwanda. *International Journal of Higher Education, 2*(2), 1–12.

MacSwan, J. (2017). A multilingual perspective on translanguaging. *American Educational Research Journal, 54*(1), 167–201.

Martínez, R. A. (2010). Spanglish as a literacy tool: Toward an understanding of the potential role of Spanish-English code-switching in the development of academic literacy. *Research in the Teaching of English, 45*(2), 124–149.

Mazak, C. M., & Herbas-Donoso, C. (2015). Translanguaging practices at a bilingual university: A case study of a science classroom. *International Journal of Bilingual Education and Bilingualism, 18*(6), 698–714.

Mazak, C. M. (2017). Introduction: Theorizing translanguaging practices in higher education. In C. Mazak & K. S. Carroll (Eds.), *Translanguaging in higher education: Beyond monolingual ideologies* (pp. 1–10). Tonawanda, NY: Multilingual Matters.

MEXT. (2020). *Global 30 Project-Establishing university network for internationalization-.* Retrieved from https://www.mext.go.jp/en/policy/education/highered/title02/detail02/sdetail02/1373894.htm.

Mokgwathi, T., & Webb, V. (2013). The educational effects of code-switching in the classroom–Benefits and setbacks: A case of selected senior secondary schools in Botswana. *Language Matters: Studies in the Languages of Africa, 44*(3), 108–125.

Koh, M. & Kim, M. (2019). No. of int'l students rises to all-time high in S. Korea. *PULSE.* Retrieved from https://pulsenews.co.kr/view.php?year=2019&no=680611.

Otheguy, R., García, O., & Reid, W. (2015). Clarifying translanguaging and deconstructing named languages: A perspective from linguistics. *Applied Linguistics Review, 63,* 281–307.

Rose, H., & McKinley, J. (2018). Japan's English-medium instruction initiatives and the globalization of higher education. *Higher Education, 75*(1), 111–129.

Schiffrin, D. (1987). *Discourse markers.* Cambridge University Press.

Tsou, W., & Kao, S.-M. (2017). Overview of EMI development. In W. Tsou & S.-M. Kao (Eds.), *English as a medium of instruction in higher education: Implementations and classroom practices in Taiwan* (pp. 3–18). Singapore: Springer.

Turnbull, B. (2018). Is there a potential for a translanguaging approach to English education in Japan? Perspectives of tertiary learners and teachers. *JALT Journal, 40*(2), 101–134.

Williams, C. (1994). *Arfarniad o Ddulliau Dysgu ac Addysgu yng Nghyd-destun AddysgUwchradd Ddwyieithog,* [An evaluation of teaching and learning methods in the context of bilingual secondary education]. Unpublished Doctoral Dissertation (University of Wales, Bangor).

Shin-Mei Kao is a full professor at Foreign Languages & Literature Department, National Cheng Kung University, Taiwan. Her research interests include multilingualism, English as a lingua franca in education for learners of all ages, discourse analysis, and language assessment. She is co-editor of E*nglish as a medium of instruction in higher education: Implementations and classroom practices in Taiwan* (Springer), and *Resources for teaching English for specific purposes* (Bookman). Currently she is a teacher trainer and supervisor for the national bilingual education project of Taiwan.

Wenli Tsou is a Full Professor in the Department of Foreign Languages & Literature, and currently Director of the Foreign Language Center at National Cheng Kung University, Taiwan. She received her PhD in Foreign and Second Language Education from the State University of New York at Buffalo, US. She is the project leader of the National Cheng Kung University ESP and EMI programs. She is also the leading figure of bilingual education in Taiwan, helping with its teacher training and curriculum design. Her research interests include teacher training, ESP, English as a Lingua Franca, Content and Language Integrated Learning and English as a Medium of Instruction. Her current research projects have focused on the links between transdiciplinary teaching and translanguaging of bilingual education and EMI. She chairs the 13th International Conference of English as a Lingua Franca and has co-edited the following books: *English as a Medium of Instruction in Higher Education: Implementations & classroom practices in Taiwan* (2017, Springer), *Exploring CLIL: A Resource Book* (2018, Bookman) and *Resources for Teaching English for Specific Purposes* (2014, Bookman).

Fay Chen is an Assistant Professor of the Foreign Language Center at National Cheng Kung University, Taiwan. She received her PhD from the same university. She is a member of the NCKU bilingual education project team, helping with CLIL teacher training and curriculum design. Her research interests include teacher training, ESP, English as a Lingua Franca, Content and Language Integrated Learning (CLIL) and English as a Medium of Instruction (EMI). Her current research has focused on CLIL materials development, translanguaging, and scaffolding strategies in compulsory education.

Chapter 6
Strategic Use of L1 in Chinese EMI Classrooms: A Translanguaging Perspective

Yi Zhang and Rining (Tony) Wei

Abstract Bilingual education (BE) for majority-language students in China usually refers to using English as a medium of instruction in part or all of the instruction time of a non-language subject. Coupled with the spread of BE programmes, there seems to be a monolingual tendency in English-medium instruction (EMI) settings, which disapproves of the use of teachers' and students' first language (L1) resources. The present study aims to contribute some empirical evidence concerning teachers' strategic use of L1, an important under-investigated topic in the Chinese EMI context, and explore its pedagogical potentials from a translanguaging perspective. The data were derived from EMI lessons delivered by content teachers at one university in the East China region, which has been actively implementing EMI against the backdrop of educational internationalisation. Based upon the transcripts of the sampled video-recorded EMI classrooms, four types of strategic use of L1 were identified: adopting L1 for domain-specific knowledge, complementing English with L1, L1 recast, and utilizing L1 for localized knowledge. These strategies reflected a translanguaging practice that mobilises L1 and other localized knowledge for pedagogically sound teaching practices. Policy implications to move away from the monolingual paradigm were also discussed for the focal university and its counterparts.

1 Introduction

The continuing development of bilingual education in North America and Europe over the last decade (e.g. Coyle et al., 2010; Mehisto, 2012) has prompted the rise of strong forms of bilingual education (Baker, 2006) beyond these continents (cf. Kim & Lee, 2020; Wei & Feng, 2015; Yang, 2015). One strong form of bilingual education in the Chinese mainland, commonly known as Chinese–English bilingual education where English is used as a medium of instruction in non-language subject-matter

Y. Zhang · R. (Tony) Wei (✉)
Department of Applied Linguistics, Xi'an Jiaotong-Liverpool University, Suzhou, China

Y. Zhang
e-mail: Yi.Zhang01@xjtlu.edu.cn

courses, has received scholarly attention in the past decade. Chinese-English bilingual education at the tertiary level is often referred to as English-medium instruction (EMI) (cf. Zhao & Dixon, 2017). In terms of exposure to instruction through the target language (English in this case), we distinguish between very-high-exposure EMI and other categories of EMI, which is consistent with the categorisation for Content and Language Integrated Learning (CLIL) programmes in China (see Wei, 2013).

Important topics concerning Chinese–English bilingual education in the Chinese context have been explored, which range from classroom pedagogy (e.g. Hoare, 2010) to different stakeholder groups including parents (e.g. Wei, 2011), students (e.g. Kong & Wei, 2019; Tong & Shi, 2012; Wei, Ma, & Feng, 2017), and teachers (e.g. Kong et al., 2011). However, EMI research is still in "the infancy stage" (Wei et al., 2017, p. 54); it is worth noting that the academic discussion about EMI has unfortunately been "long on claims and short on empirical research" (Wei, 2011: 482). The present study aims to contribute some empirical evidence concerning teachers' use of L1, an important topic under-investigated in the Chinese context. The importance of this topic can be reflected in the fact that some conceptual models (e.g. Baetens Beardsmore, 2009; Baker, 1996) have listed teachers' classroom language use (including possible L1 use) as one of the key factors impinging upon the effectiveness of any EMI programme. As only a very limited number of studies (e.g. Wang & Curdt-Christiansen, 2019) have examined teachers' use of L1 in the Chinese context, our study endeavours to contribute more empirical data to this topic.

In the remainder of this chapter, before reviewing the relevant literature, we first present an introduction to the wider context (e.g. local language policy relating to EMI). After reporting upon the specific research setting (viz. one Sino-foreign university) and the methods and procedures employed in this study, we present findings on the main types of L1 adoption by the two non-native English speaking EMI teachers in an undergraduate applied linguistics module, and conclude with their language-in-education policy implications and possible directions for future research. Specifically, we situate our findings of L1 adoption via the perspective of translanguaging (García & Li, 2014), and argue that L1 use by the EMI teachers is often strategic and extend beyond purely linguistic concerns, so as to cater for optimal pedagogical practices.

2   National and Local Policy Documents Relating to EMI

The provision of bilingual education involving a foreign medium of instruction (e.g. EMI or French-medium instruction) for majority-language students in China had been far from uncommon prior to the founding of the People's Republic of China (henceforth China) in 1949 (cf. Chen & Jin, 2003; Fu, 1986). Although this provision was discontinued by the Communist regime in the early 1950s, it began to return to the public education sector half a century later (Wei, 2011), when Shanghai became the first region in the Chinese mainland to experiment with EMI (more often called "Chinese-English bilingual education" in local policy documents).

At the pre-tertiary level, there have been two waves of development. The first wave started in Shanghai in 1999 as a regional government-organised endeavour at public schools (Wei, 2009), began to stall since 2005 (Wei, 2013) and has to date come to a halt. The second wave of EMI, sometimes labelled as CLIL (Gong, 2015), has been promoted by local governments in some cities (e.g. Zhangjiagang City, in Jiangsu Province) and by many schools (Kong & Wei, 2019). Overall speaking, pre-tertiary EMI at best has received official endorsement from the regional level.

In sharp contrast, since 2001, EMI at the tertiary level has gained consistent policy support from state departments (e.g. the Ministry of Finance). In the very first national-level policy document where EMI and other foreign-language medium instruction are mentioned, it is proposed that "actively promoting teaching through foreign languages such as English" be one of the twelve guidelines to improve the undergraduate-level teaching quality nationwide (Ministry of Education, 2001); under this general guideline, more specific measures are proposed; one measure is that some majors are encouraged to "take the lead and try their best to teach 5%–10% of their courses through a foreign language for the next three years to come"; another measure is to allow "universities and majors that do not yet have the resources to teach through a foreign language verbally" to "use foreign-medium teaching materials in part of courses with the verbal teaching medium still being Chinese" (Ministry of Education, 2001). It is noteworthy that this policy document does not impose uniform requirements on all universities and majors, but instead, it allows under-resourced institutions to provide EMI in a phased manner; however, the flexibility allowed in the above-cited document is seldom mentioned, and the Ministry of Education' intentions are often misrepresented in the English-language literature (see Wei, 2013 for a critique of the unfortunate lack of precision in recounting the policy measures). Since the promulgation of the 2001 document, consistent policy documents (e.g. Ministry of Education, 2004, 2009; Ministry of Education & Ministry of Finance, 2010) have been issued, lending support—financial and otherwise—to the promotion of EMI in universities. Although no statistics from government sources are available to show how many universities out of the 2500+ Chinese tertiary institutions offer EMI, one survey of the websites of "key" universities (i.e. all of the 116 institutions included in Project 211 by the Ministry of Education) finds that over 80% of them claimed to provide EMI courses (Kong, 2017). As regards whether there is a guiding policy document concerning EMI, the answer varies from university to university (Wei, 2019); at the university where the present study was conducted, there is a language policy document designating English as the main teaching medium (see also the **Research Setting** section below).

3   Literature Review

Teachers' use of L1 is an important and complex research topic in bilingualism research (as well as in the wider field of applied linguistics). There are two major competing theoretical frameworks: the interactionist perspective and the sociocultural theory one (Ellis, 2018). The former underscores the need for ensuring that students receive maximum exposure to L2 input, while the latter sees the L1 as a useful cognitive tool for scaffolding L2 production and for private speech on the part of students. More recent research on L1 use has shifted to a translanguaging perspective (Canagarajah, 2011; García & Li, 2014) which suggests that bilingual/multilingual language users access "different linguistic features or various modes of what are described as autonomous languages, in order to maximize communicative potential" (García, 2009, p. 140). Instead of viewing languages as separate linguistic systems, a translanguaging perspective does not strictly distinguish between languages but argues that all meaning-making resources, either linguistically or via other semiotic means, form our communicative repertoire in various types of communication events.

Researchers respectively informed by these frameworks have formed two camps. Those in one camp argue against the use of the L1 in foreign language and bilingual education contexts; for example, Ellis (1984) maintains that the teacher should use the students' L1 as little as possible in order to maximise students' exposure to L2 input; the three assumptions underlying two-way bilingual immersion programmes delineated by Cummins (2005) are (1) instruction should be exclusively in the target language (viz. L2), (2) translation should be avoided, and (3) the two languages should be kept strictly separate. In contrast, researchers in the other camp argue for the value of L1 when used in a judicious manner; for instance, Cook (2001) recommends that teachers use the L1 to explain grammar, organise tasks, discipline student, and implement tests, who argues that code-switching is a natural and normal phenomenon in settings where speakers have a shared language. Based on a re-analysis of the teacher's discourse data collected in the 1980s during a Science lesson at an Anglo-Chinese secondary school in Hong Kong SAR of China, Lin (2009) vividly illustrates the positive role of L1 in a supposedly EMI classroom and argues for flexible use of code-switching and/or code-mixing in teaching subject matter through a foreign language. Most recently, García-Mateus and Palmer (2017, p. 245) argue that strictly separating the language of instruction appears to inhibit both emergent bilinguals' development of positive identities and their willingness to take linguistic risks and engage in critical discussions.

Given the importance of this research topic, many empirical studies have investigated teachers' L1 use in the past four decades. However, most of the extant studies taking place in settings ranging from L2 learning classrooms (e.g. Mahboob & Lin, 2016) to content-based EMI classrooms (e.g. Tavares, 2015 for the subject of mathematics) have been conducted outside the Chinese mainland, where the number of English learners/users already exceeded 390 million in 2000 according to the best available government statistics (Wei & Su, 2012). There is evidence indicating that this number of English-knowing Chinese bilinguals is on the rise (cf. Wei & Su, 2015). In other words, the Chinese mainland represents an important but under-investigated context for the investigation of teachers' L1 use in EMI classrooms; until now, empirical research on teachers' L1 use in EMI classrooms has been very limited. Only two recent studies from within the Chinese mainland are highly relevant to the present study.

The first study, Wang (2019), addresses the reality and complexity of emergent translanguaging in foreign language classrooms, by focussing on a group of international students studying Mandarin Chinese (Putonghua) as a foreign language (CFL) programmes in Beijing. She identifies three types of translanguaging pedagogy in CFL classrooms: (1) explanatory strategies, which are initiated by teachers so as to provide cognitive or metalinguistic scaffolding for meaning-making activities (e.g. explaining and elaborating grammar rules and lexical uses, translating new words, and interpreting cultural meaning), (2) managerial strategies which are also initiated by teachers in order to provide operational classroom instructions (e.g. giving instructions for an activity, giving feedback, praising, disapproving, checking the comprehension of learning content, and planning assignments), and (3) interpersonal strategies which are mostly initiated by students who often interact with each other using multiple languages to translate questions raised by teachers to classmates sitting nearby. Her study reveals the huge challenges posed to the monolingual teaching approach, which prevails in most CFL classrooms, by the influx of international students into the often linguistically diverse classrooms where the students do not share the same L1. Although in the CFL classroom, the language (English) which the teachers resorted to was not the international students' L1, it was a vehicle language other than the target language (Chinese). In this sense, Wang's (2019) study is relevant to our study, which concerns to what extent the teachers resorted to a vehicle language (students' L1 Chinese) that is different from the target language (English) in an EMI setting.

The second study, Wang and Curdt-Christiansen (2019), examines the practices of Chinese–English bilingual education in an undergraduate Business Management Programme at one university in the Chinese mainland. This study, notwithstanding being a classroom ethnography with few statistics, reveals that translanguaging is a prominent phenomenon in almost all subject courses in the focal university. These researchers suggest that translanguaging practices can be largely grouped into four categories: bilingual label quest, simultaneous code-mixing, cross-language recapping, and dual-language substantiation. While Wang and Curdt-Christiansen (2019, p. 331) acknowledge that "flexible practices" in terms of exposure to English are implemented, they simply report that it is "difficult to quantify the respective percentages of English or Chinese used in any one class or course" (p. 326) in their focal university. We argue that the EMI practices in Wang and Curdt-Christiansen's (2019) study fall within the medium to high[1]-exposure EMI category, based on what is

---

[1] In EMI programmes, the percentage of instruction time through L2 English in the total instruction time is divided into four categories: low (about 5–15%), medium (about 15–50%), high (about 50–85%), and very high (over 85%) (cf. Wei, 2013).

implied by these authors (e.g. the name changing of the programme from All-English to bilingual education) and our understanding of the local Chinese university context. In other words, in very-high exposure EMI settings, to date there has been no research on teachers' use of L1.

Accordingly, we seek to address this research question: in very-high exposure EMI settings, what types of L1 use can be identified?

4   The Study

4.1   Research Setting

The present study took place in Xi'an Jiaotong-Liverpool University (XJTLU), which, established in 2006, is the largest Sino-foreign institution in China. In the academic year of 2020–21, it has attracted nearly 5,500 students from within China and abroad to commence their studies, amongst who over 4,400 are freshman undergraduates. XJTLU aspires to be a research-led international university, in keeping with the spirit of its parents, Xi'an Jiaotong University (China) and the University of Liverpool (UK). It has dual degree awarding powers, from the Chinese Ministry of Education and from the University of Liverpool. A student who completes his/her undergraduate study will receive both a Chinese degree and a UK degree. Unsurprisingly, in XJTLU's policy documents; for instance, in *Framework for Undergraduate Programmes*, it is stipulated that "All modules at levels 0, 1, 2, and 3 must be taught and assessed in English. Exemptions may be permitted at level 0. Language modules may be taught and assessed in the relevant language."; similarly in *Framework for Postgraduate Programmes*, the requirement that "The language of teaching and assessment shall be English" can be found.

XJTLU, similar to many of its counterparts examined in previous studies (e.g. Wang & Curdt-Christiansen, 2019; Wu et al., 2010) falls within the category of *yiben* (一本) or first-tier universities[2]; in other words, it has quality students recruited from the competitive national college entrance examination. However, XJTLU also differs from its counterparts in earlier research in two ways. First, it is a Sino-foreign university, which is similar to a private joint venture company in terms of governance, rather than a public education institution. Second, regarding history which is usually considered as a core attribute of an institution's prestige, our focal university enjoys

---

[2]Generally speaking, tertiary institutions in China can be categorised into three types: *yiben* (一本, first-tier), *erben* (二本, second tier), and *sanben* (三本, third tier). The first tier universities are elite public-funded institutions with a primary focus on research; this category includes all the Project 211 universities surveyed by Kong (2017). The second tier universities, which constitute the bulk of the Chinese tertiary education system, include public-funded institutions of lower prestige and usually with a primary focus on teaching. The third tier institutions are normally accredited private colleges dedicated to training students for employment after their undergraduate education. It is widely believed that these tiers create a complex layering of resource allocation.

a shorter history (i.e. around 15 years) compared with the university in Tong and Shi's (2012) case study which has a history of over 100 years.

4.2 Participants and Data Collection

The present study, conducted over one academic semester from September to December 2019, was the first part of a larger project that is still on-going. Both authors worked at the same department in the university and co-taught the module, ENG 115 *English as a Global Language*. A total of 50 Year 2 undergraduate students were formally enrolled in this Level 1 module, and another 28 MA TESOL students at XJTLU audited the lecture part of this undergraduate module as part of their post-graduate additional learning activities. None of these students were international students, and they shared a common L1, Mandarin Chinese. It was anticipated that the presence of international students in the classrooms of ENG115 might affect the teachers' use of L1 in XJTLU's EMI setting. In the second part of the above-mentioned larger project that is taking place at the time of writing, data from a total of 74 undergraduates enrolled in ENG115 in the current semester are now being collected, amongst whom two are international students with little knowledge in Chinese.

With the purpose of investigating the use of L1 (Chinese) in an EMI context, we adopted an emic research approach and immersed ourselves into the teaching context by documenting our own teaching practice. During one academic semester, ten lectures (2 h each) and ten seminars (1 h each) were recorded, accounting for a total of 30 h of teaching. The first author (teacher 1) taught the first four lectures and seminars and the second author (teacher 2) completed the remaining sessions. Both teachers, with Mandarin Chinese as their L1, have had tertiary EMI teaching experience over four years in China and overseas, and are experts in terms of the subject knowledge of applied linguistics as well as English in an academic context and beyond. The spoken data of two teachers were transcribed for further analysis in terms of how L1 was applied during teaching.

4.3 Data Analysis

Analyzing the transcript of the spoken data, we focused on the instances of L1 Chinese adoptions amid lectures and seminars which were mainly taught in English, compatible with the overarching EMI context of the university. Inspired by the previous studies of Wang (2019) and Wang and Curdt-Christiansen (2019), the sampled cases of L1 use were further coded based on the emerging themes guided by teachers' communicative purposes, leading to the generation of four major types of L1 use. The data analysis was conducted by multiple rounds of examining, highlighting and annotating the transcript. The first author coded the data, which were later checked by the second author. For any uncertain coding, both authors discussed these cases and reached a final agreement.

5 Findings

5.1 Types of L1 Use in an EMI Context

In the 30 h of teaching sessions, it was observed that both teachers involved were flexible regarding the use of L1 during teaching. At first glance, the instances of L1 use seem random, as they were identified in various scenarios, such as in the process of theory/terminology explanations, demonstrating examples, checking students' understanding of both linguistically or domain-specific challenging expressions or concepts. However, a more in-depth analysis reveals four major types of L1 use that reflect the teachers' communicative and pedagogical purposes. In the following sections, we discuss these four main types of L1 by demonstrating corresponding excerpts of teaching by both subject-matter teachers.

5.2 Adopting L1 for Domain-Specific Knowledge

In many cases, both teachers have adopted L1 Chinese when terminologies, notions and important concepts specifically related to the field of applied linguistics or the module ENG 115 were introduced. For instance, the teacher would introduce a terminology in the field of applied linguistics in English first, and then immediately provide the matching Chinese of this terminology. In other words, the translated part of the English information is "domain-specific" to the target subject-matter. The example below demonstrates a typical case of adopting L1 for domain-specific knowledge as the teacher explains the statistical terminologies of conducting qualitative and quantitative applied linguistics research (Example 1).

Example 1
Teacher 2: "Do they publish more qualitative or quantitative study? The findings of this research provide you with some messages, although this research covers this period, OK? Quite some time ago, but it can still send you a rough idea. They want to look at the proportion of qualitative research, 质性, 质性研究 *(qualitative, qualitative research)*. I've talked about quantitative research, 量化研究 *(quantitative research)*."

(11/11/2019)
    In the example above, the teachers explained the terms of "qualitative research" and "quantitative research" in statistics that are related to empirical applied linguistics research in English first and provided the matching Chinese expressions adjacent

to English. These cases of L1 adoptions are short in terms of utterance length and targeted at terminologies, notions and concepts of applied linguistics and the module content. This quick alternation of language choices provides both linguistic and subject-matter knowledge support for the students, thus avoiding potential misunderstandings or missing of information due to unfamiliarity with the English expressions or related knowledge of empirical applied linguistics research. At the same time, terminologies and notions that are more related to the module and its textbook information, rather than applied linguistics knowledge, were also provided with matching Chinese, such as another example below:

Example 2

Teacher 1: "Well, here's a new word, a history of apartheid. Apartheid is 种族隔离 *(segregation of races)*."

(10/14/2019)

In Example 2, L1 was adopted for a specific terminology, "apartheid", which was mentioned in the module textbook. This expression is not specifically related to applied linguistics research; nevertheless, the teacher made a decision for L1 use as the focal terminology potentially may pose challenges to the students' understanding of the lecture. A similar type of L1 use has been observed in the study by Wang and Curdt-Christiansen (2019) as "bilingual label request." We intentionally modified this category by highlighting the focal feature of domain-specific, as well as avoiding the possible implied duality of language choices.

In the retrospective investigation, it became clearer to us that both teachers were making decisions of adopting this type of L1 use based on the level of complexity of the terminologies, notions and concepts related to the module, as well as their ongoing observation of students' classroom reactions. In other words, such decisions were made owning to the teachers' expert knowledge of the subject matter as well as their awareness of the students' here-and-now learning experience.

5.3   Complementing English with L1

The teachers often complemented EMI lectures and seminars with L1. This practice refers to the strategy of adopting both English and Chinese for separate parts of utterances during teaching. In other words, the teacher would produce a string of utterances in both languages with each responsible for different information. To follow and understand the teachers on such occasions, the students would need to combine information from both languages for a full understanding of meaning. The example below shows a representative case of such practice.

Example 3

Teacher 1: "These are the ASEAN countries. And I presume that you know their working language is English. I skip Thailand, Indonesia, Burma, and 老挝 (Laos), Cambodia, 越南 (Vietnam). OK."

(10/28/2019)

The case above clearly shows that the teacher constantly alternated between English and Chinese in his utterances. The two languages carry different information, and only by combining the utterances from both languages can students perceive the message entirely. This type of L1 use can often be identified when the teachers were attempting to provide examples to further illustrate a concept or terminology. In some cases, the use of L1 can be quite intensive with longer utterances and higher frequencies of language alternation, as the teachers endeavor to situate theories and concepts via real-life examples (see Example 4 below).

Example 4

Teacher 2: "Very small *p* means that, wow, 真的差异会存在或者关系会存在 *(indeed, differences or association exist)*, but how big is the difference or how strong is the association? Look at r, r is the effect size here. 在这里要举一个例子, 让你看看如果不汇报这个r会有什么后果呢? *(Here I shall provide one example, to show you what the consequences are if this r is not reported.)* 假设这个研究没有汇报effect size这一栏, 你只看到一堆p, 就会有一个错觉 *(Let's assume that this study does not generate this column for effect sizes, and you will have an illusion)*: 比如说, 前面三个城市, 这个是它跟全国的比较, 这个是它跟全国的比较, 这个是它跟全国的比较, one-sample t-test 的结果 *(Take the first three cities as examples: This is the comparison between its mean and the national average [Teacher pointing to the column of results for City X]; this is the comparison between its mean and the national average [Teacher pointing to the column of results for City Y]; this is the comparison between its mean and the national average [Teacher pointing to the column of results for City Z]; each of these columns contains the results from a one-sample t-test.).* 你看到这三个同样的p 觉得, 这三个城市给你的感觉是同等厉害, 因为它的p一样嘛 *(If you are only given the same three p values, the illusion is that these three cities are equally impressive).* This is a misunderstanding. If you have effect size, you will notice that 谁更厉害 *(which is more impressive)*? The effect size range is between zero to one; the bigger the effect size, the larger the effect."

(11/11/2019)

In Example 4, the teacher applied L1 for the purpose of utilizing real-life examples to explain the concept of "effect size." Different from the features of the first type of L1 adoption, the teacher used L1 for the most part of his utterance, with only a few English expressions inserted, such as "effect size" and "t-test". The above example, as explained by the teacher, was produced also due to the convenience of explanation from the teacher's point of view. In other words, as a bilingual himself, the teacher deliberately chose to shuttle between languages for more efficient teaching to his judgment.

This second type of L1 use is similar to the notion of "complementary code-switching" which can be found in multilingual signage (e.g. Sebba, 2013) or other communicative practices by multilinguals (Zhang, 2021). Similarly, in the case of teaching within an EMI context, the use of complementary languages is transient and flexible, and it is constantly shaped and utilized by the teachers. Ultimately, the purpose of such language alternation was to further ensure students' optimal under-standing of the taught content, considering their current English language proficiency and subject-matter knowledge.

5.4 L1 Recast

Another type of Chinese adoption is L1 recast, which refers to the situation when an utterance was firstly produced in English and then repeated in Chinese. This type of L1 adoption is the least frequent one of the identified categories. In some cases, the teachers would provide an utterance, which is usually longer and not domain-specific (different from the first type "adopting L1 for domain-specific knowledge"), and then offer an identical sentence in Chinese. At first sight, this is similar to Wang and Curdt-Christiansen's (2019) notion of "cross-language recapping"; however, different from the bilingual education context described in Wang and Curdt-Christiansen's (2019) study, no instances of starting classes with L1 Chinese or utterances longer than single sentences were identified in our EMI context. Instances of this type of L1 use are demonstrated in Examples 5 and 6 below:

Example 5
Teacher 1: "So there are various reasons for people to choose to learn, to put English importance in language policy. For example, Georgia, guys you know the conflicts of Georgia and Russia? 格鲁吉亚跟俄国不是打过吗? You guys don't read newspapers at all."

(9/26/2019)

Example 6
Teacher 2: "This sounds like criticising for the sake of criticising. 为了批评而批评. Who told you that this cannot be used as a noun? This is something abstract. Of course, it can be used as an entity."

(12/5/2019)
In Example 5, we can see that the teacher provided L1 recast of his previous utter-ance in English as "Georgia, guys you know the conflicts of Georgia and Russia?" and immediately provided a similar Chinese version which is "格鲁吉亚跟俄国不是打过吗" (*Didn't Georgia have a conflict with Russia?*) for the students. Specifically, the teacher was trying to explain language choice issues due to political reasons by providing an example of language use and political conflicts between Georgia and Russia. A recast of the English information was offered in Chinese, yet the content of the information is not directly related to that of the subject-matter. Similarly, Teacher 2 also provided an L1 recast immediately after his use of an English saying "criticising for the sake of criticising" to aid students' understanding. In both exam-ples, the teachers were offering real-life examples in L1 to better facilitate students' comprehension of applied linguistics knowledge as well as the module content. It is

worth mentioning that we deliberately avoid the use of "translation" as the L1 recast does not necessarily "match" the English counterpart. In other words, the teachers were not "fixed" on providing the exact matching linguistic codes in the L1, but focused more on the convey of meaning. Only a few cases were identified for this type of L1 use. This is possibly due to the context of total-exposure EMI, which is contrasted from previous findings of bilingual education and high-exposure EMI context (e.g. Wang, 2019; Wang & Curdt-Christiansen, 2019) where use of L1 has been observed with higher frequency and often in longer utterances, often serving as translation of English content.

5.4.1 Utilizing L1 for Localized Knowledge

The last distinctive type of L1 usage is utilizing Chinese for localized knowledge. This specifically referred to the situation in which the teachers applied examples from the localized Chinese context in L1 to explain English information. This type of L1 adoptions often happened when the teachers attempted to explain complex concepts or theories in applied linguistics in general or research methods. Since the module was designed for Year 2 undergraduate students, they were not yet fully exposed to rigorous study of theories or research; thus, supplementing teaching content with contextualized local knowledge in L1 was deemed helpful by both teachers. A distinction was made against the notion of "dual-language substantiation" by Wang and Curdt-Christiansen (2019) as we would like to avoid the assumption of "duality" of language use in an EMI context as opposed to a bilingual education or high-exposure EMI situation. An example is provided below:

Example 7
Teacher 2: "… It has specific meaning, similar to 情 and 理. She developed the Chinese concept of 情 and 理, meaning I would like to persuade you with reasoning, with 理, also with 情, with empathy, with sympathy, OK? … 动之以情, 晓之以理."

(10/31/2019)
   The context of the above excerpt was that Teacher 2 was explaining the concept of pathos, ethos and logos and how they were represented and analyzed in a research paper. In his explanation, he utilized the traditional notions of 情, meaning empathy and 理, meaning reasoning in Chinese culture to facilitate students' learning. 情 and 理 as the close matching alternatives of pathos, ethos and logos were utilized as familiar concepts to these Chinese students. It is potentially a pedagogically sound practice to enhance the students' understanding of the originally distant notions and concept. In addition, the teacher proceeded with further explications of 情 and 理 by presenting a well-known Chinese saying "动之以情, 晓之以理", meaning "persuade someone sentimentally and rationally." In this case, the strategy of L1 adoption was extended beyond simple linguistic accessibility and comprehension, and also activation of local knowledge from the students.

This type of L1 use may extend well beyond the students' knowledge of traditional Chinese culture or history, but also the popular culture of younger generations who are internet-savvy. For instance, Teacher 1 referred to a popular singer/rapper "吴亦凡" (Kris Wu) when he was explaining features of African American Vernacular English (AAVE) to the students, demonstrated in the following example:

Example 8
Teacher 1: "For us, who are in a foreign English context, the most cases we hear about the AAEE is either from movies, TV series or rap songs, right? So they have a lot of that, OK? I was listening to the song called 皇帝的新衣. Anyone heard this before? OK. Check it out. It's a rap song that disses (meaning "trash") 吴亦, er, Kris Wu."

(10/14/2019)

In the above example, Teacher 1 mentioned "Kris Wu" (吴亦凡)—the famous singer and rapper familiar to most Chinese students—and a rap song related to him (i.e. "皇帝的新衣"—The Emperor's New Clothes), to illustrate features of AAVE. With students' localized knowledge of this singer, as well as related characteristics of hip-hop and rap music, the teacher was in the hope of facilitating students' understanding of AAVE.

In this way, utilizing both English and Chinese is no longer as simplistic as traditional code-switching or code-mixing in response to students' lack of L2, but a good practice of teaching that reflects a translanguaging perspective (Canagarajah, 2011; García & Li, 2014). The students' knowledge of Chinese culture in this example are equally important, if not more, compared with purely linguistic knowledge of Chinese and English. Contradictory with full English immersion, localized knowledge from Chinese, both linguistically and socioculturally, became facilitative resources for learning and teaching in the focal EMI context.

6   Conclusion: Using L1 via a Translanguaging Perspective

The study reveals the strategic use of L1 by subject-matter teachers in a typical EMI classroom in China. Compared with previous research of bilingual education in the Chinese mainland (e.g. Wang, 2019; Wang & Curdt-Christiansen, 2019), English is considered as the academic language for all subjects in the focal institute. The amount of L2 English use, although remains difficult to quantify, was obviously high due to the total exposure EMI language policy and internationalization of the institute in terms of its composition of students and staff, arrangement of teaching, and other relevant factors. Nevertheless, adoptions of L1 were observed in the teaching of the two subject-matter teachers as they strategically shuttled between L1 and L2 for better pedagogical purposes to their understanding (Canagarajah, 2011).

Four types of L1 use, namely adopting L1 for domain-specific knowledge, complementing English with L1, L1 recast and utilizing L1 for localized knowledge were identified from the transcript of teaching by both teachers. Bearing the overarching structure of EMI in mind, the teachers utilized L1 for linguistic, domains-specific and localized knowledge to facilitate teaching sessions in English. This flexible shuttling among languages can be conceptualized via translanguaging (García & Li, 2014). It is also noteworthy that among the four main types of L1 adoptions as translanguaging practices, the motivations of such practices are not always foregrounded with the assumption of students' lack of English proficiency (Yu, 2017). In other words, it is not a "compromise" when using L1, but a pedagogical decision for better teaching practices, such as the example of utilizing L1 for local knowledge. Such conceptualization and practices of translanguaging demonstrate the value of L1 in EMI teaching and push beyond the existing monolingual views on language use in bilingual education and EMI classes (Wang & Curdt-Christiansen, 2019).

On the other hand, subject-matter teachers, as experts in the field as well as proficient English language users, took initiatives of translanguaging practices and explored practical space of L1 use to facilitate content delivery, notwithstanding the current English-only language policy of the institute. Many cases of L1 adoptions, such as complementing English with L1, could also be attributed to the teachers' choice of convenient delivery in teaching as a deliberate decision. Being capable bilingual/multilingual themselves, the teachers in the EMI context play an important role in language choices and practices at the meso level. While some of the previous studies focus on translanguaging practices of bilingual education students (e.g. Wang, 2019), our study further reveals the dynamic role of teachers in negotiating L1 resources in a (total-exposure) EMI context. The study contributes to the literature of translanguaging practices in the Chinese mainland and specifically demonstrates the strategic and flexible L1 adoptions in a rarely researched context of EMI focusing on subject-matter teachers.

As a final note, we would like to emphasize that L1 adoptions in content-based instruction are not always focused purely on linguistic issues. It is clear that other purposes, if not more important, manifested through the use of L1 have been considered and realized by the two teachers in our study. These findings are compatible with the core views of translanguaging that flexible and strategic choices of languages from one's meaning-making repertoire extend beyond linguistic codes, and reaches further to the realization of communicative functions, ideologies, pedagogical applications and more. To put L1 use in a translanguaging perspective, as demonstrated in our study, captures a more complete picture of functions and values of linguistic and other semiotic resources of language use and beyond, such as the students' localized knowledge. The translanguaging practices demonstrated by the two teachers provide practical and flexible space of L1 use to facilitate content-based instruction, which is beneficial for students' learning experience. It is hoped that our findings could enable policy-makers, at the focal institute or in similar international universities, to allow more flexibility concerning teachers' L1 use in EMI classrooms, so as to move beyond the monolingual paradigm when formulating language policies.

In previous studies, researchers have pointed out that the continuing desire of EMI by officials in the Chinese mainland may impede the translanguaging practices and further negative influences on students' English learning proficiency (Ren et al.,

2016; Zhao & Dixon, 2017). Some researchers (e.g. Wang & Curdt-Christiansen, 2019), also argue for a preference of bilingual education over EMI, as the former model has been investigated with facilitative translanguaging practices. We argue, however, that translanguaging practices are also evidenced in the EMI context for better teaching practices, and that resources beyond linguistic considerations are mobilized by subject-matter teachers. Yet we realize that such translanguaging cases may run into challenges in an international university, since classes with a globalized student body may require more knowledge, linguistically and beyond, from the teachers, and it is difficult to find capable teachers that may attend to every student's linguistic repertoire or other related knowledge. This, however, requires more strategic management of teachers' linguistic resources and careful design of module content that responds to students of diverse backgrounds.

In addition, we realize that the implementation of EMI requires effort beyond teaching practices and processes. According to Dafouz and Smit's (2020) ROAD-MAPPING framework, other factors, ranging from policy-making discussion of the role of English, the inter-relationship between academic literacies and academic (disciplinary) culture, various agents involved, to the ongoing influence of internationalisation and glocalisation, need to be further explored and analysed for future EMI development. One obvious direction of inquiry, which was not included in this chapter due to space constraints, is the research of the communication and contestant between the language policy establishment by the stakeholders and the actual practice of language use by EMI teachers. In this chapter, we have mainly focused on the teachers as agents that carried out EMI practices, yet the following are other important agents that require further scholarly attention: the administrative faculty who designs the language policy within and beyond classroom teaching (e.g. Wei & Feng, 2015), parents who possess certain views and expectations regarding the internationalisation of the higher education market (e.g. Wei, 2011), and the macro linguistic environment and legislation of the state (e.g. Wei & Xiong, 2011). When the above various agents were considered simultaneously, a more complete picture could be provided in an attempt to explain the current EMI practices as demonstrated in our chapter. As EMI practitioners and researchers of translanguging, we are in hope of furthering the inquiries relating to EMI via a complex and dynamic framework, such as ROAD-MAPPING, in future research.

References

Baetens Beardsmore, H. (2009). Bilingual education: Factors and variables. In O. García (Ed.), *Bilingual education in the 21st century: A global perspective* (pp. 137–158). Malden, MA: Wiley-Blackwell.

Baker, C. (1996). *Foundations* (Subsequent Ed.). Multilingual Matters.

Baker, C. (2006). *Foundations* (4th Ed.). Multilingual Matters.

Canagarajah, S. (2011). Codemeshing in academic writing: Identifying teachable strategies of translanguaging. *The Modern Language Journal, 95*(3), 401–417. https://doi.org/10.1111/j.1540-4781.2011.01207.x

Chen, K., & Jin, L. (2003). *Shanghai jindai jiaoyushi* [A history of modern education in Shanghai]. Shanghai: Shanghai Education Publishing House.

Cook, V. (2001). Using the first language in the classroom. *Canadian Modern Language Review, 57*, 402–423. https://doi.org/10.3138/cmlr.57.3.402

Coyle, D., Hood, P., & Marsh, D. (2010). *CLIL: Content and language integrated learning.* Cambridge: Cambridge University Press.

Dafouz, E., & Smit, U. (2020). *ROAD-MAPPING English medium education in the internationalised university.* Cham: Palgrave Macmillan.

Ellis, R. (1984). *Classroom second language development.* Oxford: Pergamon.

Ellis, R. (2018). *Use of the Ll in the foreign language classroom.* Public Lecture at Shanghai International Studies University.

Fu, K. (1986). *Zhongguo waiyu jiaoyu shi* [History of foreign language education in China]. Shanghai: Shanghai Foreign Language Education Press.

García, O. (2009). Education, multilingualism and translanguaging in the 21st century. In A. Mohanty, M. Panda, R. Phillipson, & T. Skutnabb-Kangas (Eds.), *Multilingual education for social justice: Globalising the local* (pp. 128–145). New Delhi: Orient Blackswan.

García, O., & Li, W. (2014). *Translanguaging: Language, bilingualism and education.* Palgrave Pivot.

García-Mateus, S., & Palmer, D. (2017). Translanguaging pedagogies for positive identities in two-way dual language bilingual education. *Journal of Language, Identity & Education, 16*(4), 245–255. https://doi.org/10.1080/15348458.2017.1329016

Gong, H. (2015). CLIL liupai jiqi dui woguo jichu yingyu jiaoyu de qishi [CLIL and its implications for basic English language teaching in China]. *Jiangsu Jiaoyu [Jiangsu Education], 6*, 8–12.

Hoare, P. (2010). Content-based language teaching in China: Contextual influences on implementation. *Journal of Multilingual and Multicultural Development, 31*(1), 69–86. https://doi.org/10.1080/01434630903367207

Kim, H. K., & Lee, S. (2020). Multiple roles of language teachers in supporting CLIL. *English Teaching & Learning, 44*(2), 109–126. https://doi.org/10.1007/s42321-020-00050-6

Kong M. (2017). *The role of English in key Chinese universities: English-medium instruction, international cooperation, and English-language websites* (Unpublished master's thesis). The University of Liverpool, Liverpool, England.

Kong, M., & Wei, R. (2019). EFL learners' attitudes toward English-medium instruction in China: The influence of sociobiographical variables. *Linguistics and Education, 52*, 44–51. https://doi.org/10.1016/j.linged.2019.03.005

Kong, S., Hoare, P., & Chi, Y. (2011). Immersion education in China: Teachers' perspectives. *Frontiers of Education in China, 6*(1), 68–91. https://doi.org/10.1007/s11516-011-0122-6

Lin, M. Y. (2009). Chaoyue jiaoxue yuyan zhengce de yuyan chuncui zhuyi: Tanjiu Xianggang zhongxue kexue ketang de shuangyu jiaoxuefa [Beyond linguistic purism: Bilingual classroom strategies in science lessons in Hong Kong]. In L. M. Yu (Ed.), *Quanqiu Shijiao xia de Zhongguo Shuangyu Jiaoxue* [Bilingual instruction in China: A global perspective] (pp. 181–198). Beijing: Foreign Language Teaching and Research Press.

Mahboob, A., & Lin, A. (2016). Using local languages in English language classrooms. In H. Widodo & W. Renandya (Eds.), *English language teaching today: Linking theory and practice* (pp. 25–40). New York: Springer.

Mehisto, P. (2012). *Excellence in bilingual education: A guide for school principals* (Illustrated Ed.). Cambridge University Press.

Ministry of Education. (2001). Guanyu jiaqiang gaodeng xuexiao benke jiaoxue gongzuo tigao jiaoxue zhiliang de ruogan yijian [Guidelines for Strengthening Undergraduate Programs and Enhancing the Quality of Teaching]. Retrieved from http://www.moe.edu.cn/edoas/website18/level3.jsp?tablename=29infoid=254. Accessed 6 May, 2007.

Ministry of Education. (2004). *Putong Gaodeng Xuexiao Benke Jiaoxue GongzuoShuiping Pinggu fang'an (Shixing)* [Assessment scheme for the teaching quality of undergraduate programmes (trial version)]. Retrieved from http://www.moe.gov.cn/srcsite/A08/s7056/200408/t20040818 148778.html

Ministry of Education. (2009). *Jiaoyubu Gongbu Jing Pizhun Sheli De Waiji RenyuanZinv Xuexiao Mingdan* [List of schools authorized by the Ministry to EnrolChildren of Expatriates]. Retrieved from http://www.moe.edu.cn/publicfiles/business/htmlfiles/moe/s3119/201002/82560.html

Ministry of Education and Ministry of Finance. (2010). Guanyu pizhun 2010 niandushuangyu jiaoxue shifan kecheng jianshe xiangmu de tongzhi [Circular on theapproval of the bilingual education demonstration courses for the academic year of 2010]. Retrieved from http://old.moe. gov.cn//publicfiles/business/htmlfiles/moe/s3850/201008/xxgk93899.html Accessed 22 March 2011.

Ren, W., Chen, Y., & Lin, C.-Y. (2016). University students' perceptions of ELF in mainland China and Taiwan. *System, 56*, 13–27. https://doi.org/10.1016/j.system.2015.11.004

Sebba, M. (2013). Multilingualism in written discourse: An approach to the analysis of multilingual texts. *International Journal of Bilingualism, 17*(1), 97–118. https://doi.org/10.1177/136700691 2438301

Tavares, N. J. (2015). How strategic use of L1 in an L2-medium mathematics classroom facilitates L2 interaction and comprehension. *International Journal of Bilingual Education and Bilingualism, 18*(3), 319–335. https://doi.org/10.1080/13670050.2014.988115

Tong, F., & Shi, Q. (2012). Chinese-English bilingual education in China: A case study of college science majors. *International Journal of Bilingual Education and Bilingualism, 15*(2), 165–182. https://doi.org/10.1080/13670050.2011.607921

Wang, D. (2019). Translanguaging in Chinese foreign language classrooms: Students and teachers' attitudes and practices. *International Journal of Bilingual Education and Bilingualism, 22*(2), 138–149. https://doi.org/10.1080/13670050.2016.1231773

Wang, W., & Curdt-Christiansen, X. L. (2019). Translanguaging in a Chinese-English bilingual education programme: A university-classroom ethnography. *International Journal of Bilingual Education and Bilingualism, 22*(3), 322–337. https://doi.org/10.1080/13670050.2018.1526254

Wei, R. (2009). Shuangyu jiaoxue de qunze jichu jiqi chengxiao: Laizi yixiang jiazhang wenjuan diaocha de shizheng [Parental support for and efficacy of bilingual education in Shanghai: Evidence from two schools]. *Zhongxiaoxue Yingyu Jiaoxue Yu Yanjiu [English Teaching & Research Notes], 2*(31–35), 40.

Wei, R. (2011). Parental support for Chinese-English bilingual education: A survey of parents of primary and secondary students in Shanghai. *Journal of Multilingual and Multicultural Development, 32*(5), 481–496. https://doi.org/10.1080/01434632.2011.592588

Wei, R. (2013). Chinese-English bilingual education in China: Model, momentum, and driving forces. *Asian EFL Journal, 15*(4), 183–199.

Wei, R. (2019). *Students' L1 and English-medium instruction (EMI) in Chinese universities: Preventing English monolingualism with language policies.* Public Lecture at Southeast University, Nanjing, China.

Wei, R., & Feng, J. (2015). Implementing CLIL for young learners in an EFL context beyond Europe: Grassroots support and language policy in China. *English Today, 31*(1), 55–60. https:// doi.org/10.1017/S0266078414000558

Wei, R., Feng, J., & Ma, Q. (2017). College students' perspectives regarding EMI and their English learning motivational intensity. In J. Zhao & Q. Dixon (Eds.), *English-medium instruction in Chinese Universities: Perspectives, discourse and evaluation* (pp. 45–58). London: Routledge.

Wei, R., & Xiong, J. (2011). Woguo hanying shuangyu jiaoxue de hefaxing de tantao [On the legitimacy of Chinese-English bilingual education in China]. *Shijie Jiaoyu Xinxi [Journal of World Education], (6)*, 37–40.

Wei, R., & Su, J. (2012). The statistics of English in China: An analysis of the best available data from government sources. *English Today, 28*(3), 10–14. https://doi.org/10.1017/S02660784120 00235

Wei, R., & Su, J. (2015). Surveying the English language across China. *World Englishes, 34*(2), 175–189.

Wu, P., Wang, S., Jiang, X., Guan, Y., & Li, X. (2010). *Gaodeng xuexiao shuangyu jiaoxue de xianzhuang yanjiu he shijian tansuo* [Bilingual education in tertiary institutions: Current research and exploration]. Beijing, China: Higher Education Press.

Yang, W. (2015). Content and language integrated learning next in Asia: Evidence of learners' achievement in CLIL education from a Taiwan tertiary degree programme. *International Journal of Bilingual Education and Bilingualism, 18*(4), 361–382. https://doi.org/10.1080/13670050.2014.904840

Yu. (2017). *Zhongguo shuangyu jiaoxue fazhan guiji lvetan* [A study on Chinese bilingual education history]. *Waiyu jiaoxue lilun yu shijian [Foreign Language Learning Theory and Practice], 2*, 57–61.

Zhang, Y. (2021). English as a linguistic resource. *English Today, 37*(1), 34–41. https://doi.org/10.1017/S0266078419000324

Zhao, J., & Dixon, L. Q. (Eds.). (2017). *English-medium instruction in Chinese universities: Perspectives, discourse and evaluation* (1st Ed.). Routledge.

Yi Zhang Ph.D., teaches courses related to sociolinguistics, English for Specific Purposes and methods of English language teaching for both undergraduate and postgraduate levels, as an Assistant Professor at the Department of Applied Linguistics, Xi'an Jiaotong-Liverpool University. His main research interests include sociolinguistics, discourse analysis, multilingualism, computer-mediated communication and L2 teacher education. He has published in various journals including *Language@internet, Discourse, Context & Media, International Multilingual Research Journal* and *English Today*. He also frequently serves as a guest reviewer for international journals such as *Discourse, Context & Media, Lingua* and *TESOL Quarterly*, etc.

Rining Wei (Tony) Ph.D., teaches courses related to bilingualism and research methods at undergraduate and postgraduate levels, at the Department of Applied Linguistics, Xi'an Jiaotong-Liverpool University. He has supervised master's and doctoral dissertation projects covering topics such as English for Specific Purposes (ESP) and Teaching English to Speakers of Other Languages (TESOL). His major areas of research are bilingual education, bilingualism for the older population, Content and Language Integrated Learning (CLIL), TESOL, and quantitative methodology. He has published in journals including *Asian EFL Journal, English Today, IEEE Transactions on Professional Communication, Journal of Multilingual and Multicultural Development, Journalism, Sage Open*, and *World Englishes*. He has served as a manuscript reviewer for reputable journals such as *Modern Language Journal* and *International Journal of Bilingual Education and Bilingualism*, as a book proposal reviewer for academic publishers (e.g. Bloomsbury, Routledge), and recently as a lead guest editor co-editing three special issues for the 2021 Global English Education China Assembly.

Part IV
Classrooms and Students' Practices and Perspectives

Chapter 7
Translanguaging Practices in EMI Settings from the Perspective of Student Agency: An Example from Vietnamese Higher Education

Phuong Le Hoang Ngo

Abstract This chapter aims to explore translanguaging practices in an EMI programme at a Vietnamese university. More specifically, the chapter focuses on how students enact their agency in using their linguistic repertoires during assessed oral presentations to make meaning and construct content knowledge with their lecturers and classmates, who all are Vietnamese. Data were collected within a semester from an ethnographically informed approach, with classroom observations, interviews, focus groups, and other supplemented sources of data. The findings highlight the fact that students' dynamic use of languages contributes to generating bottom-up policy at classroom level, which may or may not adhere to the top-down policy. Based on the findings and discussion, recommendations regarding EMI implementations and EMI pedagogical practices for lecturers are proposed.

Keywords EMI translanguaging · Vietnam · ROADMAPPING · Student agency · Presentation

1 Introduction

Our time of globalisation has led to the phenomenon of internationalisation of Higher Education (HE). Universities around the world have adopted a wide range of strategies to internationalise their institutions, one of which is the introduction of English-medium instruction (EMI) programmes. During the last few decades, there has been a striking increase in the number of EMI programmes worldwide (Dafouz & Smit, 2020; Doiz, Lasagasbater, & Sierra, 2013; Wachter & Maiworm, 2014).

As a large-scale language-in-education policy, the use of English as the medium of instruction (MoI) has been realised differently in various contexts, simply because HE is "not a monolithic and potentially homogeneous phenomenon" (Smit, 2018, p. 387). Instead, each institution is constructed by its own cultural, political, structural, and economic features; hence, it is problematic to simply define EMI as the delivery of

P. Le Hoang Ngo (✉)
Faculty of English, University of Foreign Languages, Hue University, Hue, Vietnam
e-mail: nlhphuong@hueuni.edu.vn

© The Author(s), under exclusive license to Springer Nature Singapore Pte Ltd. 2021
W. Tsou and W. Baker (eds.), *English-Medium Instruction Translanguaging Practices in Asia*, https://doi.org/10.1007/978-981-16-3001-9_7

content subjects through English. Apparently, what may be considered as a typical EMI programme in one educational setting may not in another context. For example, EMI may be seen as "the use of English language to teach academic subjects in countries or jurisdictions where the first language of the majority of the population is not English" (Dearden, 2014, p. 2). This definition is shared by EMI Oxford Research Group and many other researchers, but it only includes EMI in non-Anglophone settings. The problem, therefore, appears when it comes to the analysis of English use in increasingly international campuses in English-speaking countries like UK or Australia. In these settings, a considerable number of students are from different linguistic backgrounds studying the same course via English. Meanwhile, Murata and Iino (2018) conceptualise EMI contexts as settings where "English is used as a lingua franca for content learning/teaching among students and teachers from different linguacultural backgrounds" (p. 404). While this definition includes Anglophone settings, it fails to acknowledge the rising popularity of EMI programmes in which lecturers and students share the same mother tongue and culture.

The study presented in this chapter follows the conceptualisation of EMI proposed by Dafouz and Smit (2016), which introduces the label of English-Medium Education in Multilingual University Setting (EMEMUS). This term explicitly describes the sociolinguistic in question, recognising the particular role that English plays in an academic context, while at the same time, underlining the multilingual nature of HE no matter whether that multilingualism reflects a top-down or bottom-up practice (Dafouz & Smit, 2020). Accordingly, in this study, a programme is defined as EMI if English is [among] the language[s] of: (1) classroom interaction between lecturers and students, (2) teaching and learning materials, and (3) assessment. This way of conceptualising EMI reflects the current situation in many Vietnamese universities where EMI is introduced among domestic students and staff—with the occasional appearance of foreign students and staff. Linguistic homogeneity among these stakeholders, thus, affects how English and other languages—in this case mainly Vietnamese—are used in real classroom practices.

2   Literature Review

2.1   The Implementation of EMI Policy in Vietnamese Higher Education

Internationalisation has been considered as a strategic approach to supporting the development and reform of Vietnamese HE system (Tran & Nguyen, 2018). Among various strategies of internationalisation, the adoption and promotion of EMI is a key agenda, with the first programmes established in the country during the early 1990s (Nguyen, Walkinshaw, & Pham, 2017). Since then, the number of EMI programmes in Vietnamese universities has sharply increased. Several governmental policies and projects have effectively mandated EMI adoption in Higher Education Institutions

(HEIs). Among the most influential and large-scale initiatives is the Prime Ministerial Decision number 1400/QĐ-TTg (30 September 2008), which launched a national scheme on foreign language teaching and learning from 2008 to 2020 (Vietnamese Government, 2008). This is often known as the National Foreign Languages Project 2020 (NFLP2020) under the responsibility of the Vietnamese Ministry of Education and Training. The goal of using English as a MoI in Vietnamese education is stated, either explicitly or implicitly, under the term of "bilingual programmes" or "foreign language" as follows:

> … encourage education institutions to become more proactive in constructing and implementing bilingual programmes which aim to enhance their own training capacity (p.2)

> … construct and implement other teaching and learning programmes in English for Mathematics and other subjects that are suitable for high schools. (p.3)

> … construct and implement teaching programmes in foreign language for some subjects at basic and major levels within college and university systems; and also select some key factors at senior college level to apply teaching programmes in foreign language. (p.3)

While the NFLP2020 policy generally addresses the use of English in teaching content subjects at different education levels, another prominent governmental policy specifically directed at HEIs is the Higher Education Reform Agenda (HERA), issued in 2005 (Vietnamese Government, 2005). One of its aims is to construct a more capable educational system at tertiary level by highlighting the crucial role of English in the quality improvement of training programmes, the expansion of education networks, and the exchange of academic staffs and students.

Under that governmental support, Vietnamese HEIs have implemented two types of EMI programmes, namely foreign and domestic programmes (Nguyen et al., 2017). As their names imply, foreign programmes refer to those which have input from foreign partner universities regarding curriculum, materials, and assessment. Meanwhile, domestic programmes—with reference to correlative overseas programmes—are those completely developed, administered and delivered by Vietnamese universities (ibid.). It should be noted that a large number of these programmes are delivered among Vietnamese lecturers and students, hence creating a linguistic homogeneity in classroom contexts where all the participants share the same mother tongue. The use of Vietnamese, therefore, is expected in these EMI classes.

Regardless of its increasing popularity, EMI has not been extensively researched in Vietnamese context. Especially, the currently limited number of existing empirical studies have mainly focused on stakeholders' beliefs about EMI. A recurring theme has been revealed that lecturers face different challenges in EMI implementation, such as language use, language proficiency, teaching methodologies, or professional development activities (Nguyen et al., 2017; Tran & Nguyen, 2018; Vu & Burns, 2014). When it comes to students, their inadequate English language proficiency and their ability to follow EMI lessons have been found problematic in several studies (Nguyen, Hamid, & Moni, 2016; Le, 2012; Vu & Burns, 2014). However, what actually takes place inside an EMI classroom is under-researched, and therefore, similar to what happens in many other EMI contexts, classroom practices "are still relatively unknown" (Cots, 2013, p. 110) in the context of Vietnamese HE. Especially, few studies to date have examined how students employ their language resources, including both Vietnamese and English, for meaning-making and knowledge co-construction in their class practices via naturally occurring data. This gap, therefore, is addressed in the current chapter.

2.2   *The ROAD-MAPPING Framework and Student Agency*

As stated earlier, there is a great diversity of current EMI practices, and the actual policies that shape local practice of EMI provision "ha[ve] been less consistently well-articulated" (Ryan, 2018, p. 17). The use of English in EMI policy is strongly linked to a nexus of patterns creating a specific HE entity, such as disciplinary areas, nature of programme, or student and staff availability. In capturing this multi-faceted nature of the implementation and practice of EMI, Dafouz and Smit (2016) have proposed a holistic and dynamic framework named ROAD-MAPPING. They suggest that when investigating an EMEMUS programme, it is necessary to take a look into six core areas of that entity, including: (1) The Roles of English in relation to other languages (RO), (2) Academic Disciplines (AD), (3) Agents (A), (4) Practices and Processes (PP) and (6) Internationalisation and Glocalisation (ING). The first dimension, Roles of English (RO) is derived from the ecological perspective that considers different functions of English in relation to other existing languages within a respective setting. The second dimension, Academic Disciplines, encompasses the characteristics of disciplinary practices. The dimension of (language) Management (M) addresses language policy statements, declarations, and documents that can "manipulate the language situation" (Spolsky, 2004, p. 8) and come in a myriad of shapes and sizes. Dimension four—Agents—is an umbrella term including all the social players involved in an EMI setting, ranging from an individual (teachers, students, administrators, etc.) to collective entities (faculty, student union, etc.). Fifthly, Practices and Processes refers to the actual teaching and learning activities that construct and are constructed by a specific EMI entity. Finally, the sixth dimension, INternationalisation and Glocalisation, encapsulates a variety of international, global, national and local forces and interests that HEIs need to address.

Clearly seen in Fig. 1, the six components of ROAD-MAPPING intersect with one another and interact dynamically. Entry point to a specific multilingual university can be granted through any of the six abovementioned dimensions via discourses—the central and methodological point of access. Various forms of discourses can be used to examine a specific EMI setting, including classroom discourses, interviews, discussions, policy documents, and notes, just to name a few.

As mentioned earlier, the aim of this current study is to investigate how students enact their agency in using their language resources in an EMI setting. Accordingly, the focused dimension of ROAD-MAPPING herein is Agents and its interrelation with the Roles of English and Practices and Processes. Students' agency in their

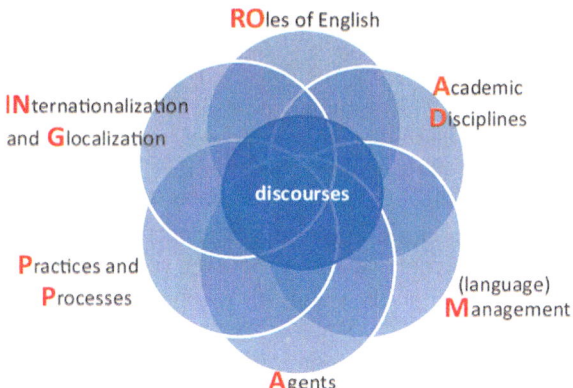

Fig. 1 The ROAD-MAPPING framework (Dafouz & Smit, 2016, p. 404)

EMI engagement can be seen through the way they contribute to the interpretation and implementation of the EMI policy at a classroom level. They can also enact their agency via a number of learning strategies they adopt for their EMI programmes, including asking questions after the lecture, reading before class, or seeking peer support (Airey & Linder, 2006; Chang, 2010; Evans & Morrison, 2011). To improve their technical vocabulary bank, they can record new words or analyse affixes and roots through "a relentless diet of disciplinary reading and listening" (Evans & Morrison, 2011, p. 203). Especially, students can challenge the monolingual orientation which directs EMI as an English-only zone. Students can refer to reading materials in their mother tongue to make sense of their English lectures or textbooks, look up unknown English vocabulary before class, or translate content from English to L1 (Hu & Lei, 2014). Students can also employ their L1 in classroom interactions with their lecturers and classmates for meaning-making and constructing the knowledge (Kang & Park, 2005; Ljosland, 2011). Their effective use of L1, or their translanguaging practices, contribute to the construction of a bi/multilingual classroom and generating grassroots policy for class practices, which may or may not adhere to the top-down policy. They take care of their own learning by making use of their language repertoires, or by acts of "pupil-directed translanguaging" (Lewis, Jones, & Baker, 2012a). In other words, student agency in EMI settings can be seen through their dynamic translanguaging practices in classroom practices.

2.3 A Brief Overview of Translanguaging Practices in Bi/Multilingual Classrooms

The employment of a speaker's language resources for meaning-making and knowledge construction, either in a planned or spontaneous manner, significantly constructs teaching and learning activities in bi/multilingual settings, including EMI contexts.

This dynamic use of an individual's linguistic repertoire is referred in the literature as "translanguaging". Traditionally, bilingual education has "insisted on the separation of the two languages" to help learners acquire a new linguistic system more easily (Jacobson & Faltis, 1990, p. 4). In that meaning, the two languages are supposed to be kept strictly separate. Cummins (2005, p. 588) refers to this as "two solitudes", while a multilingual/bilingual student/teacher is compared as "two monolinguals in one body" (Gravelle, 1996, p. 11). Challenging these socially and politically defined boundaries of languages and their hierarchy, the newer field of translanguaging underlines "both the complex and fluid language practices of bilinguals, as well as the pedagogical approaches that leverage those practices" (García & Lin, 2016, p. 1). Since first coined by Welsh researchers in the 1980s, this term has been increasingly employed to capture the complexity of linguistic practices for a variety of purposes, especially in education (see reviews by Lewis, Jones, & Baker, 2012b; Otheguy, García, & Reid, 2015). The rising popularity of translanguaging in educational context can be seen as "emancipation from many negative ideas about bilinguals and bilingualism" (Lewis et al., 2012b). That is to say, the separation of languages in classrooms has gradually been replaced by the recognition of students' linguistic repertoires as valuable resources for learning, with a number of studies investigating the concept of translanguaging and its pedagogical values (Blackedge & Creese, 2010; García, 2009; García & Li, 2014; Lewis et al., 2012b). Generally defined, translanguaging is "the deployment of a speaker's full linguistic repertoire without regard for watchful adherence to the socially and politically defined boundaries of named (and usually national and state) languages" (Otheguy et al., 2015, p. 283). Multilingual/bilingual speakers can "shuttle between languages, treating the diverse languages that form their repertoire as an integrated system" (Canagarajah, 2011, p. 401). In other words, a translanguaging approach recognises the dynamics and functional integration of languages in the mental processes of understanding, speaking, literacy, and learning (Lewis et al., 2012b, p. 652).

Translanguaging has been recognised as having special values in bilingual/multilingual pedagogy. This is because, as Hornberger (2005) states,

> bi/multilinguals' learning is maximized when [students] are allowed and enabled to draw from across all their existing language skills (in two+ languages), rather than being constrained and inhibited from doing so by monolingual instructional assumptions and practices (p.607).

Accordingly, instead of avoiding L1 use, teachers should be guided to involve the L1 as a rich resource for their teaching through translanguaging practices. García (2009) regards translanguaging as "a powerful mechanism to construct understandings, to include others, and to mediate understanding across language groups" (pp. 307–308). Therefore, she argues that teachers should be aware of its value instead of believing that only monolingual ways of speaking are good and valuable (ibid., p. 308). Baker (2011) similarly underscores educational advantages of translanguaging as a pedagogical practice, suggesting that in a bilingual classroom the teacher can allow a student to use both languages, but in a planned, developmental and strategic manner, to maximize a student's linguistic and cognitive capability, and to reflect that language is sociocultural both in content and process (p.290).

García (2009) posits that "children translanguage constantly to co-construct leaning, to include others, and to mediate understandings" (p. 304). This statement refers specifically to children at kindergarten, yet its value is applicable to bilingual learners of different ages. García and Li (2014) dedicate one chapter in their book to discuss students' translanguaging to learn, with empirical evidence to support that students translanguage in writing, or in combination of reading and writing. Additionally, they report that students who are still in the beginning process of acquiring the additional language tend to use translanguaging to support and expand their existing knowledge, whereas more experienced students do it for their knowledge enhancement (p. 86). Lewis et al. (2012a) describes "pupil-directed translanguaging" as those translanguaging activities in which learners work independently with little support from teachers to complete the given tasks by using all languages available to them. For example, they can search for information in second language (L2), discuss the content in both L1 and L2, and complete the written work in their L1. Translanguaging, consequently, can empower students, and "move[s] the teacher and the learner toward a more "dynamic and participatory engagement" in knowledge construction" (García & Li, 2014, p. 112).

While existing empirical studies in EMI translanguaging have focused significantly on teachers' perceptions and practices (e.g. Cahyani, de Courcy, & Barnett, 2018; Lin & Wu, 2015; Lo, 2015; Pun & Macaro, 2019; Tavares, 2015), how students dynamically employ their linguistics repertoires remains under-researched. Accordingly, for this chapter, it is of interest to investigate these "pupil-directed translanguaging" activities in the context of EMI in Vietnamese HE. To be more specific, the chapter seeks to investigate translanguaging practices from the perspective of student agency. By observing and analysing students' assessed presentations in two EMI modules, the study aims to underline how students enact their agency in using their linguistic repertoires to make meaning and co-construct content knowledge with their Vietnamese lecturers and classmates.

3 Methodology

3.1 Research Context

The data to develop the argument of this chapter are obtained from a doctoral research project that aimed to investigate a specific EMI programme in International Studies of a regional university in central Vietnam. All the lecturers in the department are Vietnamese, and most of them have a degree abroad, at either an undergraduate or a postgraduate level. They all have a high proficiency in English and feel more comfortable to teach disciplinary modules in EMI. Similarly, all the students in the department are Vietnamese, but they do not need to sit a screening language test before enrolling in the programme.

The programme includes a total of 138–140 credits, consisting of two main packages: general education (49 credits) and disciplinary education (89–91 credits). General education modules, such as "The history of Vietnamese Communist Party" or "Marxism theory", are delivered in Vietnamese and conform to the framework of the Ministry of Education and Training. Meanwhile, for EMI, students start to attend one to two courses of basic disciplinary knowledge in their first year, and the number of these modules increases as students progress in their programme. Additionally, during the first five semesters, students are required to attend the modules of General English skills from level 1 to level 5, including Writing, Speaking, Listening and Reading. Some courses of English for Specific Purposes (ESP), such as English for Economics, English for Politics, or English for Law, are also available as substitute modules if students do not take English level 5. The total number of credits students have to achieve within 4 years of study means that most of the semesters are fully packed with more than 10 modules per each. This tight schedule undeniably has a marked influence on students' learning strategies and their classroom practices to achieve the best results.

3.2   Data Collection

Data were collected within a semester from an ethnographically informed approach, with classroom observations, interviews, focus groups, and other supplemented sources of data. Four modules were observed for the whole semester, yet for the purpose of this chapter, only data collected in two modules where students had to deliver assessed oral presentations are discussed. A total of 12 recorded classes was acquired from these two modules with about 17 h of data. The first one, "The diplomatic relation between the USA and Vietnam", was for fourth-year students while "Introduction to global politics" was for second-year students. All student participants were from 19 to 22, and they had studied English for at least 8 years. As stated earlier, they did not take a screening test, and during my fieldwork, most of them revealed their lack of confidence in learning content subjects through English only. Meanwhile, both teachers were female and had their MA study abroad in Australia and New Zealand. They both preferred English as the MoI, as they were trained in EMI postgraduate programmes and their teaching materials were mainly in English. However, Teacher 1 (T1) allowed her fourth-year students to be flexible with their language use. Translanguaging practices, therefore, were strongly encouraged in students' group presentations. Meanwhile, Teacher 2 (T2) required her second-year students to use English only in their assessed individual presentation. The difference in the two guidelines above can be partially explained by two reasons. First, T1 was more experienced than T2, and hence could recognise the necessity of an ad hoc language policy in her class. By the time of the fieldwork, her fourth-year students had studied a few modules with her in the previous semesters. Therefore, she was

Table 1 The observed modules

No.	Lecturer	Years of teaching experience	Module	Level of students	Student number
1	T1	11	The diplomatic relation between the USA and Vietnam	Fourth-year students	41
2	T2	5	Introduction to global politics	Second-year students	36

aware of their language proficiency. Meanwhile, T2 just came back from her two-year study in New Zealand and that was the first semester she started teaching again. That may have had a considerable influence on her expectation of students' level (Table 1).

The two lecturers were interviewed and 14 students—numbered as S01 to S14—also participated in three focus groups. All of these were conducted in Vietnamese, although regularly the participants switched to English for terms like "assignments" or "presentation". Besides, other supplementary sources of information were also gathered. They included site documents (teaching and learning materials, syllabus, etc.) and research diary.

3.3 Data Analysis

Transcribed data of recorded classrooms were named as CR.T1 and CR.T2, interviews as IN.T1 and IN.T2, and focus groups with students as FG.01, FG.02, FG.03.

This study employed thematic analysis (TA) as the primary method of analysis. The interview, focus group and classroom observation data were analysed using the same procedure of six phases recommended by Braun and Clarke (2006, p. 87), including: (1) familiarising oneself with his/her data, (2) generating initial codes, (3) searching for themes, (4) reviewing themes, (5) defining themes, and (6) producing the report. Samples of transcriptions, translations, and coding were sent to an external researcher to ensure the dependability of this study.

4 Findings

4.1 Students' Translanguaging Practices During Group Presentations

In T1's class, students had to come up with a group project related to the topics covered in lectures and presented the idea in class. As mentioned earlier, students were explicitly allowed to independently select whatever language they felt comfortable and hence, they continuously switched between English and Vietnamese. Students could either choose to use L1 as the main presentation language, or switch to Vietnamese only when the content is too difficult for them to fully explain in English. However, it should be noted that there was no explicit guideline on how much English or Vietnamese students should use in their presentation. When talking about this policy, T1 explained:

Extract 1. IN.T1
There is no section for language in my assessment criteria, just not to make students stressed. I will encourage, encourage students to speak English, but I don't mark if the presentation is in English or in Vietnamese. […] Teaching in English is our wish, but this is a content area, and it has disciplinary knowledge. This is a laborious degree, very difficult.

Remarkably, if any students could manage to speak English, they would attempt to do it. They would select Vietnamese not because they were too lazy to think, but because they were aware that their English proficiency might influence the content they delivered, as a student revealed in the focus groups:

Extract 2. FG.02. Student S06
I want to explain more, but my English is limited. It's not enough. But when we can present in Vietnamese, if we see a blank expression in our friends' faces, we can make it easier for them to understand.

This point can be seen in Extract 3, where students, instead of struggling in English to express her ideas, decided to shuttle between L2 and L1 for the sake of meaning conveying. This is a typical episode when students translanguaged for learning. Here, in line 1 and 2, the student was lost for words in English although she had already prepared the content at home. The main part of her discourse in the first two lines was "ah", accompanied with a number of short pauses. In line 3, after a 2-second pause, she decided to switch to Vietnamese and her presentation became much smoother and more fluent. The slides were still in English (Fig. 2), and the student maintained a balanced cooperation between what she said and what was shown in the slide. Here, there was a shuttle of languages in speakers' and listeners' minds to analyse the information delivered in both audio and visual channels.

Fig. 2 An example of students' PowerPoint slides

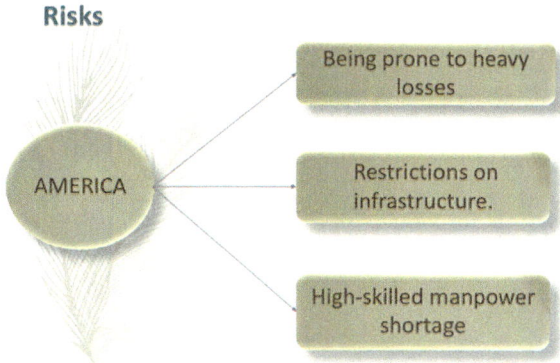

Risks

AMERICA

Being prone to heavy losses

Restrictions on infrastructure.

High-skilled manpower shortage

Extract 3. CR.T1.03

1 S1   and ah ah and ah ah (.) I will (.) ah present (.) ah the risks for ah (.) America and (.) ah ah Vietnam in

2   this project (.) this this (.) ah ah (.) the risk of America ah ah ah (2)

3   *đây đây là những cái rủi ro mà ah Mĩ có thể gặp phải khi đầu tư vào dự án (.)*
     {these these are the risks that ah the USA can face when investing into this project}

4   *Đó là ah ah cái vấn đề thu hồi vốn của Mĩ là sẽ khó khăn (.)*
     {it is ah ah its payback will be difficult}

5   *Thứ hai là cơ sở hạ tầng ở Việt Nam là vẫn còn yếu kém (.) nên là gây khó khăn ah cho Mĩ khi mà (.)*
     {secondly the infrastructure in Vietnam is still underdeveloped (.) so it is difficult for the USA when}

6   *Mĩ tiến hành dự án (.)*
     {the USA starts the project}

7   *Và thứ ba là (.) cái trình độ mà (.) cái trình độ lao động là còn thấp nên gây khó khăn cho Mĩ khi mà*
     {And thirdly (.) the level that (.) the work level is still low so it causes difficulties for the USA when}

8   *tiến hành ah cái (.) dự án này (.)*
     {conducting ah this (.) project}

In groups with various language proficiency, each individual member could also have their own language choice. It was common for a presentation to be delivered in English by one speaker, and then in Vietnamese by the next speaker. Similarly, each team selected the language for PowerPoint slides based on their own linguistic repertoire. Students expressed a positive attitude towards this translanguaging practice:

Extract 4. FG.01. Student S02

In classes like the one of T1, we are allowed to present the outline in English, the slides in English, but we should explain and present in Vietnamese so everyone can understand. If not, if we are asked to explain in English, no one will understand @ @

CAUSES OF DUMPING

Intentional dumping:

- Producers in one country are trying to stay competitive with producers in another country.
- Producers in one country are trying to eliminate the producers in another country and gain a larger share of the world market.
- Producers can make more profit by dividing sales into domestic and foreign markets, then charging each market whatever price the buyers are willing to pay.

➢ CHÍNH PHỦ
•Thúc đẩy phát triển kinh tế.
•Cung cấp một môi trường chính sách thuận lợi để tăng khả năng cạnh tranh toàn cầu
• Thúc đẩy quan hệ hợp tác và sự kéo theo phát triển của các ngành dịch vụ liên quan.

Fig. 3 Two PPT slides—CR.T1.04

An interesting example for students' language choice in T1's class is a project presentation about "dumping". Figure 3 represents the employment of both English and Vietnamese in students' slides. When introducing the background of dumping, student S1 had both the slides and her talk in L2. This part was quite theoretical and the English information presented could be found in journal articles or on the Internet. Furthermore, compared to her classmates, S1 was observed to prefer using English to Vietnamese. The next student, S2, switched to Vietnamese in her slide design and her talk without any advanced notice. After that introduction part, the group applied what they had learnt to proposing their project of "ProShrimp", an imaginative company founded and invested by a US corporation. The group had to ask for their classmates' participation in discussing the feasibility of this project by role playing a meeting between the company representative and local Vietnamese people. For this second part, the slides and talk were done in Vietnamese. In Extract 5, student S3 played the role of Proshrimp Company representative from the US and explained in English that she would use Vietnamese to communicate with her potential Vietnamese partners. After that, she switched to Vietnamese.

Extract 5. CR.T1.04

1 S3   hello everybody (.)
2   I'm Birdy (.) the representative of ah Proshrimp (.) Company (.)
3   well (.) I'm from the US but I want everyone to understand ah more clear about
4   our project (.) so I will present the project in Vietnamese (.) are you ok? (.)
5 Class @@ ok
6 S3   đầu tiên thì (.) nhằm đáp ứng nhu cầu của ah người dân người dân nuôi tôm cả trong tỉnh
        {first (.) to meet the demand of people people who build shrimp farm in this province}
7   và ngoài tỉnh (.) tức là đáp ứng được nhu cầu và chất lượng của con tôm giống thì ah (.)
        {as other provinces (.) I mean to meet the demand and the quality of shrimp breeding ah}

It is apparent from the example above that S3 felt free to select what could maximise the quality of her presentation from her linguistic repertoires. S3 began her presentation in English (lines 1–4), but then explained that she would use Vietnamese for the rest of her talk because she wanted everyone to understand her talk clearly. That is to say, S3 took into consideration the need to make her language choice fit well in that situation. At the end of S3's talk about ProShrimp, T1 questioned the use of Vietnamese by comparing the identity of Proshrimp and the use of language associated with that identity (Extract 6). T1's laughter (line 3) and comment on S3's Vietnamese proficiency (line 5) indicated her attention to the use of Vietnamese in this context. S3's response in line 6 functioned as a rebuttal against T1's statement "You speak Vietnamese fluently"—claiming that her choice of using Vietnamese in that setting was a deliberate and prepared act. It is interesting to see how the students empowered their L1 through this role play because normally in real life, that kind of meeting between an American company and local people would often take place in English with an English-Vietnamese translator.

Extract 6. CR.T1.04

1	T1	so Proshrimp is an American company (.) or a Vietnamese company?
2	S3	American
3	T1	[@@]
4	Class	[@@]
5	T1	you speak vietnamese fluently
6	S3	*không phải mô cô (.) do học Tiếng Việt cấp tốc* {no Mrs (.) I learnt Vietnamese intensively}

4.2 Students' Translanguaging Practices During Individual Presentations

While students presented in groups in the class of Teacher T1, individual presentation was assessed in the class of Teacher T2. However, delivering an individual presentation in English only was considerably hard for the second-year participants given their limited linguistic proficiency. Especially, when the module content was related to Politics, which means students often had to express their understandings in the form of essays or verbal presentations. Additionally, students were requested to prepare PowerPoint slides and handouts for their audience in English. At the end of their individual presentations, students were also expected to answer two to three questions from their classmates and Teacher T2, also in English. Teacher T2 explained the reason for her regulation as below:

Extract 7. IN.T2
I had a lot of expectations before teaching these classes. Yeah but there were many contradictions between expectations and realities, because in fact I thought my students would be similar to me. When I was a student here, I learnt these subjects in

English and felt interested. But I feel like they are learning because they are obliged to learn, so I am quite disappointed.

As can be seen from Extract 7, Teacher T2 imposed the policy based on her own experience as a previous student of the department, who studied these subjects in English with much enthusiasm. She had assumed that, students would make their effort at acquiring disciplinary knowledge no matter how challenging it was, and that dictates her policy of English only in students' individual presentations. Yet even when T2 recognised that delivering individual presentation in English was stressful for students, it was too late for her to change that part of the policy because students had already started presenting in week 3, and it would be inconsistent in assessment if the language of delivery was not the same among students.

With such requirements, most students found it quite challenging to fully express their understanding of the topic presented to their classmates. In most cases, the PowerPoint slides turned out to be a reading script for presenters. Extract 8 and Fig. 4 are typical illustrations for this. There was no difference between what the student S4 verbally presented—as transcribed in the extract, and what was shown in the slide—as screenshotted in Fig. 4. She literally read everything written on her slide, without any clarification or elaboration. Moreover, it was puzzling for the audience at the same time due to a number of pronunciation problems. For example, S4 pronounced the word "range" (line 2) as /ren/, arrangements (line 3) as /əˈrenrəmənt/, or measures (line 6) as /məˈʃʊə/. Her pauses at the middle of a word also added more obstacles for comprehensibility, such as "broa(.)der" instead of "broader" (line 2), or "in(.)terrogation" instead of "interrogation" (line 8).

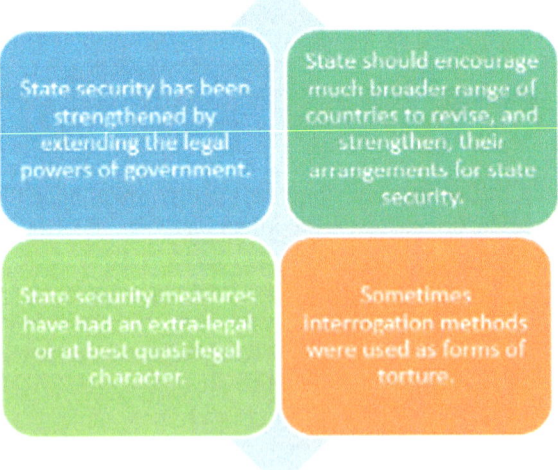

Fig. 4 A PPT slide in S4's presentation on "Counter-Terrorism"—CR.T2.05

Extract 8. CR.T2.05

1	S4	firstly ah strengthening state security ah (2)
2		State should ah encourage much broa(.)der range of countries (.) to revise (.) and
3		strengthen (.) their arrangements for state security (.)
4		State security has been strength(.)ened by (.) extending the ah legal powers of government
5		(.)
6		State security ah measures have had an extra legal or at best ah quasi legal character (2)
7		Sometimes in(.)terrogation methods were used as forms of ah torture

S4 was just among many students in T2's class to deliver their presentations in this way. Consequently, the prohibition of translanguaging practices in this kind of English-only presentation appeared to make no contribution to the knowledge construction, because the majority of students did not seem to grasp the knowledge presented by their friends. Even the speakers read the content like a machine and were totally dependent on the slides or the prepared scripts, as revealed in focus groups:

Extract 9. FG.03. Student S11

I totally don't agree with this way of T2 because honestly we only focus on what we are gonna present, not our classmates. Once we finish ours, it's all done. We don't care anymore. We spend much time preparing for this, we read, we translate, we write, then we translate again, but in class we can only English and it's super hard for us. We just read aloud what we wrote at home. It's not the ideas that we can confidently present. And then, when someone presents, we audience don't understand anything. We sit there understanding nothing about our friends' presentations.

Nonetheless, students still managed to create a space for their translanguaging practices against that language policy of T2. During the focus groups, students uncovered that for the Q&A session at the end of each presentation, the presenters and their classmates would arrange beforehand a prepared set of questions to be asked (Extract 10). They would try to find the information in both Vietnamese and English first, and then in class would use English as required to answer the questions. On the one hand, this way of doing challenged the validity of an English-only zone during students' presentation and Q&A. On the other hand, it demonstrated how students acted on their agency towards the prohibition of translanguaging practices imposed by T2. This may be linked to the concepts of "front stage" and "back stage" behaviours in sociology proposed by Goffman (1959). In this case, the presentation in class was a "front stage" performance when presenters were aware of the norms, the expectations and the class setting, with T2 and their classmates watching them. They were expected to present in English in a comprehensible way, and the audience was supposed to follow the talk so as to come up with proper questions. In order to prepare for their "front stage" appearance, students secretly had their "back stage" interaction—when the presenters and the audience were more relaxed and revealed their true selves. They admitted their fear for being reprimanded in class, employed their linguistic repertoires to complete the tasks given, and rehearsed their way of asking and answering questions naturally. The roles of the questioners and respondents in the class, therefore, were only a "front stage" performance of the roles of friends/classmates on the "back stage".

Extract 10. FG.03. Student S13
For that subject of global politics, we will arrange the questions before class in Vietnamese, sometimes if we are confident we'll do it in English as well. We will tell the presenters before class what we are going to ask them after their presentation, so they can get their answers ready. They can search for the information on the Internet, on the Vietnamese webpages.

It is apparent from the example above that students did not just passively follow what was imposed on them in terms of language use. Instead, they conduct their translanguaging practices, either explicitly or secretly, hence could make great use of their linguistic repertoires for the benefit of learning.

5   Discussion and Conclusion

The book chapter has analysed translanguaging practices from the perspective of student agency in two observed EMI modules, in which students had to deliver either individual or group presentations. This section will discuss its findings in comparison to existing literature based on the three components of the ROAD-MAPPING framework: Agents, Roles of English, and Practices and Processes. The Agents component in ROAD-MAPPING considers different individual social players in an EMI setting, including students (Dafouz & Smit, 2016). At a micro level, students' agency in EMI can be demonstrated via their way of negotiation and re-interpretation of the language policy imposed on their processes of knowledge co-construction and meaning making (Practices and Processes). Students' "complex and fluid language practices" (García & Lin, 2016, p. 1) underline the linguistic ecology of an EMI setting where English co-exists with other languages in harmony (the Roles of English). As the ROAD-MAPPING framework points out, "the functional breadth of English must be considered in relation to the complete linguistic repertoire of a specific higher education site" (Dafouz & Smit, 2016, p. 403).

In this study, there were different factors influencing teachers T1 and T2 in the way they imposed the language policy on their classes. Since those go beyond the scope of this current chapter, they were briefly touched in Extract 1 and Extract 7. However, the aforementioned examples from two modules of T1 and T2 clearly illustrate the roles of translanguaging practices from students' perspectives, no matter what the policy was. In the second module, T2's strict rule in which students had to use English only in their presentations, handouts, Q&A, and PowerPoint slides seriously limited students' learning space and impeded their meaning-making process. This monolingual orientation follows the ideological pressures that languages should be kept "pure and separate" (Lemke, 2002, p. 85), hence moving between languages is "frowned upon" in educational settings (Creese & Blackedge, 2010, p. 105). Notwithstanding this, as Laupenmühlen (2012, cited in Tavares, 2015) argues, students are naturally inclined to activate their own existing resources in L1 when dealing with tasks and concepts in L2. T2's students still enacted their agency in resorting to Vietnamese as a "hidden" strategy from their teacher. This once again reconfirms that studying via L2 does not prevent students from relying on their mother tongue in processing information (Logan-Terry & Wright, 2010).

On the other hand, in the module of T1, students independently and naturally shuttled between Vietnamese and English when presenting their group ideas or when discussing with their classmates and T1 during their presentations. Students' use of translanguaging to co-construct content knowledge was accepted by their lecturer T1, who acknowledged the existence of two languages in the programme and jointly created the space for students' translanguaging practices. Students played along two languages in meaning-making process, creating a new reality in which both English and Vietnamese operated within the dynamism of classroom practices. How much each language was used varied among students depending on individual language strength, but more importantly, the two languages collaborated and empowered the students linguistically and academically. Particularly in student talk, their translanguaging serves three important discursive functions mentioned by García and Li (2014, p. 103), including "to participate", "to elaborate ideas", and "to raise questions".

The data presented in this study highlight the crucial importance of translanguaging pedagogy via student involvement for the benefit of both learning and teaching in bilingual/multilingual settings (e.g. Doiz et al., 2013; García & Li, 2014; Lewis et al., 2012a, 2012b; Probyn, 2006). Additionally, it can be inferred from this study that L1 use in EMI classrooms is not "a deficit practice" (Probyn, 2006, p. 220), or something to feel guilty about (Creese & Blackedge, 2010). Instead, students' active use of both Vietnamese and English in this current study underscores that EMI should be seen as providing settings for the nourishment of bilingualism/multilingualism. It should not definitely be oriented towards monolingual English ideologies and practices.

From students' translanguaging practices in the investigated EMI settings, the final point to discuss here is what lecturers can do to support their students' EMI learning. It is of great importance that lecturers can provide "bilingual supportive scaffolding practices" (Doiz et al., 2013, p. 218), in which Vietnamese or any other L1 can function as a bridge for students to access the content to be acquired in English and then produce new knowledge themselves. Especially, in situations where students' language proficiency is insufficient, the "linguistic purism" with English only (Lin, 2006) may cause the simplification of content knowledge or the risk of students' failure to absorb necessary disciplinary information. Consequently, it is highly recommended that students' translanguaging practices should not be considered as negatively impacting their academic development. More importantly, there should be trainings or activities to raise lecturers' awareness of classroom translanguaging in EMI settings. This is necessary for both pre- and in-service teacher education and can be done by providing specific examples, probably from empirical studies in the area, in which lecturers' and students' linguistic repertoires are valued and employed in an appropriate way to enhance learning opportunities. A taxonomy of translanguaging strategies and functions may also be useful for teacher trainees to accept the usefulness of different languages in their classes, while feeling assured that bilingual/multilingual practices are common in EMI programmes. However, as Ferguson (2003) suggests, the general aim of these activities is not to impose prescriptive guidelines on EMI lecturers, but to enhance their understanding of translanguaging, based on which they can make their own decision.

To sum up, the study provides useful empirical data, analysed and discussed against the ROAD-MAPPING framework, to provide insights into EMI translanguaging practices as seen through the perspectives of student agency. It highlights students' role in re-interpreting and implementing the language-in-education policy at the classroom level. The differences in two modules observed and how students in each module perceived and employed English and Vietnamese in delivering their presentations reflect the significance of translanguaging activities in knowledge co-construction and meaning-making. The key contribution of this study, therefore, is the recommendation for EMI lecturers to value students' classroom language resources and take pedagogically language-related actions (Tavares, 2015). In so doing, students are given enough learning space to construct their disciplinary knowledge dynamically and functionally with their available linguistic repertoires. Future research could build on this study by exploring EMI students' perceptions and practices of translanguaging in preparing for their classes, reading at home, reviewing for exams, or interacting with their classmates and lecturers during group discussions. Also, as the current chapter's limitation lies in the lack of focus on teachers' perspective of translanguaging practices, it may be helpful for future studies to cross-reference data from teachers and students to provide a more comprehensive picture of translanguaging in EMI classes.

Transcription Conventions

(.)	short pause
(number)	longer pause in seconds
Italic text	utterances in Vietnamese
{ }	translation
@	laughter
?	rising intonation for question

References

Airey, J., & Linder, C. (2006). Language and the experience of learning university physics in Sweden. *European Journal of Physics, 27*, 553–560. https://doi.org/10.1088/0143-0807/27/3/009.

Baker, C. (2011). *Foundations of bilingual education and bilingualism* (5th ed.). Bristol, UK: Multilingual Matters.

Blackedge, A., & Creese, A. (2010). *Multilingualism: A critical perspective*. London: Continuum International Publishing Group.

Braun, V., & Clarke, V. (2006). Using thematic analysis in psychology. *Qualitative Research in Psychology, 3*(2), 77–101.

Cahyani, H., de Courcy, M., & Barnett, J. (2018). Teachers' codeswitching in bilingual classrooms: Exploring pedagogical and sociocultural functions. International *Journal of Bilingual Education and Bilingualism, 21*(4), 465–479.

Canagarajah, S. (2011). Codemeshing in academic writing: identifying teachable strategies of translanguaging. *The Modern Language Journal, 95*, 401–417.

Chang, Y.-Y. (2010). English-medium instruction for subject courses in tertiary education: Reactions from Taiwanese undergraduate students. *Taiwan International ESP Journal, 2*(1), 55–84.

Cots, J. M. (2013). Introducing English-Medium instruction at the University of Lleida, Spain: Intervention, beliefs, and practices. In A. Doiz, D. Lasagabaster, & J. M. Sierra (Eds.), *English-Medium Instruction at Universities. Global challenges* (pp. 106–128). Bristol: Multilingual Matters.

Creese, A., & Blackledge, A. (2010). Translanguaging in the bilingual classroom: A pedagogy for learning and teaching? *Modern Language Journal, 94*, 103–115.

Cummins, J. (2005). A proposal for action: Strategies for recognising heritage language competence as a learning resource within the mainstream classroom. *Modern Language Journal, 89*, 585–592.

Dafouz, E., & Smit, U. (2020). *ROAD-MAPPING English Medium education in the internationalised university*. Palgrave Macmillan.

Dafouz, E., & Smit, U. (2016). Towards a dynamic conceptual framework for English-Medium education in multilingual university settings. *Applied Linguistics, 37*(3), 397–415.

Dearden, J. (2014). English as a medium of instruction—A growing global phenomenon. The British Council.

Doiz, A., Lasagabaster, D., & Sierra, J. (2013). *English medium instruction at universities: Global challenges*. Bristol, UK: Multilingual Matters.

Evans, S., & Morrison, B. (2011). Meeting the challenges of English-medium higher education: The first-year experience in Hong Kong. *English for Specific Purposes, 30*, 198–208.

Ferguson, G. (2003). Classrooms code-switching in post-colonial contexts. Function, attitudes and policies. In S. Makoni & U. Meinhof (Eds.), *African and applied linguistics. AILA volume* (Vol. Review Volume 16, pp. 1–15). Amsterdam: John Benjamins.

García, O. (2009). *Bilingual education in the 21st century: A global perspective*. Oxford, UK: Wiley-Blackwell.

García, O., & Lin, Y. A. (2016). Translanguaging in bilingual education. In O. García, A. Lin, & S. May (Eds.), *Bilingual and multilingual education (Encyclopedia of Language and Education)* (pp. 117–130). Switzerland: Springer.

García, O., & Li, W. (2014). *Translanguaging. Language, bilingualism and education*. Basingstoke: Palgrave Macmillan UK.

Gravelle, M. (1996). *Supporting bilingual learners in schools*. Stoke-on-Trent, UK: Trentham Books.

Goffman, E. (1959). *The presentation of self in everyday life*. Harmondsworth: Penguin Press.

Hornberger, N. (2005). Opening and filling up implementational and ideological spaces in heritage language education. *Modern Language Journal, 89*(4), 605–609.

Hu, G., & Lei, J. (2014). English-medium instruction in Chinese higher education: A case study. *Higher Education, 67*, 551–567.

Jacobson, R., & Faltis, C. (Eds.). (1990). *Language distribution issues in bilingual schooling*. Clevedon, UK: Multilingual Matters.

Kang, S., & Park, H. (2005). English as the medium of instruction in Korean Engineering Education. *Korean Journal of Applied Linguistics, 21*(1), 155–174.

Le, M. D. (2012). English as a medium of instruction at tertiary education system in Vietnam. *The Journal of Asia TEFL, 9*(2), 97–122.

Lemke, J. (2002). Language development and identity: Multiple timescales in the social ecology of learning. In C. Kramsch (Ed.), *Language acquisition and language socialization* (pp. 68–87). London: Continuum.

Lin, A. M. Y., & Wu, Y. (2015). 'May I speak Cantonese?' – Coconstructing a scientific proof in an EFL junior secondary science classroom. International *Journal of Bilingual Education and Bilingualism, 18*(3), 289–305. https://doi.org/10.1080/13670050.2014.988113

Lo, Y. Y. (2015). How much L1 is too much? Teachers' language use in response to students' abilities and classroom interaction in Content and Language Integrated Learning. *International Journal of Bilingual Education and Bilingualism, 18*(3), 270–288. https://doi.org/10.1080/136 70050.2014.988112

Lewis, G., Jones, B., & Baker, C. (2012a). Translanguaging: Developing its conceptualisation and contextualisation. *Educational Research and Evaluation, 18*(7), 655–670.

Lewis, G., Jones, B., & Baker, C. (2012b). Translanguaging: Origins and development from school to street and beyond. *Educational Research and Evaluation, 18*(7), 641–654. https://doi.org/10. 1080/13803611.2012.718488.

Lin, A. M. Y. (2006). Beyond linguistic purism in language-in-education policy and practice: Exploring bilingual pedagogies in a Hong Kong science classroom. *Language and Education, 20*, 287–305. https://doi.org/10.2167/le643.0.

Ljosland, R. (2011). English as an Academic Lingua Franca: Language policies and multilingual practices in a Norwegian university. *Journal of Pragmatics, 43*, 991–1004.

Logan-Terry, A., & Wright, L. (2010). Making thinking visible: An analysis of English language learners interactions with access-based science assessment items. *AccELLerate 2, 2*(4), 11–14.

Murata, K., & Iino, M. (2018). EMI in higher education. An ELF perspective. In J. Jenkins, W. Baker, & M. Dewey (Eds.), *The Routledge handbook of English as a Lingua Franca* (pp. 400–412). Abingdon and New York: Routledge.

Nguyen, T. H., Hamid, M. O., & Moni, K. (2016). English-medium instruction and self-governance in higher education: The journey of a Vietnamese university through the institutional autonomy regime. *High Education, 72*. https://doi.org/10.1007/s10734-015-9970-y.

Nguyen, T. H., Walkinshaw, I., & Pham, H. H. (2017). EMI programs in a Vietnamese University: Language, pedagogy and policy issues. In B. Fenton-Smith, P. Humphreys, & I. Walkinshaw (Eds.), *English medium instruction in higher education in Asia-Pacific: From policy to pedagogy* (pp. 37–52): Springer.

Otheguy, R., García, O., & Reid, W. (2015). Clarifying translanguaging and deconstructing named languages: A perspective from linguistics. *Applied Linguistic Review, 6*(3).

Probyn, M. (2006). Language and learning science in South Africa. *Language and Education, 20*(5), 391–414. https://doi.org/10.2167/le554.0.

Pun, J., & Macaro, E. (2019). The effect of first and second language use on question types in English medium instruction science classrooms in Hong Kong. *International Journal of Bilingual Education and Bilingualism, 22*(1), 64–77. https://doi.org/10.1080/13670050.2018.1510368

Ryan, J. (2018). Voices from the field. Email interviews with applied linguists in Asia. In R. Barnard & Z. Hasim (Eds.), *English medium instruction programmes. Perspectives from South East Asian Universities* (pp. 15–28). Abingdon & New York: Routledge.

Smit, U. (2018). Beyond monolingualism in higher education. A language policy account. In J. Jenkins, W. Baker, & M. Dewey (Eds.), *The Routledge handbook of English as a Lingua Franca* (pp. 387–399). London and New York: Routledge.

Spolsky, B. (2004). *Language policy*. Cambridge: Cambridge University Press.

Tavares, N. J. (2015). How strategic use of L1 in an L2-medium mathematics classroom facilitates L2 interaction and comprehension. *International Journal of Bilingual Education and Bilingualism, 18*(3), 319–335. https://doi.org/10.1080/13670050.2014.988115.

Tran, L. T., & Nguyen, H. T. (2018). Internationalisation of higher education in Vietnam through English Medium Instruction (EMI): Practices, tensions and implications for local language policies. In I. Liyanage (Ed.), *Multilingual education yearbook 2018* (pp. 91–106): Springer International Publishing AG.

Vietnamese Government. (2005). *Resolution No. 14/2005/NQ-CP on "Substantial and comprehensive reform of Vietnam's higher education in 2006–2020 period*. Hanoi.

Vietnamese Government. (2008). *Decision No.1400/QD-Ttg on "Teaching and learning foreign languages in the national education system, period 2008–2020"*. Hanoi.

Vu, N. T. T., & Burns, A. (2014). English as a medium of instruction: Challenges for Vietnamese tertiary lecturers. *The Journal of Asia TEFL, 11*(3), 1–31.

Wachter, B., & Maiworm, F. (2014). English-taught programmes in European higher education: The state of play in 2014. In *ACA Papers on International Cooperation in Education*. Bonn: Lemmens Medien.

Phuong Le Hoang Ngo finished her Ph.D. study at the University of Southampton, UK in 2019 and is currently a lecturer at Faculty of English, University of Foreign Languages, Hue University, Vietnam. Her research interests include English Medium Instruction (EMI), English as a Lingua Franca, language-in-education planning and policy, and teacher education. Her latest publication is Truong, T. T. L, Ngo, L. H. P, and Nguyen, X. N. C. M (2020). Assessment practices in local and international EMI programmes: Perspectives of Vietnamese students. In Phan, L. H. & Doan, B. N. (eds). *Higher Education in Market-Oriented Socialist Vietnam: New Players, Discourses, and Practices*. Palgrave MacMillan.

Chapter 8
"I Forgot the Language:" Japanese Students' Actual Multilingual Selves and Translanguaging Challenges as English Majors in Taiwan

Simon Humphries and Tomoko Yashima

Abstract Most studies on motivation and translanguaging have focused on learning Global English. This has led to a call for more research into how this lingua franca influences attitudes to languages other than English. We describe Japanese undergraduates who studied English and Chinese in Taiwan during an 11-month study abroad programme. Following a survey of their translanguaging practices in Japanese (L1), English (L2) and Chinese (L3), we interviewed them to explore motivations underlying their language choices. Extending beyond Dörnyei's *L2 motivational self* system, we used Henry's *multilingual self* analytical framework. Results indicated that, rather than striving for *ideal* multilingual selves or settling for contentedly bilingual selves, participants had *actual* multilingual selves in response to immediate needs and interests. One participant had a *contentedly trilingual self* period where he could use his three languages socially while delaying further formal study. The other participant focused on his L3 due to intrinsic motivation derived from its proximity to his L1.

Keywords L2 motivational self system · Multilingual self · L3 motivational self system · Languages other than English (LOTE) · Translanguaging · Contentedly trilingual self · Dual language study abroad (SA)

1 Introduction

1.1 Japan's Communicative English Policy Versus Yakudoku Reality

Since the 1980s, various policies in Japan attempted to improve students' English communicative competence, culminating in a directive that high school teachers deliver classes in English, in principal, from April 2013 (Tahira, 2012). However, classroom observations indicated that secondary level Japanese teachers of English

S. Humphries (✉) · T. Yashima
Faculty of Foreign Language Studies, Kansai University, Osaka, Japan
e-mail: shumphri@kansai-u.ac.jp

© The Author(s), under exclusive license to Springer Nature Singapore Pte Ltd. 2021   143
W. Tsou and W. Baker (eds.), *English-Medium Instruction Translanguaging Practices in Asia*, https://doi.org/10.1007/978-981-16-3001-9_8

(JTEs) continued to use *yakudoku*, which is a form of grammar-translation conducted in Japanese (Humphries et al., 2020). A survey of nearly 4000 secondary school JTEs by Negishi et al. (2016) supported *yakudoku*'s widespread existence. Respondents blamed student issues, time constraints, entrance examination preparation and unfamiliarity with communicative approaches. These difficult conditions and widespread *yakudoku* provoked JTE uncertainty and burnout (Humphries, 2020). Moreover, from the students' perspective, the mechanical, test-focused nature of JTE *yakudoku* caused demotivation (Kikuchi, 2015). Under this environment, where Japanese use seems to be widespread in classrooms but perceived unfavourably by the government and students, it is difficult to promote translanguaging.

At tertiary level, English and an additional foreign language is mandatory at many, but not all universities (Takahashi, 2019). Moreover, an increasing number of universities offer English as a medium of instruction (EMI) courses to prepare Japanese students for studying abroad, encourage an influx of international students, and meet government globalisation evaluation criteria (Kojima & Yashima, 2017; see Ishikawa (this volume) for details about EMI policy in Japan). We work in the English department of the Faculty of Foreign Language Studies (FFLS) in a large private university in western Japan, where the curriculum contains EMI and dual foreign languages.

1.2 Language Policy at FFLS

FFLS contains English and Chinese majors who take a four-year undergraduate course containing a compulsory study abroad (SA) in their second year. To prepare for studying overseas, all first-year English majors take compulsory content and language integrated learning (CLIL) courses in oral communication, reading, writing and SA preparation during their first two semesters (April-July and September-January). They also take two semesters studying a second foreign language. However, they do not have many opportunities to use the L2 or L3 in natural contexts. After returning to FFLS from their SA, they may select EMI courses in intercultural communication, language analysis, area studies, language education and interpreting/translation.

Most students study abroad in their target language country such as Australia for English majors or China for Chinese majors. One unique option is the dual language SA programme, where some English majors study in the country of their L3. These learners study English and their L3 in Taiwan, South Korea, Kyrgyz, Germany or France.

1.3 The Dual Language SA Programme in Taiwan

Participants in this study attended a dual language partner university in Taiwan (Kao, Tsou & Chen (this volume) outline language policy at this institution). This SA programme lasted approximately 11 months in the students' second year from end of February until mid-January. As dual language English majors needed to maintain their competitiveness after SA with peers who immersed in target language countries, they studied mainly in their L2 (approximately 60% English to 40% Chinese). There were a mix of English skills courses from the Foreign Language Centre (FLC) and undergraduate EMI content courses from the Foreign Languages and Literature Department (FLLD), where our students studied alongside Taiwanese. They also associated with international students at the university dormitory and during Chinese skills courses from the Chinese Language Centre (CLC).

As far as we know, no Japanese universities offer a dual language SA programme; moreover, SLA research has focused on monolingual English L2 learners. Therefore, there is intrinsic value to explore our learners' multilingual translanguaging and motivation.

2   Literature Review

2.1   *Monolingual Bias in Second Language Acquisition Motivation Research*

Second language acquisition (SLA) implies a research bias towards monolingual speakers adding a second language. Gardner and Lambert's (1972) concepts of instrumental and integrative motivation influenced early studies. The former motivation arises from career or test-oriented goals; whereas, the latter derives from wanting proximity to a target language community. Gardner and Lambert's work originated from the Canadian bilingual context, which led many to question the existence of integrative motivation in locations where learners had no intention of joining the target language community. In response, Dörnyei (1994) suggested a framework centred on learners and their learning environment. Moreover, for English as a foreign language (EFL) contexts such as Japan, Yashima developed the international posture construct based on students' attitudes towards the international community rather than towards a specific language group (Yashima, 2002; Yashima et al., 2004). In response to the increase in global communication, particularly using the English *lingua franca,* Dörnyei (2005) proposed the L2 Motivational Self System, which has been validated in various L2 learning contexts, especially in Japan (Hughes et al., 2020; Yashima et al., 2017). This approach, centred on the complex interaction between language learner and context, contained three components. Firstly, the ideal self, which contained a desirable self-image of the kind of L2 user that one would like to become in the future. Secondly, the ought-to self, which contained attributes that one might believe necessary to meet expectations of others. These first two components had psychological roots in self-discrepancy theory where motivation arises from desire to reduce the gap between the actual self-concept and personally relevant self-guide (ideal or ought self) (Higgins, 1987). Thirdly, the learning experience focused on motives related to the immediate learning environment (such as teacher, classmates and experience of success) (Dörnyei, 2005).

In recent years, the multilingual turn (May, 2014) has led to calls to research languages other than English (LOTEs); however, Global English continued its impact.

2.2 English Shadow

Roughly a quarter of the world population speak English to some degree (Crystal, 2008) but it is a disembodied language (Pinner, 2016). In many contexts, varieties of British or American English as foreign languages are becoming replaced by Global English, which is a basic educational skill alongside reading, writing and maths (Graddol, 2006). There is a danger that Global English has become an economic commodity leading to a loss in studying languages for cultural, linguistic or social enrichment (Ushioda, 2017). A belief in English dominance can dissuade education providers from promoting other foreign languages leading to a less diverse language curriculum (Siridetkoon & Dewaele, 2018).

Global English often influences LOTE learning. "Arguably the most important unique characteristic of the motivation to learn LOTEs is the fact that the process typically takes place in the shadow of Global English" (Dörnyei & Al-Hoorie, 2017, p. 457). When studying two foreign languages simultaneously, "crosslinguistic interaction" may occur leading to "competition for the learner's generally limited cognitive resources" (Henry, 2017, p. 553). Based on data from Hungarian teenagers studying English and German, "the clear winner appears to be World English" (Csizér & Dörnyei, 2005, p. 657). In a follow-up study in the Hungarian context, sequence of language study appeared to influence attitudes. If youngsters studied German first, it could facilitate motivation for L3 English; however, in contrast, beginning with English earlier had a negative influence on L3 German motivation (Csizér & Lukács, 2010). In Sweden, secondary school students deprioritised their L3 French as they perceived greater L2 English use-value and self-competence (Henry, 2015). Among adult learners in Poland, participants had low instrumental motivation for L3 French and their positive L2 English learning experiences led them to feel that they could not attain the same proficiency (Gabrys-Barker, 2011).

Large-scale studies based on the L2 self system can capture dominant Global English learning reasons. However, according to Dörnyei and Al-Hoorie (2017), LOTE learning motivation differs in two fundamental ways. Firstly, unlike Global English, which is a trans-national communication tool, "LOTEs are usually associated with a specific community that 'owns' the L2"; secondly, "unlike the 'default-like' nature of the universal desire to master Global English, a high level of LOTE proficiency is normally associated with very specific and personalized reasons on the part of the learner" (Dörnyei & Al-Hoorie, 2017, p. 465). Therefore, we need an emic, qualitative approach.

2.3   Nuanced Relationship with English in Asia

Despite the bleak perspective emanating from large-scale surveys where Global English tended to reduce LOTE learning motivation in Europe, a nuanced picture appeared in Asia from recent qualitative studies by Wang and Liu (2020), Siridetkoon and Dewaele (2018) and Bui and Teng (2019).

Conducting interviews across two years at a Chinese university, Wang and Liu (2020) tracked changes in motivation for L3 German learners. Initially, they had strong instrumental L3 motivation in relation to their L2 English because they felt that German gave them career-oriented advantages. However, this motivation decreased as they perceived that opportunities to use German would be remote; in contrast, English could be used widely—even with German people. Their ideal L3 selves seemed to grow during their first year of study before decreasing in the second year. In contrast, they only showed ought-to L3 self motivation for examination preparation. This ought-to motivation decreased further when it became optional in the second year causing the perception that German was desirable but not necessary. Out of five participants, one maintained a strong ought-to self motivation for financial reasons, because she wanted to study for free in Germany.

In their study at a Thai university, Siridetkoon and Dewaele (2018) discovered strong instrumental career-oriented motivation to learn L3-Asian foreign languages (Korean, Chinese or Japanese). Confident English users believed that the additional language gave them a competitive edge. Interestingly, weaker L2 users perceived a threat from non-Thai workers fluent in English, which developed a competitive L3 ought-to self. The authors claimed that this initial ought-to self transferred into an ideal L3 self for some participants who could "have access to another world" ("Mana," cited by Siridetkoon & Dewaele, 2018, p. 321). Considering language-learning experience, some participants, who had struggled in English, treated the L3 as a fresh start and became motivated by their successes. Most interviewees seemed to maintain positive attitudes towards English, but some of them put their L2 study "on hold" while focusing on the L3 (Siridetkoon & Dewaele, 2018, p. 318). Consequently, the authors suggested "English is not necessarily the bogeyman that dampens interest in other [foreign languages]" (Siridetkoon & Dewaele, 2018, p. 326).

Using semi-structured interviews, Bui and Teng (2019) explored the motivation of eight undergraduates in Hong Kong whose languages were Chinese (L1), English (L2) and Japanese (L3). Rather than language as a tool for communication, results revealed participants' cultural and linguistic interests. Japanese proximity to Chinese motivated some participants. They appreciated the closeness of Japanese and Hong Kong cultures but also compared the Japanese language favourably. "Perceived dissimilarity between their L1 and their existing L2 (English) motivated some participants in learning their L3 (Japanese) essentially because they experienced the [culturally similar] L3 as 'easier' than the L2" (Bui & Teng, 2019, p. 8). The novelty and comparative easiness of Japanese caused some stagnation in English study. In one case, learning English loanwords in Japanese provoked an L2 pronunciation decline: "The more I learn Japanese, the more bizarre my pronunciation of some

English words will become" (Timi, cited in Bui & Teng, 2019, p. 10). However, for two participants, "a clear analytic awareness of their linguistic repertoire … enabled them to explore similarities and differences between their L2 and L3" (Bui & Teng, 2019, p. 11), prompting increased motivation for both target languages.

This recognition of a linguistic repertoire, that learners possess as resources, underlies the multilingual turn in language research (May, 2014). We need to move away from the monolingual-biased deficient-learner perspective, that promulgates feelings of failure and incompleteness, towards an emergent multilingual-speaker model representing "who students already are and what they can already do as incipient multilingual communicators who are expanding their repertoires" (Ushioda, 2017, p. 478).

3   Theoretical Framework

In the concluding chapter, Baker and Tsou compare the studies in this volume using ROAD-MAPPING: Roles of English (RO), Academic Disciplines (AD), Management (M), Agents (A), Practices and Processes (PP), Internationalisation and Glocalisation (ING) (Dafouz & Smit, 2020). Although we did not use ROAD-MAPPING for our analysis, our framework aligns with Agents (students' multilingual self system) and Roles of English (translanguaging between English, Chinese and Japanese), which are outlined below.

3.1   Multilingual Selves

We explored Henry's (2017) ideal multilingual self system, which developed from the work of Dörnyei (2005) and Higgins (1987). The multilingual self system has explanatory potential based on earlier studies by Henry (2011), Kramsch and Huffmaster (2015), and Pavlenko (2006).

In his study of four cases of Swedish schoolchildren learning multiple languages, Henry (2011) noticed the complex interplay between English and other languages. One particular case ("Anton") developed a multilingual self-image as a Swedish peacekeeping officer using English, French and Russian overseas. Anton activated "a view of himself as being indomitable, focused and persevering" which insulated his L4 Russian self "from the incursions of his English speaking/using self" (Henry, 2011, p. 247).

"Judith," who was interviewed by Claire Kramsch, described living at an intersection as "a metaphor for her multilingual self" (Kramsch & Huffmaster, 2015, p. 133). She experienced parallel lives through her four languages and the kaleidoscope of feelings and emotions they aroused.

An open question, exploring if respondents sometimes felt like different people in alternate languages, in Pavlenko's (2006) survey received an almost two-thirds affirmative response rate. Similarly to Judith, multilingualism enabled people to live in different metaphorical worlds and enkindled emotions. Although anxieties such as an "inner split" could "stem from a lack of social acceptance" (Pavlenko, 2006, p. 28), many respondents described uniqueness, enjoyment and choices that arose.

Henry's (2017) model expanded Jessner's (2008) dynamic multilingual model (DMM). Rather than discrete languages, the DMM refers to language systems that are interdependent and activated according to perceived communicative needs of the multilingual speaker. As a result, "development of a multilingual repertoire … changes over time; is nonlinear; is reversible … and is complex" (Jessner, 2008, p. 272). In other words, Jessner admitted that language attrition can occur when learning multiple languages; however, he also claimed that a multilingual awareness develops that can influence the L1.

The cornerstones of Henry's (2017) model are the ideal multilingual self and contentedly bilingual self. Regarding the contentedly bilingual self, the language user feels comfortable and confident speaking the mother tongue and a second language (usually English) but not perceiving a need or having any interest in learning another language. In contrast, a harmonious relationship between additional language systems may lead to aspirations to be multilingual, which is the ideal multilingual self. The contentedly bilingual self has a demotivating effect; whereas, the ideal multilingual self "functions to generate motivational energy additional to that created by the desire to become a proficient speaker [of additional languages]" (Henry, 2017, p. 554). Henry predicted that perception of an ideal multilingual self could offset threats to L3 learning (such as from L2 English).

Currently, only three studies appear to have examined Henry's multilingual self system. Firstly, Henry and Thorsen (2018) tested the construct validity using structural equation modelling. While they validated the multilingual self system, it influenced language learning effort indirectly (via the L2 self). At the time of writing, only Takahashi (2019) and Fukui and Yashima (2021) have applied the theory emically to language learners. Both studies involved Japanese learners of English and an L3. They noted LOTEs' motivational challenges in Japan, where multilingualism is not highly valued and there are few opportunities to interact in the target language(s). However, during Takahashi's (2019) longitudinal study, "Interviewee 11" developed an ideal multilingual self as an academic reading work in their original languages and disseminating knowledge in English and French. Interviewee 11 also displayed intrinsic motivation for reading foreign languages and appreciating linguistic and cultural diversity. In the study by Fukui and Yashima (2021), two Japanese participants studying English (L2) and Chinese (L3) struggled during their 10-month SA at a university in Taiwan. Both learners developed ideal L2 and L3 selves, which helped them sustain language-learning motivation. The authors advised that exposure to multilingual speakers from Thailand seemed to stimulate the emergence of an ideal multilingual self for one of the participants ("Haruka"). In fact, that multilingual friendship community provided a nurturing environment for Haruka to practise with these L3 Chinese speakers, where she felt less anxiety over mistakes and confidence that they could use their L2 English to smoothen communication gaps.

3.2   Translanguaging

As Henry and Thorsen (2018) admitted that the multilingual self is an abstract concept, we grounded our study in our participants' translanguaging. Translanguaging also needs defining as it "means different things for different researchers in different contexts" (Mazak, 2016). We treat translanguaging as "a trans-semiotic system with many meaning-making signs, primarily linguistic ones that combine to make up a person's semiotic repertoire" (Garcia & Li, 2014, p.14). Unlike the concept of shuttling between languages in codeswitching (Garcia & Li, 2014), translanguaging channels a single internal integrated system of language resources. We view the permeable nature of languages and continuum from *becoming multilingual* to *being multilingual* (Cenoz & Gorter, 2015). Individuals are becoming multilingual through formal study and being multilingual through using their languages. Translanguaging captures the full continuum as multilingual learners/users employ their resources to learn and communicate.

Most translanguaging studies have focused on challenging existing monolingual ideologies in favour of inclusive instruction for linguistic minorities at primary and secondary schools, but studies at tertiary level are rare and often situated in multilingual contexts (Carroll, 2016). Japan has traditionally been thought of as a linguistically homogeneous society even by Japanese themselves (Turnbull, 2020). We are unaware of any translanguaging studies of participants from a perceived monolingual country (Japan) studying English and an L3 (Chinese) in the L3 setting (Taiwan). Moreover, translanguaging studies of university students have tended to focus on attitudes towards and acceptance of the practice in pedagogy (Moody, Chowdbury and Eslami 2019; Rivera & Mazak, 2017). As far as we know, no study uses translanguaging as a starting point for conceptualising multilingual motivation. To fill this gap, we researched the following questions:

1.   What patterns emerged in participants' translanguaging? (To what extent did they use each of their languages in different contexts?)
2.   What evidence emerged of multilingual motivation?

4   Data Collection and Analysis

In order to capture the complex dynamic systems (Larsen-Freeman, 2014) nature of translanguaging and motivation during their SA, we collected data in three phases. In the first two phases, the participants answered Japanese online surveys in July and December during their SA, where they estimated weekly minutes used for each language (Japanese, English and Chinese) academically and socially. At the end of the December survey, participants could submit their contact details for a follow-up interview. We received permission from two males (pseudonyms Oji and Naoki). After their SA, the second author interviewed them in Japanese using a semi-structured approach based on their survey responses and the research questions. Oji's interview lasted 39 min and Naoki's was 55 min. An independent bilingual person transcribed and translated the audio files into English.

We analysed the participants as two intrinsic cases (Stake, 1995) from perspectives of their translanguaging patterns and underlying motivations.

5 Case Study 1: Oji

Oji was sociable and his multilingual self emerged from his desire to talk to people from all nationalities. His motivation therefore arose from his translanguaging experience; in contrast, he had vague ideal L3 self orientation for studying in Taiwan or continuing to study Chinese.

5.1 Pre-Taiwan Motivation

Rather than a strong integrative or ideal L3 self orientations to go to Taiwan, Oji developed a nebulous interest during his first year in FFLS. Originally, he planned to study in Oceania. Moreover, he admitted that he barely passed his two Chinese courses during his first semester. This experience encouraged him to "work hard for the second semester." Subsequently, he increased both grades to high pass. This success seemed to stimulate intrinsic motivation: "I felt that I improved a lot. I thought that Chinese was interesting." Despite his improvement, he still did not appear to develop discernible integrativeness.

Oji's first reasons for choosing Taiwan were "the period was long and it was cheap." He then appeared to investigate superficially about cuisine:

> Frankly speaking, I wanted to go to a country where I could eat nice food. I knew that the food is nice in Australia and New Zealand, but I didn't know about Taiwan. When I asked people about it, they told me that the food was nice there too.

Oji also noted Taiwan's geographic proximity. However, he did not reveal any cultural or linguistic interest. He only said "I could learn two languages" without describing alignment with future personal visions.

5.2 Translanguaging Patterns in Taiwan

Oji's translanguaging patterns altered during his SA-year as his Chinese speaking ability improved leading to a wider social circle. During the first month (February/March), he socialised with Japanese people. Partly, they "were only together as Japanese" because they had arrived before other nationalities. Oji's Japanese-speaking friends formed a supportive community as they struggled with new life in Taiwan ("food and climate") and language: "we had no idea what people were talking about in class." Chinese immersion caused problems during these initial months. In Japan, Oji "learned Chinese in Japanese" but in Taiwan "learned Chinese in Chinese from the very beginning."

From April/May onwards, Oji spoke English with fellow international students. He mentioned a Taiwanese-American acquaintance for whom "English is more his native language" but the biggest impact came from a South Korean friend (pseudonym: *Ji-Sung*). They became friends after Oji used English to teach Chinese to Ji-Sung. Oji discovered that the South Korean was bilingual (Korean and English) and that they lived in the same dorm. Ji-Sung became Oji's ideal L2-self role model: "because his English was good, I often copied his English and used it." Their friendship strengthened as Oji's English improved: "at the beginning, I was saying [the acquaintanceship] was good for English studying, but later on, I started to like him as a friend, so we went out for meals together." Oji admitted that this friendship improved his English, which led to a change in their communication. "At the beginning … even though I was speaking slowly, he listened to me patiently … He was blah blah blah, while I was quiet. But later on we were both laughing." Their communication became as natural as L1 interaction: "I was speaking with him the same way as I spoke to Japanese" and they remained friends post-SA. In contrast, they did not use their L3: "[Ji-Sung] had to study Chinese, but he said it was difficult. Then he gave up. Since then we spoke English."

The turning point in Oji's L2 and L3 language use came "after 3 or 4 months, around the summer holiday, I started to have confidence over speaking both Chinese and English." Until this moment, Oji tended to stay with Ji-Sung at the dorm speaking English. Although Oji's L2 improved through this social interaction, he increased his Chinese proficiency through formal study initially. As he progressed through proficiency levels, he grasped the grammar. Consequently, he could experiment linguistically, even if he did not understand content: "I realised how to make sentences in Chinese. I didn't know much vocabulary, but I could tell what grammar people were using … I didn't understand anything, but I was just rambling." From summer onwards, Oji switched his Chinese language use from studying to socialising: "I just did what I wanted for another six months, because until then, I just studied and studied. I started to hang out more." He was aware of his lexical limitations but prioritised using his existing knowledge without worrying about making mistakes:

> I thought myself I am fine with words I learned for this year, I would try to build up my vocabulary after I get back to Japan. I made up sentences using what I had learned when I spoke to Taiwanese people and asked them if I was correct. They said it was OK even if grammar was wrong, but I kept doing my own way.

We could describe Oji as contentedly trilingual during that final half-year. He had an adequate recreational level of English and Chinese without striving for higher proficiency.

5.3   *Multilingual Motivation*

As indicated above, Oji did not appear to have a vivid ideal multilingual or ideal L3 self for his SA in Taiwan. When asked about a future career using Chinese or English, he lacked a clear vision. He had studied some subjects towards a teaching licence, but felt "saturated" from extra study. He decided that he "might give up" and was "not keen on becoming a teacher." He said instead "if there's a long-term internship in Taiwan when I'm in the 4th or 3rd year, I'd like to go." To probe further for instrumental motivation, the interviewer asked if Chinese could be a selling point for job-hunting, Oji agreed, but indicated that he needed to improve further for this to become a reality: "If I can speak Chinese like I can for English, I feel that things will change."

Oji's aim to bring his Chinese to a similar level to his English was closest that he came to an ideal multilingual self. He mentioned this as a reason for studying Chinese harder during the earlier part of his SA "I didn't want only English to be better." Alternatively, he felt relaxed regarding pressure to learn two languages simultaneously. He agreed that he was motivated to learn both and claimed: "I never felt [that it was] hard." He used the languages differently and they seemed to reflect different aspects of his personality. He used English socially with international students but studied Chinese formally. He explained "because using English and Chinese is a separate thing. I used English when I was with my friends. I used Chinese in class and when I was alone and rambling."

Oji felt that he had a solid foundation in English from high school; therefore, he was relaxed about improving it. From one perspective, Oji developed an ought-to self from wanting to compete with local Taiwanese students. "At first, I felt I was defeated. I was thinking how I could take this class, but later on I thought I could do it if I tried hard. My motivation went high, so I took time to study." However, using English socially rather than academically remained Oji's main motivation. "We didn't have many chances to use English we learned in classes. I don't think English class helped me to improve my English, but it improved a lot through talking to my friends in my daily life." Oji failed an English literature class, but he reasoned that local students had learned "old grammar" previously. This insulated him from any disappointment: "I ended up unable to write the report and dropped out. I felt never mind."

Oji strove towards ideal foreign language selves for listening. "When Chinese spoke with their speed, it was hard to catch. I didn't understand what they were saying." This was a problem for Oji, because he wanted to interact: "I could say what I was thinking about, but it was really hard to catch someone's opinions." In contrast, for English, Oji's ideal self for listening stemmed from his frustration when he streamed English dramas during his SA: "English native speakers in films and dramas speak English fast and use slang. That is a difficult part. I want to do something about it." Through watching dramas and talking to friends, Oji's English listening skills improved, contributing to an overall 220-point increase in his TOEIC after his time in Taiwan (from 650 to 870).

Oji maintained a multilingual motivation without giving up on either target language, because he perceived their intra-linguistic proximity: "English is closer to Chinese or some parts are connected." He felt that his mother tongue lacked this symbiosis: "only Japanese is different." His English grammar learning experience boosted his Chinese-learning confidence:

> When I learned English, I saw "subject-verb-object-complement" (SVOC) for the first time … [and] I felt English was different from Japanese … but when I saw [SVOC] in Chinese, it was just like what I did in English. I didn't feel like I was bad at Chinese, because I did it once in English.

After returning from SA, as an English major, Oji needed to continue studying his L2, but he maintained his L3 motivation and took a Chinese elective class. He still maintained his ideal multilingual self, where Chinese would reach the same level as English. "I do like [studying languages]. I feel like I should study Chinese mainly. I will study English when I have time."

6 Case Study 2: Naoki

Unlike Oji, Naoki seemed to struggle socially, but developed intrinsic motivation to study Chinese lexicogrammar. He had studied English for ought-to L2 self reasons that weakened during his SA. As a result, when he returned to Japan, he switched his major to Chinese.

6.1 Pre-Taiwan Motivation

Naoki did not appear to have a strong language-oriented ideal self for studying in FFLS or Taiwan. Instead, he had a character-strengthening ought-to self. "I wanted to change something and I wanted to go abroad." Specifically, he wanted to become more open-minded. "Going abroad could change me from the conservative narrow-minded me."

Rather than an integrative motivation to study in Taiwan, Naoki chose the destination based on an emergent interest in Chinese. Although we tend to associate international posture with English as a lingua franca, Naoki noticed Chinese's global status. "The main reason is that I felt that in the future Chinese will be the international language as well as English." Rather than discussing the international community beyond Japan, Naoki noted numbers of Chinese in his home country: "I can see Chinese people everywhere."

Despite Naoki's abstract reasons for going to Taiwan, his translanguaging patterns indicated that he studied hard.

6.2   Translanguaging Patterns in Taiwan

Naoki immersed himself in both foreign languages during SA. He only spoke his L1 for approximately 15 min per week to his family in Japan and sometimes read news in Japanese. He did not seem to socialise with Japanese speakers leading to a perceived deterioration in his mother tongue. "I spoke to foreigners in English and Chinese every day in my daily life … so Japanese started to fade in me … I would say simply I forgot the language."

Naoki tended to use Chinese more than English, particularly for studying. During the first half of SA, he estimated reading Chinese for eight hours per week (opposed to one hour in English). He explained that English classes had less homework, but also noted effort involved in learning the new language: "there were many words I didn't know. I was a new learner, so it took a long time … I couldn't read sentences." In addition to studying and speaking, he immersed himself in Chinese dramas and felt successful: "learning Chinese was fast." After returning to Japan, he continued watching Chinese dramas and speaking to Taiwanese friends online.

Naoki's English facilitated his Chinese immersion. He noted that Chinese textbooks contained English translations, but his L2 also helped him to interact with his best friend and members of a university society.

Naoki interacted primarily with a Filipino-Taiwanese (pseudonym: Manny). Manny's L1 was Chinese, but he studied English (L2) and Spanish (L3) in Taiwan. Naoki used his smartphone texting app in English to arrange meeting Manny. When they met, they talked in Naoki's foreign languages. "Mostly I spoke with him in Chinese. But when I couldn't understand … we switched to English."

After summer, Naoki joined an English-speaking society. As the only Japanese member, he made friends easily: "They welcomed me, so I got on well with them." The club members' attitude motivated Naoki's English study: "it was good because everyone studied eagerly." He added "because they were not native speakers, sometimes their English wasn't fluent, but it was good conversation practice." Although the club members aimed to present and discuss in English, they spoke Chinese socially. Naoki struggled. "Everyone kept talking for about two hours non-stop. I was very tired," but "it was good to explain about Japanese culture or food in Chinese." He consciously applied his L3 knowledge: "I practised grammar and vocabulary that I learned in class."

6.3   Multilingual Motivation

Naoki lacked a concrete ideal multilingual self. When asked about merits and demerits for studying two languages, he outlined problems. "Studying two languages is very hard. It's hard to divide time." When encouraged to suggest a merit of learning multiple languages, Naoki responded vaguely, "I can learn both" without explanation.

Unlike Oji, who noted that his English grammar facilitated learning Chinese, Naoki replied "I don't feel that [the languages help each other]." He explained "raising the amount of studying for two languages is difficult, so one of them loses out." After SA, the losing language was English: "I study Chinese hard but I don't study English much recently."

No ideal L2 self emerged during interviews. Instead, his ought-to L2 self wanted to pass English as a high stakes' examination subject. "I just did [English study] because I was told to." His pre-university L2-learning experience was not pleasurable: "I didn't enjoy [English study] at all in high school." Therefore, after passing to enter FFLS, a test vacuum emerged that dissolved any instrumental English motivation. Naoki also admitted that he had no intention to take the TOEIC or TOEFL, but had a foundation for further study. "I can catch English words and I can speak, so there's no pain to keep studying English."

In contrast to Naoki's negative secondary school L2-learning experience, he developed intrinsic motivation for his L3 during SA. "Once I went to Taiwan, I found how interesting Chinese is. That's why I changed my major to Chinese." He felt L3-proximity: "Chinese is closer to Japanese." He contrasted L3-learning pleasure with L2-learning endurance. "I enjoy myself, so I feel Chinese is close. I would say English is not so close. I learn it mechanically. I don't enjoy learning it." He described the structure of language and listening, but felt closest to the Chinese writing system. Japanese uses similar characters called *kanji*. He enjoyed exploring similarities and differences. "Chinese kanji is close to Japanese kanji, but slightly different. The vocabularies' meanings are sometimes the same but even the same words have very different meanings."

As mentioned earlier, Naoki lacked a language-oriented ideal self before entering FFLS and his SA, also he was ambiguous about his post-graduation future. For example, when asked about graduate school, he responded vaguely: "I'll think about it." Regarding future career options, Naoki contemplated work related to China but his thoughts were nebulous. "I don't know yet, but in future, I want to work using Chinese and something connected to food or environmental problems."

Naoki had joined an internship "for a big company" unconnected to language use. "Nothing to do with Chinese. In the internship, I could experience what the company is doing." As with his SA-reasons, he was self-reflective. "I felt it was difficult to work with others to do something together." He also found it difficult to make friends in FFLS after changing majors to Chinese. "It is hard to join friendship groups that were already made. I can't get close to them." Therefore, despite the pleasure found from studying Chinese, Naoki faced social uncertainties, which may have hindered conceptualisation of an ideal self.

7   Discussion

The first research question explored participants' translanguaging patterns. In both cases, they increased their speaking scope from the summer of their SA onwards.

Before summer, they both focused on improving their Chinese through formal study. Naoki, in particular, immersed himself in Chinese reading. Oji also studied Chinese conscientiously sometimes, but during the initial period tended to speak Japanese and English socially. From summer onwards, their L2 English facilitated their Chinese-speaking. Oji noticed and applied similarities from English grammar, which gave him the confidence to experiment with spoken Chinese. English provided a communication gateway for Naoki by substituting Chinese knowledge gaps in conversations with his Filipino-Taiwanese friend and, more importantly, making new Taiwanese friends in an English-speaking society. In other words, their L2 proficiency simultaneously facilitated aspects of being multilingual and becoming multilingual (Cenoz & Gorter, 2015) as they developed their multilingual repertoire (Garcia & Li, 2014).

The second research question searched for evidence of multilingual motivation. When they selected Taiwan, neither participant displayed integrative motivation (Gardner & Lambert, 1972). Naoki showed signs of international posture (Yashima, 2002) towards Chinese as an international language. Oji chose Taiwan based on practical reasons such as long duration of SA, low cost, good food and proximity to Japan.

Neither participant indicated a vivid ideal multilingual self (Henry, 2017), but similarly to participants from studies by Pavlenko (2006) and Kramsch and Huffmaster (2015) each language evoked different feelings. Like some participants in the study by Siridetkoon and Dewaele (2018), Naoki had unfavourable learning experiences in English, which contrasted with his intrinsic motivation studying Chinese and consequently influenced his decision to switch majors. During his schooldays, like many other young Japanese, he had been demotivated by the mechanical nature of English study aimed at entrance examinations (Kikuchi, 2015). Ought-to motivation tends to dissipate when the external requirement clears (Dörnyei, 2005), which was the case for Naoki too. His English motivation decreased after passing the university entrance examination. In contrast, like participants in the study by Bui and Teng (2019), Naoki felt L3-proximity, that he had never felt towards his L2, and appreciated exploring similarities and differences between Chinese and Japanese writing systems. After his SA, Naoki developed a vague instrumentally oriented ideal L3 self for China-related future employment. However, his linguistic intrinsic motivation overshadowed any career-oriented ideal L3 self. Specifically, his L3-interest may have stimulated some consideration of future employment connected to China but not vice-versa.

Evidence from Oji supports Jessner's (2008) assertion that learning multiple languages is complex, dynamic and non-linear. During the final six months of his SA, Oji displayed elements of Henry's (2017) contentedly bilingual self because he lacked motivation to study hard at Chinese. However, he also lacked motivation to study hard at English. At this point, Oji felt confident at English and had reached a functional Chinese speaking level. Specifically, he had moved along the continuum towards being multilingual (Cenoz & Gorter, 2015). Although aware of his limitations, he wanted to use his restricted time in Taiwan to socialise with different nationalities. During this period, we could describe him as a contentedly trilingual speaker, where he chose to defer energy for conscientious language study until after his SA.

Aside from contentment speaking during those six months, Oji showed the desire to improve. For example, he contemplated his weakness at listening in both foreign languages and felt pride, after SA, for increasing his English listening score. During the beginning of SA, Oji had strong motivation to improve his speaking proficiency in both foreign languages. From one perspective, he had an ideal L2 self that emulated the fluency of his Korean friend and accepted his weaker Chinese. However, he frequently mentioned his desire to improve his Chinese to the same level as English, which indicated an ideal multilingual self that prevented him from ceasing studying his L3 after SA.

Differences in their multilingual motivations can be explained partially by crosslinguistic interaction (Henry, 2017) and how they translanguaged using their existing linguistic repertoires (Garcia & Li, 2014). Naoki struggled with two foreign languages and claimed to forget his mother tongue while in Taiwan. Japanese and English lost out as he focused his cognitive resources on Chinese. In contrast, Oji did not seem to perceive any difficulty, because he felt comfortable translanguaging with existing cognitive resources during his SA. While he studied Chinese formally, English represented his social language, learnt naturally through friendships and online dramas. English helped him to structure his Chinese output.

7.1 *Pedagogical Implications*

When sustaining learners' motivation is an issue in mandatory L2-(usually English) instruction (e.g., Kikuchi, 2015) a dual language SA programme where English majors study their L2 in the country of their L3 is a truly unique pedagogical intervention. As we have shown, what learners gain from their translanguaging experiences is beyond anything measured by proficiency tests in L2 and L3. Increased language awareness as seen in the conscious use of learning strategies to deal with two foreign languages simultaneously, deployment of languages to develop and maintain social relationships, differential emotional attachment to the two languages with deeper cultural insights—all of these create crucial opportunities for their multilingual multicultural development—the kind of learning that classrooms alone could not have created. The richness of experiences demonstrates the benefit of dual foreign language teaching. Although it was not the scope of this chapter, the choice of an Asian language in addition to the Western one may have implications that need to be investigated.

8 Conclusions

This was a unique intrinsic case study (Stake, 1995) that examined multilingual motivation of two Japanese learners of Chinese and English based on their reported translanguaging patterns. In contrast to LOTE-motivation studies in Europe (Csizér & Dörnyei, 2005; Csizér & Lukács, 2010; Gabrys-Barker, 2011; Henry, 2015), the L3 did not lose to Global English for either participant. Instead, English seemed to facilitate Chinese, albeit in different ways. Similarly to Bui and Teng (2019), learner experience seemed to play a strong role in their L3-motivation and, as suggested by Dörnyei and Al-Hoorie (2017), our participants had specific and personalised reasons that differ from the default-like nature of Global English motivation. In effect, their motivation arose from the context for social and intrinsic reasons, but they seemed to lack clear integrative or instrumental motivation. Higgins (1987) outlined that motivation could arise as individuals sought to eliminate the discrepancy between their actual selves and their ideal selves. In our study, rather than striving towards future ideal multilingual selves, our participants reacted to the moment. Specifically, their actual selves were multilingual, influenced by their translanguaging and intrinsic linguistic interest.

As far as we know, no other Japanese universities have successfully implemented a dual language SA programme where English majors study their L2 in the country of their L3. Both participants seemed to benefit and transform from the experience. We hope to see more dual-language SA programmes and research into multilingual motivation that uses translanguaging as the starting point.

Acknowledgements This work is financially supported by JSPS KAKENHI grant numbers 17K02995, 17K02994 and 21K00721.

References

Bui, G., & Teng, F. (2019). Exploring complexity in L2 and L3 motivational systems: A dynamic systems theory perspective. *The Language Learning Journal*. https://doi.org/10.1080/09571736. 2019.1610032

Carroll, K. S. (2016) Concluding remarks: Prestige planning and translanguaging in higher education. In C. M. Mazak & K. S. Carroll (Eds.), *Translanguaging in higher education: Beyond monolingual ideologies* [Kindle version]. Retrieved from https://www.amazon.co.jp/Catherine-M-Mazak-ebook/dp/B01MTFC28U/ref=tmm_kin_swatch_0?_encoding=UTF8&qid=&sr=.

Cenoz, J., & Gorter, D. (2015). Towards a holistic approach in the study of multilingual education. In J. Cenoz & D. Gorter (Eds.), *Multilingual education: Between language learning and translanguaging* (pp. 1–15). Cambridge University Press.

Crystal, D. (2008). Two thousand million? *English Today, 24*(1), 3–6.

Csizér, K., & Dörnyei, Z. (2005). Language learners' motivational profiles and their motivated learning behavior. *Language Learning, 55*(4), 613–659.

Csizér, K., & Lukács, G. (2010). The comparative analysis of motivation, attitudes and selves: The case of english and German in Hungary. *System, 38*(1), 1–13.

Dafouz, E., & Smit, U. (2020). *ROAD-MAPPING english medium education in the internationalised university*. Cham, Switzerland: Palgrave Macmillan UK.

Dörnyei, Z. (1994). Motivation and motivating in the foreign language classroom. *The Modern Language Journal, 78*(3), 273–284.

Dörnyei, Z. (2005). *The psychology of the language learner: Individual differences in second language acquisition*. Lawrence Erlbaum.

Dörnyei, Z., & Al-Hoorie, A. H. (2017). The motivational foundation of learning languages other than global english: Theoretical issues and research directions. *The Modern Language Journal, 101*(3), 455–468.

Gabrys-Barker, D. (2011). Appraisal systems in L2 versus L3 learning experiences. *International Journal of Multilingualism, 8*(2), 81–97.

Garcia, O., & Li, W. (2014). *Translanguaging: Language, bilingualism and education*. Palgrave Macmillan.

Gardner, R. C., & Lambert, W. E. (1972). *Attitudes and motivation in second language learning*. Rowley, MA: Newbury House.

Graddol, D. (2006). *English next: Why global english may mean the end of "English as a foreign language."* London, UK: British Council.

Fukui, H., & Yashima, T. (2021). Exploring evolving motivation to learn two languages simultaneously in a study-abroad context. *The Modern Language Journal*. https://doi.org/10.1111/modl.12695

Henry, A. (2011). Examining the impact of L2 English on L3 selves: A case study. *International Journal of Multilingualism, 8*(3), 235–255.

Henry, A. (2015). The dynamics of possible selves. In Z. Dörnyei, P. D. MacIntyre, & A. Henry (Eds.), *Motivational dynamics in language learning* (pp. 83–94). Multilingual Matters.

Henry, A. (2017). L2 motivation and multilingual identities. *The Modern Language Journal, 101*(3), 548–565.

Henry, A., & Thorsen, C. (2018). The ideal multilingual self: Validity, influences on motivation, and role in a multilingual education. *International Journal of Multilingualism, 15*(4), 349–364.

Higgins, E. T. (1987). Self-discrepancy: A theory relating self and affect. *Psychological Review, 94*(3), 319–340.

Hughes, L. S., Vye, S., & Ray, D. (2020). The L2 motivational self system: A replication study. *JALT Journal, 42*(1), 5–28.

Humphries, S. (2020). "Please teach me how to teach:" The emotional impact of educational change. In C. Gkonou, J.-M. Dewaele, & J. King (Eds.), *The emotional rollercoaster of language teaching* (pp. 150–172). Multilingual Matters.

Humphries, S., Akamatsu, N., Tanaka, T., & Burns, A. (2020). Silence in Japanese classrooms: Activities and factors in capacities to speak english. In J. King & S. Harumi (Eds.), *East Asian perspectives on silence in english language education* (pp. 123–143). Multilingual Matters.

Jessner, U. (2008). A DST model of multilingualism and the role of metalinguistic awareness. *The Modern Language Journal, 92*(2), 270–283.

Kikuchi, K. (2015). *Demotivation in second language acquisition: Insights from Japan*. Multilingual Matters.

Kramsch, C., & Huffmaster, M. (2015). Multilingual practices in foreign language study. In J. Cenoz & D. Gorter (Eds.), *Multilingual education: Between language learning and translanguaging* (pp. 114–136). Cambridge University Press.

Kojima, N., & Yashima, T. (2017). Motivation in english medium instruction classrooms from the perspective of self-determination theory and the ideal self. *JACET Journal, 61*, 23–39.

Larsen-Freeman, D. (2014). Ten "lessons" from complex dynamic systems theory: What is on offer. In Z. Dörnyei, P. D. MacIntyre, & A. Henry (Eds.), *Motivational dynamics in language learning* (pp. 11–19). Multilingual Matters.

May, S. (2014). Disciplinary divides, knowledge construction, and the multilingual turn. In S. May (Ed.), *The multilingual turn* (pp. 7–31). Routledge.

Mazak, C. M. (2016). Introduction: Theorizing translanguaging practices in higher education. In C. M. Mazak & K. S. Carroll (Eds.), *Translanguaging in higher education: Beyond monolingual ideologies* [Kindle version]. Retrieved from https://www.amazon.co.jp/Catherine-M-Mazak-ebook/dp/B01MTFC28U/ref=tmm_kin_swatch_0?_encoding=UTF8&qid=&sr=.

Moody, S., Chowdhury, M., & Eslami, Z. (2019). Graduate students' perceptions of translanguaging. *English Teaching & Learning, 43*(1), 85–103.

Negishi, M., Sakai, H., Shigematsu, K., Takagi, A. & Kudo, Y. (2016). *Chuukou no eigo shidou ni kansuru jittai chousa 2015 [Survey of actual English teaching situation in secondary schools 2015].* Tokyo: Benesse Educational Research and Development Institute.

Pavlenko, A. (2006). Bilingual selves. In A. Pavlenko (Ed.), *Bilingual minds: Emotional experience, expression and representation* (pp. 1–33). Multilingual Matters.

Pinner, R. S. (2016). *Reconceptualising authenticity for english as a global language.* Multilingual Matters.

Rivera, A. J., & Mazak, C. M. (2017). Analyzing student perceptions on translanguaging: A case study of a Puerto Rican university classroom. *How, 24*(1), 122–138.

Siridetkoon, P., & Dewaele, J.-M. (2018). Ideal self and ought-to self of simultaneous learners of multiple foreign languages. *International Journal of Multilingualism, 15*(4), 313–328.

Stake, R. E. (1995). *The art of case study research.* Sage.

Takahashi, C. (2019). Developing the ideal multilingual self in the era of global english: A case in the Japanese context. *The Language Learning Journal.* https://doi.org/10.1080/09571736.2019.1606272

Tahira, M. (2012). Behind MEXT's new course of study guidelines. *The Language Teacher, 36*(3), 3–8.

Turnbull, B. (2020). Beyond bilingualism in Japan: Examining the translingual trends of a "monolingual" nation. *International Journal of Bilingualism, 24*(4), 634–650.

Ushioda, E. (2017). The impact of global English on motivation to learn other languages: Towards an ideal multilingual self. *Modern Language Journal, 101*(3), 469–482.

Wang, T., & Liu, Y. (2020). Dynamic L3 selves: A longitudinal study of five university L3 learners' motivational trajectories in China. *The Language Learning Journal, 48*(2), 201–212.

Yashima, T. (2002). Willingness to communicate in a second language: The Japanese EFL context. *The Modern Language Journal, 86*(1), 54–66.

Yashima, T., Zenuk-Nishide, L., & Shimizu, K. (2004). Influence of attitudes and affect on willingness to communicate and L2 communication. *Language Learning, 54*(1), 119–152.

Yashima, T., Nishida, R., & Mizumoto, A. (2017). Influence of learner beliefs and gender on the motivating power of L2 selves. *The Modern Language Journal, 101*(4), 691–711.

Chapter 9
Translanguaging in EMI Higher Education in Taiwan: Learner Perception and Agency

Yi-Ping Huang

Abstract Although English-medium instruction (EMI) has attracted considerable attention in higher education, it has not widely addressed the notion of learner agency. Through a qualitative case study exploring the perspectives of local and international students in an English-taught program in business in a private university in Taiwan, this chapter explores the use of native languages in classroom interaction in translanguaging practices as well as learner perception and agency in an English as a lingua franca (ELF) context. Data, gathered from interviews and supplemented by observations, weekly journals, and artifacts, were initially analyzed based on (Carspecken in Critical ethnography in educational research: a theoretical and practical guide. Routledge, 1996) reconstructive analysis and later through (Larsen-Freeman in Modern Lang J 103:61–79, 2019) Complex Dynamic Systems Theory on learner agency. This chapter shows the EFL context in the target programs affords translanguaging as a natural yet limited practice and that the use of different resources reflects learner enactment of their agency. The positive consequence of students' translanguaging motivates them to continue to engage in translanguaging practices. As such, creating an encouraging environment is a necessary condition for students' translanguaging. This chapter hence concludes by highlighting the primacy of raising professors' and policy makers' awareness of translanguaging pedagogy.

1 Introduction

This chapter explores translanguaging as well as learner perception and agency in an English as a lingua franca (ELF) environment through a qualitative case study on the perspectives of local and international students in a business English-medium instruction (EMI) program taught in English in higher education (HE) in Taiwan. The chapter focuses on one form of translanguaging, that is, the use of native languages in classroom interaction. The study was situated in one Taiwanese private university where half of the student population in the college is international students, thereby

Y.-P. Huang (✉)
National Chengchi University, Taipei, Taiwan, ROC
e-mail: yiphuang@nccu.edu.tw

necessitating the use of ELF. The following research questions were investigated: how do the professors in an EMI program use native languages in translanguaging? How do the learners perceive it? How do the learners use their native languages in translanguaging?

2 Internationalization of Higher Education in Taiwan

After becoming a member of the World Trade Organization (WTO) in 2002, Taiwan experienced great diversity in the higher education landscape as it tried to make education services accessible for citizens from other WTO member countries. Since then, national and institutional policies have been enacted to "internationalize" university campuses in Taiwan. At the national level, the Ministry of Education (2001) stipulates two significant mechanisms to internationalize education—recruiting international students and offering English-medium instruction (EMI) courses. The government has enacted two significant projects to increase the international competiveness of Taiwanese universities, including The Aim for the Top University Project (2005–2017) and Higher Education SPROUT Project (2018–2022) (Ministry of Education, 2019a). Incentives (scholarships for studying in Taiwan) and assistance (teachers' professional development) have also been provided to attract international students and encourage professors to use EMI.

The above mechanisms regulate the institutional policy, and hence, at the institutional level, incentive policies have been made to encourage EMI courses or programs, including offering subsidies or increasing hourly pay at the rate of 1.5 or 2 times the normal rate for one or two EMI course(s) per semester. Professional training, in the popular form of workshops given by the British Council or local peers, is provided every semester or during vacations. Some universities even collaborate with American or Australian institutes to provide professors intensive professional training abroad. On the other hand, EMI in universities is mandatory such that each college is required to offer one EMI course per semester. With these mechanisms, it is not surprising that the number of overseas students doubled from 2012 to 2019 (Ministry of Education, 2019b) and that the number of EMI courses expanded at a rate of 18% (Chung & Lo, 2016).

These mechanisms reflect that internationalization in Taiwan, to a large extent, has become Englishization, given the high social status of English in Chinese society; and the reality of English as a lingua franca in commerce, education, and engineering. But what does EMI mean in Taiwan? From the policy-making perspective, EMI in Taiwan suggests using English as a medium of instruction, and in some cases, even English-only instruction; that is, many university policies stipulate that English alone can be the medium of instruction in class likely because professors should not "sail under false colors"—use Mandarin—if subsidies were implemented. A few universities even hold penalty policies when professors adopt a language of instruction other than English. Such perspectives, however, neglect ELF as multilingual communication in practice. In line with Jenkins' (2019) argument that the meaning of "E" in "EMI" is ELF in nature rather than English and that ELF is as "multilingual communication in which English is available as a contact language of choice, but is not necessarily chosen" (p. 6), this study defines EMI as using ELF as multilingual franca to achieve communicative purposes. It reasons that professors and students in EMI contexts translanguage (e.g., Jenkins, 2019) or value the use of Mandarin and diverse modes to scaffold content learning (e.g., Huang, 2012). The policy-practice discrepancy, indeed, deserves further attention, and our focus will be on both local and international students' perceptions of translanguaging and its relation to learner agency.

3   Translanguaging as a Meaning-Making Process

In this chapter, translanguaging is defined as a meaning-making process during which a bilingual or multilingual speaker selectively utilizes semiotic resources (i.e. linguistic resources and multimodalities) to achieve an aim (e.g., sharing experiences and understandings). This definition has four theoretical and practical implications. First, it reconceptualizes students in the EMI program in Taiwan not as language learners but more importantly as language users (e.g., bilinguals/multilinguals). We assume that the language development of bilinguals or multilinguals is dynamic; that is, students may select to use the two named languages even though they may not be fully competent in these languages (Canagarajah, 2013; Garcia & Kleyn, 2016). Garcia and Kleyn explain that translanguaging is "*the development of a speaker's full linguistic repertoire, which does not in any way correspond to the socially and politically defined boundaries of named languages*" (p. 14, *italics* in the original). The alternation of language choice "acknowledges that the linguistic features and practices of bilinguals from a unitary linguistic system that interacts in dynamic ways with each other" (p. 16). As such, translanguaging becomes a developmental process through which the two languages are used in a dynamic way, suggesting that language alternation or the use of the L1 is *natural* in reality and even *empowering* and *enabling* in pedagogy.

Second, this chapter does not regard translanguaging as merely language alternation, but more importantly language is viewed as "only one semiotic resource among many, such as symbols, icons, and images" (Canagarajah, 2013, p. 7). As Canagarajah argues, "All semiotic resources work together for meaning; separating them into different systems may distort meaning, violating their ecological embeddedness and interconnection" (p. 7). Translanguaging thus becomes a meaning-making process through which multiple resources and multimodalities are used to achieve understanding. This notion is also what Lin (2016) means by "trans-semiotizing" so as to "cover the use of multimodalities or multiple semiotics (meaning-making systems including languages, visuals, gestures, diagrams, etc.) to do the conceptual work of learning and to expand the meaning-making/communicative repertoires of learners" (p. 184). In this view, translanguaging has the effect of "message abundancy" (Gibbons, 2009, p. 156) that helps students understand content knowledge.

Third, taking the fluid and dynamic view of language (use/learning), we reconceptualize EMI practices as contact zones in which bilinguals/multilinguals use semiotic resource/repertoire to achieve understanding. English is used as one semiotic resource/repertoire in communicative practices. As such, the "E" in EMI refers to ELF rather than EFL (English as a foreign language) (see Jenkins, 2019).

Fourth, translanguaging is a social practice, given that "[s]emiotic resources are embedded in a social and physical environment, aligning with contextual features such as participants, objects, the human body, and the setting for meaning" (Canagarajah, 2013, p. 7). In this view, it is significant for researchers to uncover the individual, social, and contextual affordances in order to understand how semiotic resources/repertoire are selectively used. As Biesta and Tedder (2007) argue, "One *achieves by means of* an environment, not simply *in* an environment" (p. 137). The achievement through an environment highlights the importance of learner agency, which is discussed in the following section.

4 Translanguaging as Embodiment of Learner Agency

Translanguaging as a meaning-making practice presumes learner agency—one's ability to act and achieve in the world (see Larsen-Freeman, 2019). In line with Larsen-Freeman's development of Complex Dynamic Systems Theory (CDST) on learner agency, this chapter uses learner agency to refer to students' determination and goal-oriented actions in the world; it is adaptive, emerging, and spatially temporally situated. These characteristics are important because they emphasize that learner agency cannot be understood without consideration of learners' relation with others in a specific situation. Likewise, time in the system and the elements of the system interact dynamically with one another across time and space. As such, learner agency develops and evolves from an initial condition, which might not be the same as time and context change. The take-away is that learner agency is adaptive and dynamic.

Moreover, we propose that learner agency has four dimensions that guide our analysis: behavior, cognition, emotion, and identity. Learner agency does not involve the power to *will* but rather the ability to *act* or *achieve*. It involves the use of diverse semiotic resources/repertoires for specific purposes. Also, action includes not simply behavior but also decision-making rationales behind the act, given that agents can perceive and assign relevance to contextual affordance (van Lier, 2008). In addition to the behavioral and cognitive elements, we hypothesize that an agent is also emotionally engaged in the context; that is, when they feel welcomed by the community, they tend to achieve academic and social success (Townley et al., 2013). This emotional engagement is a so-called "sense of community" (SOC), defined by McMillan and Chavis (1986), as "a feeling that members have of belonging, a feeling that members matter to one another and to the group, and a shared faith that members' needs will be met through their commitment to be together" (p. 9). Having SOC suggests the last important construct of learner agency—identity. As Larsen-Freeman (2019) expresses, learner agency refers to a learner's choice of "deploy[ing] one's semiotic resources to position oneself as one would wish in a multilingual world" (p. 62). Taken together, this chapter assumes that learners demonstrate their agency to show what they wish to be/become in a community that makes them feel satisfied and recognized.

Translanguaging and learner agency are under-researched in the EMI context. To our knowledge, only Toth and Paulsrud (2017) investigated translanguaging and learner agency in Swedish schools and found that translanguaging has both positive and negative effects depending on the perspectives of students and teachers. In Chap. 7, Ng explored how students in higher education in Vietnam demonstrated their agency through translanguaging in order to negotiate and reinterpret the language policy imposed on their meaning-making processes. In line with these studies' focus on language choice in translanguaging, this chapter aims to examine the use of native languages in classroom interaction from the local and international students' perspectives in an ELF context in higher education in Taiwan. As such, it explores the three components of the ROAD-MAPPING framework (Dafouz & Smit, 2016, 2020): agents (students and professors), and Practices and Processes (lectures and group work).

5   The Qualitative Case Study

This chapter presents findings from a qualitative case study on an undergraduate business EMI program in the International College of a private university in Taiwan over the course of two academic years. This college consists of six undergraduate programs and one graduate program. It has approximately 1,000 students, with more than half of the students coming from abroad, specifically 61 different countries. It stipulates that all the students must have sufficient English abilities; that is, a minimum language requirement of approximately TOEFL iBT 61 or its equivalent. Students failing to demonstrate their English proficiency must take an English test given by the College, and those who fail it must take intensive English courses. International students may be concurrently taking intensive Mandarin courses.

Regarding the policy of instructional language, the Mandarin version of the on-line brochure uses the term "English-taught program," but when it is situated in this particular business program, "English-only instruction" is used. In contrast, on the departmental website, information about "English-only instruction" is absent; instead, the keywords are "English-taught program," "English communication skills," and "multicultural environment." As such, it is unclear whether languages other than English are allowed in practice.

Participants included three local and three international students who were juniors when they volunteered to participate in the study. Their demographic information is presented in Table 1. These participants were recruited based on participation willingness and nationality. The target university and program were chosen not because students used translanguaging and demonstrated agency but because they represented

Table 1 Personal profiles of the participants

Name	Gender	Age	Nationality	Native language	Length of learning english (year)	Language proficiency
Sandy	F	20	Taiwan	Mandarin	10	B1
Charlie	M	20	Taiwan	Mandarin	15–19	N.A.[a]
Angela	F	22	Taiwan	Mandarin	>20	N.A
Leo	M	27	Germany	German	15–19	Pass exam[b]
Max	M	22	Mexico	Spanish	8	B2
William	M	25	South Korea	Korean	10	B2

[a] N.A = Not applicable (the participants did not provide the information)
[b] Pass exam = passed the test given by the International College.

a specific type of ELF context—in which half of the student population in class was international students and hence ELF was a common tool for communication.

Multiple data collection methods were used for the purpose of triangulation and trustworthiness (Carspecken, 1996; Yin, 2017). The major data sources include students' semi-structured interviews, supplemented by classroom observations, weekly journals, and artifacts. Nine to twelve interviews were conducted with each participant for approximately one to two hours each time. The exact number of interviews depended on the openness and eloquence of the participant. These interviews aimed to understand students' reasons for entering the EMI program, language-learning and language-use experiences, teacher instruction, and their changes across time. Interviews were conducted in a language with which the participants felt comfortable; most local students chose Mandarin and international students chose English. With students' permission, one of their courses was chosen for observation once by the researcher who became a passive observer to avoid interruption of teaching. The participants were instructed to complete a language-use journal weekly for a semester. Journal were kept primarily in English with occasional Mandarin. Also, artifacts such as departmental website information were included in data collection.

Data were analyzed based on Carspecken's (1996) reconstructive analysis that allows the researcher to uncover hidden meanings. The researcher began with reading and reconstructing the meaning of student interviews, class observations, and artifacts, from which initial coding was used to label significant concepts (e.g., language use, language learning, and cross-cultural communication). Then, current literature on translanguaging and learner agency was read to re-interpret and re-code the data. In the end, the codes with high frequency were reorganized to develop a coding scheme to depict the relationship between translanguaging and learner agency (i.e. modes, semiotic resources, language choice, non-linguistic choice, action, reason, identity, and emotional engagement).

6 Results

The findings are discussed in two regards: the use of native languages in lectures and in group work because they represent the most popular practices in the program.

6.1 The Use of Native Languages in Lectures

Lecture is a common approach by the professors in the program to convey critical academic concepts to students. In this paper, it is extended to include instructors' provision of the presentation and their interaction with students in class and during breaktime. Below teachers' use of native languages will be presented, followed by students' perceptions of it as well as students' own use of their native languages in translanguaging practices.

6.1.1 Professors' Use of Native Languages and Students' Perceptions

According to our interviews and observations, all the professors in this EMI program primarily used English in class, including on the PowerPoint slides. The virtual use of English may reflect the promotion of English-only instruction in the program. It may suggest that the instructor deemed English as the only common language for effective communication as local students had studied English for more than a decade yet international students might have just begun to learn Mandarin after being admitted to the program. The dominance of English use was accepted by the local students likely because they desired to improve their English ability, which, they believe, could be done by immersing themselves in this ELF context. Likewise, the participants reported thinking it made little sense for them to translate content in Mandarin if they were required to complete academic work in English. Professors' translanguaging appeared limited due to the assumption of ELF for diverse audiences, the implicit influence of the English-only instruction policy, and learners' immersion-language-learning beliefs.

Like the professors in Kao, Tsou, and Chen's study in Chap. 5, the professors in this study also adopted instructional and interactional strategies; that is, they occasionally adopted Mandarin primarily at the word or phrasal level when it could scaffold local students' understanding of the concept or when the concept was related to Chinese culture. For example, in the class observation of Sandy, the instructor explained the term "grey market goods" shown on the PowerPoint slide by defining it in English followed by saying "grey market goods" in Mandarin–"shuǐhuò":

Excerpt 1

> Having you ever heard of grey market? Some people may spell gray, some people spell grey, they are pretty much the same…. We want to describe purchases from grey markets. We call it shuǐhuò. Shuǐhuò means it's not a legal, unauthorized product.

Unlike Kao, Tsou, and Chen's finding that the professors completed sentences in one language before using another and usually with discourse signals (e.g., <u>so</u>), Sandy's professor embedded the Mandarin technical term in a simple syntactic structure (i.e. we call it.), with the pronoun *it* helping students understand that shuǐhuò refers to grey markets (instructional strategy). The Mandarin technical term was then used as an interactional strategy to deliver content at a conversational pace without any interruption. As Kao, Tsou, and Chen pointed out, this interactional strategy successfully got Sandy's attention as she wrote the term down in Mandarin in the textbook, fulfilling Sandy's thirst for knowledge and reflecting her self-reported identity as a good student who concentrated on lectures.

The occasional use of Mandarin was not only accepted by the local students but also international students. Although Mandarin is not the common language, international students considered it a significant language to learn because they were living in the context where Mandarin is used as the L1 and because Mainland China is a leading business market. As such, the instructor would use Mandarin and sometimes pinyin to satisfy the needs of both local and international students. Likewise, William noted in his weekly journal that he learnt the cultural difference of how to address professors when writing Mandarin and English email:

Excerpt 2

> We had to send him our assignment by E-mail. And he said "the title of E-mail should be 'Dear Professor Chao'. Many Taiwanese write 'Dear teacher' because of Chinese expression "Qīn'ài de lǎoshī" (the traditional version of Mandarin) but it is wrong in English.

His description showed his understanding of the email genre of the two languages. Using Mandarin characters is a way to demonstrate and practice Mandarin as well as to craft his self-reported identity as a good student who applied content from lectures.

In addition, during the breaktime between classes, the instructor used English with international students but Mandarin with local students in response to their request to clarify exam/assignment requirements and unclear academic concepts. The instructor would chat with international students in Mandarin and local students in English, depending on which language the learner used. Indeed, language choice reflects the instructor's attempt to address students' needs and interests as shown in prior literature (Mazak & Carroll, 2017) as well as their attempt to bond with students.

In addition to Mandarin, professors tended to use the target countries' native language with visual aids (the target companies' logos or images) to draw students' attention and introduce business in diverse cultures. For instance, in excerpt 3, the professor introduced a beer brand "Kodomo no nomimono" to emphasize Japan's creativity in marketing as the company targets children as future customers by using photos,[1] a video clip, and questions:

Excerpt 3

> T: In Japan, according to um the statistics, they have the most-the variation in terms of their beer flavours. (Showing a photo with diverse kinds of Japanese beers) You have to go to Japan. When I went to Japan several years ago, I was very surprised about you know how creative they put in beers…. These are some famous Japanese brands. (Showing a photo with diverse kinds of Japanese beers) And this is vending machine for beers…. You can buy beers anything, anywhere because vending machines are everywhere. (Showing a photo of a vending machine full of Japanese beers) And what is it? This is a label from a beer bottle. (Pointing to a child's image on the label of the beer bottle and photos of children who are drinking "fake beer") Are they adults? They are children, right? So, why do they have children's pictures on the bottle? Do they allow children to have beers? …. This kind of drink is called Kodomo no nomimono. (A video clip about this beer in Japanese)
>
> Ss: Nà qíshí méiyǒu jiǔjīng! (It's actually not alcohol!) (whispered in Mandarin)
>
> T: So-But it's not rea::l beer I can tell you. Otherwise, it's not legal. It's like-a fake beer. It tastes-like sparkling… So, it looks like beer but not really alcoholic… But why do they make to make this for children?.... They help children enjoy that. When they grow up, they can drink beer for sure I guess. Different countries, different cultures have different practices in terms of their foods…. kanpai (In Japanese pronunciation) What does that mean? Cheers. Bottoms up. Usually when you cheer your friends, you need to empty your cup. kanpai That's a very collectivist culture….How can Heineken compete with it?....

Sticking to the principle of authenticity, the instructor chose images of different beers in Japan, videos in Japanese, and the brand name in Japanese. The instructor did not explain the content of video likely because it was not important. Instead, she used it as a way to visualize the product, establish rapport, and engage students in thinking. An important simple Japanese word like "Kodomo no nomimono" was pronounced and written in Roman pinyin to help students understand the brand name. "Kanpai" was pronounced and explained with synonyms of cheers and bottoms up to facilitate students' understanding of the term in Japanese and relating it to business. The professor's use of image and video successfully gained some students' attention as they exclaimed in Mandarin, "Nà qíshí méiyǒu jiǔjīng" (It's actually not alcoholic!).

In general, the professors tended to explain concepts not with the L1 support but with the usage of diverse modes (PowerPoint slides, videos, and realia), semiotic resources (e.g., graphics, figures, and formula), non-linguistic resources (e.g., body language and voice change), and space (e.g., rearrangement of class). Professors' translanguaging mostly intended to increase students' understanding of the concepts especially via visual aids in the PowerPoint presentation. In class observation of Sandy, we found that the instructor explained the basic pricing concept through texts (written words), aural aids (spoken words), and a diagram (a box divided into three

---

[1] Descriptions of photos were given since copyright permission of images use could not be obtained.

levels, the top of which points to price ceiling and the bottom price floor)[2] to show the relationships between price ceiling and floor. As she explained in excerpt 4:

Excerpt 4

> So here for basic pricing concepts. Usually you need to understand your cost struc-ture…While there'll be some price is too low, you cannot afford. If there's anything lower than that, I will be broke. You'll know the ceiling of your price. If anything's over that, you will not survive also because you will not compete with it. Usually ceiling and floor-usually we have some room for you to manipulate your price.

Instead of using the abstract written texts (minimum/maximum price), the instructor chose to use objects "floor" and "ceiling" to help students visualize the lowest and highest price and talked about the consequence if the price is set too low or too high for the learner to understand the primacy of price ceiling and floor. In so doing, the professor's translanguaging affords different opportunities for the learner to make sense of the technical term.

Another way for the professor to increase students' understanding of the concept was the use of non-linguistic resources (e.g., body language and voice change) and classroom space, which can be illustrated by the instructor of the etiquette course—an effective one that all the participants held in high regard. They all mentioned that setting the table using real plates, spoons, forks, glasses, and napkins helped them visualize and remember Western manners. As Charlie expressed, "It's (The course) is impressive because she set the table for us by bringing forks, plates- and tell us how to place (the knife, fork) after eating meat in this country…. She just shows us" (IN1). According to the participants, this instructor's translanguaging practice not only successfully fulfilled students' needs for knowledge but also engaged them in thinking and becoming active participants in class and in the world.

6.1.2 Students' Use of Native Languages in Translanguaging

Students' use of native languages can be observed in conversations among themselves while professors were lecturing. For instance, in our class observations, Charlie, a Taiwanese male student who was not afraid of using English, mostly read the textbook, underlined important points, and looked up difficult words (in Mandarin) in a dictionary. He was asked by a local student in Mandarin if they could use "evaluation" to express "high regard" when reporting on a company. He looked it up in the dictionary to answer the question. Indeed, students' language choices suggest the principle of effectiveness and efficiency.

Another common practice of using native languages occurred during the break-time between classes. Students from the same nations mostly talked in their native languages and used English while talking to their international peers. Occasionally, participants would use a second foreign language in communication in hopes of

---

[2]Descriptions of the diagram were given since copyright permission of image use could not be obtained.

improving their language skills. For example, Max, a Mexican male student who deemed learning culture as a foundation for learning a language, aimed to acquire Mandarin and so he often talked to locals in Mandarin. To him, it was a way to familiarize himself with local students and make them become "open" to a foreigner. Similarly, Charlie, a Taiwanese male who wanted to learn a new foreign language to increase his competitiveness, often talked to the Latinos in Spanish. Using interlocutors' native languages reflects learners' interest in their languages or cultures, and hence it was easier to establish rapport for further interaction than speaking in English.

In particular, using native languages for the learner is not simply a means to learn a new language or make friends but also an attempt to accurately convey ideas. Learners reported that the meaning of a word in different languages gave different feelings and so they preferred using the interlocutors' native languages or their own when they wanted the interlocutors to understand the meaning or when they had a strong feeling. For instance, Max used the word "hypocrite" in English to describe a local student's behavior but he insisted that the meaning of "hypocrite" in English is different from that in Mandarin. In order for his interlocutor to understand him, he used an on-line dictionary to find the word in Mandarin "wèijūnzǐ."

6.2   The Use of Native Languages in Group Work

Group work—collaboration with peers from diverse ethnic or linguistic groups—is considered a popular way to cultivate learners' "ability to communicate and work as a team player" and "to recognize the situation and analyze for solution rationally" (department homepage). In the research settings analyzed for this project, group work usually took the form of in-class and out-of-class discussions. Unlike passive roles in lectures, students are compelled to communicate in group discussions especially when instructors require students from different nations to work together. This context affords more student use of native languages in translanguaging practice than lectures.

Choice of language and/or semiotic resources (e.g., on-line dictionaries or websites, graphics, and drawing) illustrated students' translanguaging practices in group work as well as their agency. Most often when learners did not have the vocabulary or technical words to express their ideas in English, they used an on-line dictionary, checked their own notes, or surfed websites to find the exact word in English. They would also use body language or realia to enable others to determine what they wanted to express. In so doing, they satisfied the need to convey ideas accurately. The sense of achievement—learning a new word in English—encouraged most students (especially Asians who sometimes positioned themselves as EFL learners) to take risks in the future. Additionally, learners might use the same strategies to learn a new word or phrase in a foreign language. For example, Max, a Mexican student who enjoyed learning about cultures, asked Leo how to say "varnish" in German in an in-class group discussion (Leo, Class Observation). Such conversations may show learners' interest in others' languages or cultures, thereby establishing rapport to facilitate later interaction.

In group work, the learners used drawings to illustrate the ideas they wanted to convey. For example, in thinking about the components of a chair, Ron drew how two pieces of wood were joined together in his textbook:

Excerpt 5

> Leo: A wooden chair. (drawing how two pieces of wood were joined)
>
> Sue: .
>
> Leo: Ya! Glue- a special glue. A wood glue.
>
> Max nail.

His drawing enabled his groupmate to propose an idea, leading him to realize a component of a wooden chair is glue. Drawing enabled the learner to visualize the image of a chair to help brainstorm ideas in group discussion.

Much more often, learners sought help from co-nationals especially those with good English speaking abilities or those who can speak the interlocutors' native languages. One translanguaging practice is that the learners might not know the concept in English, and their co-nationals would translate it in English or in their native languages. As Charlie expressed, "Basically we used English to express our own opinions. But if there's any difficulty due to a language barrier, we asked those who understand to translate in their native languages" (IN1). Angela also explained, "They (the Latinos) would discuss first before talking to me because they all speak Spanish" (IN2).

Other than co-nationals, those who understood Mandarin also used English to help local students. As in the observation of Leo's in-class group discussion, the female local student, Mary, a less proficient English speaker asked a question in Mandarin and Ron, the male German student with better English proficiency, translated it in English to help the conversation continue to complete the task:

Excerpt 6

> Mary: Yóuqī zěnme jiǎng (How to say "paint"?)
>
> Leo: Paint…. what kind of chair…

Another practice is that the student who is perceived to have better spoken English skills plays the role of translator or even negotiator in these collaborations; that is, native languages were used among co-nationals in group discussions before learners selected a co-national to convey their ideas to international peers. This language choice was often observed when students were unfamiliar with one another (at the beginning of the program), when they had sophisticated ideas, or when they expressed disagreement and gave a new suggestion. For example, Sandy explained that due to her personality and better spoken English, she would be responsible for translating Chinese-mediated discussions among the local peers to international peers in

English: "Maybe, it was because that my English was better…. I think that I was the one who always talked…. Maybe, they [my Taiwanese groupmates] felt that I just could express my thought faster" (IN1). Her groupmate, Angela, collaborated this idea by explaining, "I'm talkative myself so I usually gathered local students' ideas and passed them to those who are better at English speaking to communicate with international students. I didn't take the role as a speaker because I was not confident" (IN1).

Although learners' English abilities and confidence in using English increased as time went by, they might still have chosen not to communicate with international peers in English directly; they still preferred translanguaging for effectiveness and efficiency. For example, Angela emphasized that she was able to talk to international peers after getting to know about them, yet she may still choose not to do so for effectiveness and efficiency. As she said, "I think it's faster. It's efficient. Everyone does what he or she is good at" (IN1). Since some students emphasized the primacy of learning English via the program, the researcher asked them if they thought using their native languages suggested constrained chance to practice English (the detrimental view of the L1 use). They did not think so. Completing tasks and gaining good grades outweighed English practice. As the less proficient Korean student, William, explained:

Excerpt 7

> But discussion isn't practice time. Discussion is the time when we need to (discuss) something important…. This is not practice, the most important thing is that we have to make the completion about our project. So I better speak to someone who can understand, who I can understand. So, during the discussion, which more complicate. I encounter with that problem, because I don't understand what this person say, so there's no way to conversation during the discussion, so I better speak to the other guy. Like, I met this person in the street during lunch time, I try, I ask him again and again. I can make this kind of effort, but this is discussion time, we don't have much time. So it's a big problem.
>
> (IN10)

The deliberate language choice along with the task assignment served as a way to achieve a task—an important problem-solving strategy to be cultivated in the business world.

Interestingly, using native languages appeared to strengthen sense of community (SOC), thereby increasing learner agency. As Angela expressed, "They speak fast… and I can't speak that fast, but others can; otherwise, ours will not be heard when they are balalabla" (IN2). Their language choice suggests a power negotiation in which students leveraged their native languages and advantages to finish the group work. It is no wonder that Angela used "mutualism" to describe how each learner could work together and benefit the whole group. This analogy illustrates that learners' language or semiotic choices in group work reflects their goal-oriented action, which is reiterated when learners discovered such practice can get work done efficiently and effectively. As Max expressed, "The second year was easier because you already have friends. And then eventually you always, like you can see it right now, right now we have a group that we always work together and stuff" (IN2). Now in most of the group work activities, learners worked with regular group members because they had already worked together for a long time.

Another way to increase learner agency via SOC is teasing—a lubricant in maintaining groupmates' relationships especially for international peers as they might use Mandarin to make fun of those who understand Mandarin, especially local students. For example, excerpt 8 shows that while brainstorming for BOM (Bill of Materials), Leo teased his Taiwanese groupmate about her physical appearance:

Excerpt 8

> Leo: How about cupcake? It's easier.
>
> Mary: Butter
>
> Leo: Nánguài nǐ zhème pang (No wonder you are so heavy)
>
> Mary: Ei:: (as if protesting)
>
> (All the female groupmates were laughing.)
>
> Sue: What kind of cupcakes?
>
> Mary: Mango, strawberry

Leo and Mary were groupmates for several courses, so they had a good friendship as a foundation for Leo to joke about her physical appearance. Mary did not stop contributing because of his teasing. Instead, she remained concentrated and even exclaimed, "Ā wǒ zhīdàole" in Mandarin ("Oh! I see!") as if she understood the concepts discussed.

7   Discussion

This book chapter aimed to explore one form translanguaging—usage of native languages in classroom interaction—as well as learner perception and agency from local and international students' perspectives in an ELF context—that is, the EMI business program in a private university in Taiwan. The results showed that the ELF context in the target program affords translanguaging as a natural yet limited practice (Practices and Processes) and that the use of different resources reflects learners' enactment of their agency (Agent). When translanguaging is affirmed, it increases learners' desire to keep translanguaging and hence nurtures learner agency. It is also the learner's recognition of the instructor's translanguaging that enables the learner to take action. The implication of the embodiment of translanguaging as agency and learners' perception is discussed in terms of four components of learner agency (behaviour, cognition, emotion, and identity), professors' translanguaging, student perception of it, and the condition of translanguaging.

The two significant components of learner agency—behavior and action—can be shown from the result that students' translanguaging practice was a purposeful act. It was more abundant in group activities than in lectures probably because more space and time were given. In lectures, students' translanguaging practice often took the form of the L1 for effective, efficient and accurate communication or a new foreign language for cultural and language learning. In collaborative activities, it was embodied by language choices (e.g., the L1), semiotic resources (e.g., drawing), and non-linguistic resources (e.g., body language). All of these resources enabled the learner to make sense of complex concepts as, for example, the L1 enabled the learner to explore complex concepts and drawing enabled the whole group to brainstorm the components of "a wooden chair." Although compared with the prior literature (Canagarajah, 2013; Lin, 2016), the results did not reveal a detailed process or multimodality of translanguaging, which may be due to the nature of tasks or the fact that the original design was not for translanguaging. As such, future research can focus on group tasks of the local and international learners to further understand the development of the learner's translanguaging.

The third significant element in learner agency—identity—can be discussed in two ways. First, students' translanguaging practices indicated a process of becoming for the learner. To be more specific, the learner's translanguaging practice suggested the transformation of a novice into a business professional as the learner employed cooperation strategies and public speaking skills in translanguaging. Moreover, some students would translanguage to foreground a part of their identity—being playful or being an active language learner. For example, Leo and Max liked to tease peers by using Mandarin to maintain good rapport. Charlie liked to use Spanish with the Latinos to practice his language skills and to better understand Spanish-speaking cultures. Not being a speaker but an idea organizer, Angela used Mandarin to encourage the locals' voices to be heard. Indeed, recognition of students' deliberate choices in translanguaging is acknowledgement of who the learner is and who they hope to become.

The last component of learner agency shown from students' translanguaging in both lectures and group activities involved emotion—and sometimes sense of community (SOC). In lectures, the use of the L1, according to the participant, helped them establish and enhance friendships, through which they gained cultural and linguistic knowledge. In collaborative activities, translanguaging helped interlocutors create friendships (membership), had a reciprocal symbiosis (influence), held task completion as a common goal (fulfilment of needs), and enabled groupmates to bond together (shared emotional connection) as indicated in McMillan and Chavis (1986). Recognition of the primacy of emotional engagement requires the professor to create a condition in which students' needs can be satisfied, goals completed, bonds established, influence exerted, and membership gained.

In addition, professors' translanguaging also reflects their attempt to address four dimensions of learner agency: behavior, cognition, identity, and emotion. Selection of languages (e.g., Mandarin and Japanese), semiotic resources (e.g., visual-aural aids, realias, and videos), non-linguistic resource (body language and voice change) and spatial arrangement in professors' translanguaging shows the instructors' attempts to grab students' attention, engage students' thinking, and enhance students' understanding of concepts, regulations, and cultures. Moreover, professors' usage of diverse languages or cultural images also shows their attempts to acknowledge students' identity, establish rapport, and engage students emotionally. As such, behavior, cognition, identity, and emotion can be considered in future studies of translanguaging practice.

It is significant for scholars to reflect on the condition of translanguaging practices and learner agency. First, students' translanguaging practices were strengthened by the positive consequences of translanguaging. In lectures, students' use of the L1 or a new foreign language was affirmed when students achieved their purposes, empowering them to keep translanguaging. In group work, translanguaging practices enabled learners to work efficiently and effectively and to gain good grades, which helped learners find the same groupmates and use the same strategies to complete tasks in the future. As such, the process became smoother. This sense of achievement led to the reiteration of students' translanguaging practice. The evolution of students' translanguaging practice concurs with the dynamic nature of learner agency; that is, learner agency is determined by the initial condition (Larsen-Freeman, 2019).

Moreover, the abundance of translanguaging practices depends on the preliminary instructional condition, which is deeply influenced by the university language policy and stakeholders' beliefs. The analysis showed that translanguaging practices in the ELF context in Taiwan may be constrained, especially in lectures, since English was rationalized for diverse audiences, since English-only instruction may have been assumed by the stakeholders, and since learners believed that English cannot be learned without an immersion context. Whether translanguaging practices were perceived or used by the learner depends largely on the initial condition in which translanguaging practices were encouraged and its positive consequence. It reasons that awareness of translanguaging pedagogy of policy makers and instructors is necessary. Unfortunately, no participants articulated the notion of "translanguaging." Thus, it is suggested that policy makers and professors should unlearn "English-only instruction," and re-learn *why* and *how* to employ translanguaging practices so that they can become role models for the learner. Translanguaging pedagogy should be incorporated in EMI professional development in higher education in Taiwan.

8   Conclusion

This paper aimed to examine the use of native languages in classroom interaction in translanguaging as well as learner perception and agency in an ELF context in higher education by a qualitative case study of learners' perspectives in Taiwan. Four dimensions of behavior, cognition, identity, and emotion in learner agency can be used to examine translanguaging as translanguaging is the embodiment of learner agency. The finding of the restricted translanguaging practice and the fact that the original design of this study was not for translanguaging urge more scholars to explore how students translanguage in ELF contexts. Given that students' translanguaging often occurs when symbolic space is given, it is important to analyze students' translanguaging in out-of-class group discussions, in particular group tasks, and in the Power-Point presentations. The reasons behind students' translanguaging is also important for scholars to understand because it shapes the learner's use of translanguaging. Moreover, it is also pedagogically significant to investigate how professors' translanguage, for what purposes, and how students perceive such translanguaging as there may be a discrepancy between student and professor perceptions. Last, according to van Lier (2008), learner agency did not lead to academic success and so the relationship among translanguaging, learner agency, and academic success is worth exploring in the future. Such results can benefit future design of translanguaging practices for professional development in ELF contexts in higher education.

References

Biesta, G., & Tedder, M. (2007). Agency and learning in the lifecourse: Towards an ecological perspective. *Studies in the Education of Adults, 39*, 132–149.

Canagarajah, S. (2013). *Translingual practice: Global Englishes and cosmopolitan relations.* Routledge.

Carspecken, P. F. (1996). *Critical ethnography in educational research: A theoretical and practical guide.* Routledge.

Chung, C. L., & Lo, M. L. (2016). Prospect and case study of English-medium instruction of transportation courses in Taiwanese universities. *English Teaching & Learning, 40*(3), 87–121. https://doi.org/10.6330/ETL.2016.40.3.04

Dafouz, E., & Smit, U. (2016). Towards a dynamic conceptual framework for English-medium education in multilingual university settings. *Applied Linguistics, 37*(3), 397–415.

Dafouz, E., & Smit, U. (2020). *Road-Mapping English medium edication in the internationalised university.* Palgrave Macmillan.

García, O., & Kleyn, T. (2016). Translanguaging theory in education. In O. García & T. Kleyn (Eds.), *Translanguaging with multilingual students: Learning from classroom moments* (pp. 1–33). Routledge.

Gibbons, P. (2009). *English learners, academic literacy, and thinking: Learning in the challenging zone.* Heinemann.

Huang, Y. P. (2012). Design and implementation of english-medium courses in higher education in Taiwan: A qualitative case study. *English Teaching and Learning, 36*(1), 1–51. https://doi.org/10.1001/archneurol.2012.1810

Jenkins, J. (2019). English medium instruction in higher education: The role of English as a lingua franca. In X. Gao (Ed.), *Second handbook of English language teaching* (pp. 1–18). Switzerland, AG: Springer. https://doi.org/10.1007/978-3-319-58542-0_7-1

Larsen-Freeman, D. (2019). On language learner agency: A complex dynamic systems theory perspective. *The Modern Language Journal, 103*, 61–79. https://doi.org/10.1111/modl.125360 026-7902/19/61-79

Lin, A. M. Y. (2016). *Language across the curriculum & CLIL in English as an additional language (EAL) contexts: Theory and practice.* Springer.

Mazak, C., & Carroll, K. (2017). *Translanguaging in higher education: Beyond monolingual ideologies.* Multilingual Matters.

McMillan, D., & Chavis, D. (1986). Sense of community: A definition and theory. *Journal of Community Psychology, 14*, 6–23. https://doi.org/10.1002/1520-6629(198601)14:13.0.CO;2-I

Ministry of Education. (2001). *White paper on higher education.* Taipei: NIOERAR.

Ministry of Education. (2019a). *Higher education SPROUT project.* Retrieved July 30, 2020 from https://sprout.moe.edu.tw/SproutWeb/Home/Index/en.

Ministry of Education. (2019b). *Overview of foreign students in colleges and universities.* Retrieved 30 July 2020 from https://depart.moe.edu.tw/ED4500/cp.aspx?n=002F646AFF7F5492&s=1EA 96E4785E6838F.

Toth, J., & Paulstrud, B. (2017). Agency and affordance in translanguaging for learning: Case studies from English-medium instruction in Swedish schools. In B. Paulsrud, J. Rosén, B. Straszer, & A. Wedin (Eds.) *New perspectives on translanguaging and education* (pp. 189–207). Bristol, PA: Multilingual Matters.

Townley, G., Katz, J., Wandersman, A., Skiles, B., Schillaci, M. J., Timmerman, B. E., & Mousseau, T. A. (2013). Exploring the role of sense of community in the undergraduate transfer student experience. *Journal of Community Psychology, 41*(3), 277–290. https://doi.org/10.1002/jcop. 21529

van Lier, L. (2008). Agency in the classroom. In J. P. Lantolf & M. E. Poehner (Eds.), *Sociocultural theory and the teaching of second languages* (pp. 163–186). London: Equinox.

Yin, R. K. (2017). *Case study research: Design and methods* (6th ed.). Thousand Oaks, CA: SAGE.

Yi-Ping Huang is an associate professor in the Department of English at National Chengchi University, Taiwan. She was the editor-in-chief and is currently the associate editor of Taiwan Journal of TESOL. Her research interests include qualitative exploration of curriculum design, student learning, teacher identity, and teacher development in the EMI settings. Her current research project concerns CLIL curriculum design in primary education in Taiwan. Her research has been published in international journals, such as Teaching in Higher Education and Higher Education and Research Development.

Part V
Conclusion

Chapter 10
EMI and Translanguaging in Asia Through the ROAD-MAPPING Lens

Will Baker and Wenli Tsou

Abstract In this concluding chapter we provide a synthesis of the discussions and findings from the nine previous chapters included in this edited volume. To aid this process we make use of the ROAD-MAPPING framework (Dafouz and Smit in ROAD-MAPPING English medium education in the internationalised university. Palgrave Macmillan UK, Cham, Switzerland, 2020). This framework provides a structure for drawing out key elements from the chapters and also enables a comparison between the studies collected here and other EMI research that also adopts the ROAD-MAPPING framework. We begin with a detailed outline of the six interrelated and overlapping dimensions of ROAD-MAPPING: Roles of English (RO), Academic Disciplines (AD), Management (M), Agents (A), Practices and Processes (PP), Internationalisation and Glocalisation (ING). This is followed by an overview of key themes from the chapters in this volume presented according to the six dimensions of the framework. We conclude by suggesting that while there is a great deal of variety in the studies presented here, a central theme that emerges is that in EMI in Asia, English functions as a lingua franca in a multilingual environment in which translanguaging practices are always present regardless of whether they are officially sanctioned or recognised. This volume, thus, makes an original contribution in emphasising the importance of a translanguaging perspective in EMI, as well as adding to the growing body of evidence that EMI is a multilingual phenomenon.

Keywords Translanguaging · English as a lingua franca (ELF) · English medium instruction (EMI) · Higher education · ROAD-MAPPING framework · Asia

W. Baker (✉)
Centre for Global Englishes, University of Southampton, Southampton, UK
e-mail: w.baker@soton.ac.uk

W. Tsou
Department of Foreign Languages & Literature, National Cheng Kung University, Tainan, Taiwan, ROC
e-mail: wtsou@ncku.edu.tw

1 Introduction

The studies presented in this volume have provided a window into the different responses to the increasing presence of English medium instruction (EMI) in Asian higher education. While all the chapters have explored translanguaging and English as a lingua franca (ELF), they have covered a range of settings (China, Japan, Taiwan, Thailand, Vietnam), levels (theory, policy, classroom practices), perspectives (governments, universities, lecturers, international students, local students), disciplines (engineering, business, applied linguistics, international studies, languages, EAP) and approaches (shared L1 classrooms, monolingualism and multilingualism, internationalisation at home and international recruitment). As might be expected a variety of issues are highlighted concerning the relationships between translanguaging, ELF use, EMI and policy formation (Tsou, Chap. 1; Ra and Baker, Chap. 4), linguistic awareness (Ishikawa, Chap. 3), teaching practices (Baker, Chap. 2; Kao et al., Chap. 5; Zhang and Wei, Chap. 6), learner agency (Ngo, Chap. 7; Huang, Chap. 9), and student identity and motivation (Humphries and Yashima, Chap. 8).

Although this rich diversity of contexts and issues is, we feel, a strength of this edited collection, it may also be helpful to attempt a synthesis of the findings that have emerged. Therefore, to provide consistency amongst these varied studies, in this concluding chapter we will discuss some of the key themes in relation to the ROAD-MAPPING framework (Dafouz & Smit, 2020). This framework has been adopted as it recognises the complexity and diversity of EMI or EME (English medium education) programmes while also providing researchers and practitioners with a systematic framework for investigating EMI. Through identifying a number of common dimensions of EMI programmes and research it also allows meaningful comparisons between sites and research reports in accordance with those dimensions. As Dafouz and Smit write, "precisely because EMEMUS [English-Medium Education in Multilingual University Settings] is so diverse, and situated, there is a strong need to provide a conceptual frame of reference at the metalevel. This will allow researchers to understand how these and other EME realities fit into the bigger picture and how they are affected by forces operating at global and local levels simultaneously" (2020, p. 40). While ROAD-MAPPING is discussed in many of the empirical chapters (Chaps. 6, 7, 8 and 9), this was not necessarily part of the original analysis (although see Ngo, Chap. 7 for an exception). However, Dafouz and Smit propose that ROAD-MAPPING can be successfully applied retrospectively and argue for "the framework's value as a means to reframe a finalised study, providing a more detailed and in-depth embedding in EMEMUS research, which has a direct impact on how findings reached earlier can be reinterpreted and repositioned" (2020, p. 90). Furthermore, ROAD-MAPPING has been successfully applied in previous studies of EMI in Asia demonstrating its relevance (Baker & Hüttner, 2017; Bradford & Brown, 2018). We will begin with a detailed outline of the dimensions of the ROAD-MAPPING framework. This is followed by an overview of key themes from the studies in this volume presented according to the framework.

2   The ROAD-MAPPING Framework

The framework is divided into six interrelated and overlapping dimensions which are Roles of English (RO), Academic Disciplines (AD), Management (M), Agents (A), Practices and Processes (PP), Internationalisation and Glocalisation (ING) (Dafouz & Smit, 2020, p. 46). Each of the six dimensions are defined below.

- **Roles of English (RO)** "refers to the communicative functions that language fulfils in HEIs, with the focus placed on English as the implicitly or explicitly identified main medium of education" (Dafouz & Smit, 2020, p. 60). This includes the role of English as both a product and process of communication and the relationship between English and other languages.
- **Academic Disciplines (AD)** "encompasses two-related notions: academic literacies and academic (disciplinary) culture" (Dafouz & Smit, 2020, p. 60). Academic literacies are related to literacy in "the diverse range of academic products (whether spoken or written) typically developed in an educational setting and conforming to socially conventionalised situated practices" (Dafouz & Smit, 2020, p. 60). Disciplinary cultures refer to "the subject specific conventions, norms and values that define different disciplinary areas" (Dafouz & Smit, 2020: 60).
- **(Language) Management (M)** "is concerned with 'direct efforts to [influence and] manipulate the language situation' (Spolsky, 2004, p. 8) in the form of language policy statements and documents" (Dafouz & Smit, 2020, p. 60).
- **Agents (A)** "dimension encompasses the different social players (whether conceptualised as individuals or as collectives, concretely or abstractly) that are engaged in EMEMUS at diverse sociopolitical, institutional and hierarchical levels" (Dafouz & Smit, 2020, p. 60). This includes students, teachers, administrators and managers but can also include institutions, and other policy making bodies such as governments.
- **Practices and Processes (PP)** is "concerned with the administrative, research and educational activities that construct and are constructed by EMEMUS realities" (Dafouz & Smit, 2020: 60). This includes areas such as "classroom discourse, teacher professional development or stages of internationalisation" (Dafouz & Smit, 2020, p. 60).
- **Internationalisation and Glocalisation (ING)** "refer to the 'the tensions but also the synergies' (Scott, 2011, p. 61) that govern twenty-first century HEIs, and portray such organisations as transnational sites where stakeholders from different social settings, linguistic and cultural backgrounds and educational models are gaining presence" (Dafouz & Smit, 2020, p. 60). This includes international, national and regional languages and communities.

The six dimensions and their interrelated nature are visualised in Fig. 1. Discourse is placed central in the model as the main point of access for researching these dimensions while also "reflecting the centrally discursive nature of the social practices that construct and are constructed dynamically in EMEMUS" (Dafouz & Smit, 2020, p. 46). This also mirrors discourse as the "point of access" in the studies in this

Fig. 1 The
ROAD-MAPPING
framework for EMEMUS
(Dafouz & Smit, 2020, p. 47)

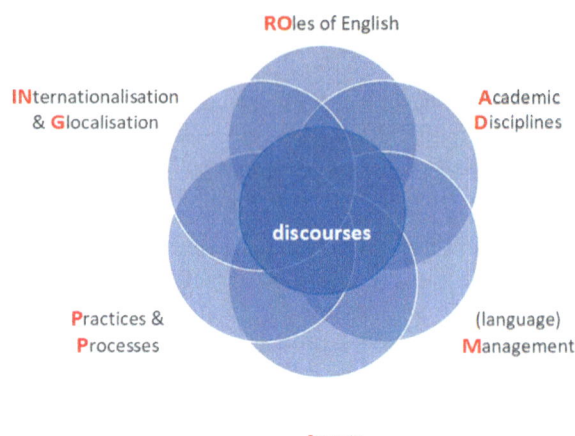

collection which made use of data from classroom discourse, interviews and policy
documents.

3   Applying ROAD-MAPPING

Beginning with the **roles of English (RO)**, due to the focus of this volume on applied
linguistics perspectives in general, and translanguaging and ELF in particular, it is
unsurprising that this dimension is a feature of all the chapters. The initial theoretical
chapters by Tsou (Chap. 1) and Baker (Chap. 2) argue that the "E" in EMI is English
used as a lingua franca. Similar to other collections of EMI studies (e.g. Fenton-
Smith, Humphrey, & Walkinshaw, 2017; Jenkins & Mauranen, 2019; Murata, 2018)
English is frequently perceived as a language of global connectivity and used in Asian
EMI for intercultural communication among speakers of different first languages.
Yet, it must also be recognised that English is also extensively used among speakers
of the same L1 in Asian EMI settings (see for example Ishikawa, Chap. 3, Zhang
and Wei, Chap. 6 and Ngo, Chap. 7). Nonetheless, here too English is used in the
fluid and variable manner associated with ELF for intercultural communication and
connections rather than adhering to a single 'native speaker' standard. In Chap. 3,
Ishikawa emphasises the multilingual dimensions of EMI, raised in the first two
chapters, through considering the role of English as a multilingua franca (EMF) in
which English is viewed as embedded in wider multilingual communicative practices.
Ishikawa also underscores the tensions between the highly variable multilingual
communicative practices in EMI and more normative ideologies that categorise and
separate languages and varieties of language in policy and agents' perceptions of
language. This tension is a theme returned to throughout this volume and all three of
the opening chapters argue that the role of English in EMI needs to be understood as
part of multilingual translanguaging practices, while recognising that this is rarely

acknowledged in pedagogy or policy. In Chap. 4, Ra and Baker zoom in on this policy dimension and illustrate how in government and university policy in Thailand the role of English is portrayed as a lingua franca to connect multilingual and multicultural groups especially in the ASEAN (Association of South East Asian Nations) region. However, they note that this diversity remains at a superficial level and English and other languages are still positioned from a normative perspective in policy with minimal recognition of multilingualism and none of translanguaging practices.

Kao et al., in Chap. 5 explain that like many settings English is associated with the internationalisation of HE in Taiwan, Furthermore, they also agree that in Taiwanese EMI settings English functions as a lingua franca. However, in examining classroom discourse they found that there was also a role for Chinese alongside English in translanguaging practices and that this was an explicit strategy employed by instructors. Similar findings in a Chinese setting are reported by Zhang and Wei in Chap. 6 who also demonstrate an explicit role for both English and Chinese in classroom practices. This is in spite of the institution investigated offering only EMI programmes and having an English only teaching policy. In Chap. 7 Ngo discusses the role of English in the internationalisation of Vietnamese HE with analogous roles identified in government policy and a particular emphasis on the belief that English can provide "higher quality" education. However, by zooming in on the roles given to English and other languages by students in classroom practices, Ngo illustrates how they resist an English-only policy and make use of their L1 resources in translanguaging practices whether condoned or not by their instructors. Humphries and Yashima, in Chap. 8 report on a rather different educational scenario in which the Japanese students in their research are English language majors studying Chinese as an additional minor language. A formal role was given to both languages in their programmes and the students spent time abroad in a Chinese L1 setting (Taiwan) EMI programme, which also included Chinese language components. Their findings show the role of both English and Chinese in international orientations of students, but also complex and varying motivations for using these languages. This reminds us that English is not the only language with a prominent global role and in their study, rather than dominating other languages, English actually facilitated learning/using Chinese. In the final chapter Huang, also examines an EMI setting in Taiwan and looks at the perceptions of the role of English and L1s for local and international students. She reports limited translanguaging practices but nonetheless identifies a role given to all the L1s present when space is provided for translanguaging. In sum, unsurprisingly, these chapters illustrate the role of English as the predominant language of instruction in EMI with English seen as the language of internationalisation in HE. However, all of the studies reported that the "E" was ELF and, crucially, a role for other languages, multilingualism and translanguaging practices; although, to varying degrees and with varying levels of formal recognition.

The chapters in this volume cover a number of **academic disciplines (AD)** including applied linguistics/TESOL, business, creative industry, engineering, international studies, and languages. Although, academic disciplines in the sense of specific disciplinary cultures are not the focus of these studies, a number of chapters do address issues of academic literacies particularly as regards spoken practices.

For instance, although Kao et al.'s (Chap. 5) findings revealed translanguaging and Chinese use, the instructors reported a preference and emphasis on disciplinary terms in English. Zhang and Wei (Chap. 6) suggest that, based on their findings, English and the L1 were used together when introducing new terminology in English that was already familiar to students in their L1. They also highlighted the use of L1 to refer to localised knowledge. Likewise, from the perspective of students, Ngo (Chap. 7) demonstrates the use of L1 in building disciplinary knowledge and terminology. In all of the studies there is agreement that the use of L1 and translanguaging practices form a vital part of teaching and learning academic content and knowledge and, as such, should be seen as an integral part of academic disciplinary cultures and literacies in EMI.

Language management (M) in the form of language policy statements and documents which are designed to directly influence language practices are dealt with in many chapters in this volume since they typically frame and contextualise the classroom practices and agent perceptions described. In Chap. 1 Tsou provides an overview of government policies in the Asian region which, like other regions, link EMI with the internationalisation of HE. However, she notes that one of the major difficulties has been an association between the English in EMI with Anglophone Englishes and academic cultures. This leads to a hierarchy of Englishes with local uses of ELF and multilingualism marginalised. There is also a monolingual ideology in policy linked to an "English only" immersion approach which Tsou argues fails to reflect the multilingual reality of EMI programmes in Asia. Both Baker (Chap. 2) and Ishikawa (Chap. 3) also agree that EMI language policies in Asia generally (Baker) and Japan in particular (Ishikawa) are orientated either explicitly or implicitly to monolingual "standard English". In Chap. 4 Ra and Baker investigate EMI policy documents in depth in the context of Thailand. Their study of government and leading EMI university policy documents suggests a positioning of English as a language for intercultural communication particularly within the ASEAN region rather than a focus on Anglophone settings. There was also some recognition of multilingualism at both government and university level. However, detailed analysis of the documents reveals a continued bias for Anglophone "standard" English, rather than a recognition of ELF, and a bilingual policy of English and Thai with little or no recognition of other languages or translanguaging practices, despite being likely features of Thai EMI classrooms. Similarly, the empirical studies in Chaps. 5, 6, 7, 8 and 9, while reflecting differing roles for English and the local L1, all report language policies that were underpinned by standard language and monolingual ideologies.

A range of **agents (A)** feature in the chapters of this book with the main focus on teachers and students but also including governments and institutions through analysis of policy documents (see language management above). However, the perspectives of administrators and managers are missing and this must be acknowledged as a limitation to the studies presented. The perspectives of instructors are provided in Chap. 5 by Kao et al. and Chap. 6 by Zhang and Wei and show a conscious use of the local L1 (Chinese) alongside English in classrooms. Kao et al. report that instructors were concerned about levels of English proficiency among local students and believed Chinese was necessary for support, while recognising that this support could not be offered to international students with different L1s. To compensate the teachers believed it was important to translate from L1 into English and were tolerant of different L1 use among students in class activities. Nonetheless, there was still a preference for content and terminology to be primarily delivered in English. In Zhang and Wei's study, despite policy stipulating English-only instruction, the teachers in their research deliberately created a translanguaging space in their classrooms where students and instructions could use their L1. Zhang and Wei argue that this was due to the instructors being competent multilinguals themselves and recognising the value of such translanguaging practices in education (and also probably supported by the instructors familiarity with current theory in applied linguistics as teachers of that subject). Importantly, they also argue that these translanguaging spaces and strategies were not viewed as compensating for linguistic deficiencies but instead as enhancing pedagogic practices.

Chapters 7 (Ngo), 8 (Humphries and Yashima) and 9 (Huang) all focus on student agency. Ngo directly employs the ROAD-MAPPING framework to examine the agency of students in an EMI programme in Vietnam. She illustrates how students resisted the English-only policy adopted for assessed individual presentations by the instructor in one of their courses and made use of their L1 resources in a way "hidden" from the teacher. In contrast, in another course where both English and L1 use were sanctioned by the teacher, a translanguaging space was created in the classroom which enabled students to openly make use of their full linguistic reper-toire. Similar findings are reported by Huang in the context of an EMI programme in Taiwan with both local and international students. Huang argues that even limited translanguaging spaces in the classroom provide opportunities for students to make use of their full linguistic repertoires and thus more fully enact their agency, which in turn, further develops student agency in regards to their own learning. Humphries and Yashima explore the links between motivation, self and translanguaging for two Japanese students studying English and Chinese during study abroad in Taiwan. Significantly this study investigated language use and motivation both in class and outside in social situations. They found a varied and fluid set of motivations and orien-tations which underpinned language choices, underscoring the importance of student agency in how they approached their language development and use. Humphries and Yashima also suggest that the two participants developed "actual" (as opposed to "ideal") multilingual selves making use of their three languages (Japanese, English and Chinese) in different ways at different times in response to the environment they found themselves in, highlighting the dynamic and complex nature of student agency.

Practices and processes (PP) are a feature of many of the chapters here with the focus on classroom activities and discourses alongside considering implications for teacher education. Practices and processes are closely intertwined with the previous exploration of roles of English and other languages, as well as stakeholder agency. A core theme that emerges from all the chapters is that other languages are present alongside English in EMI classrooms as part of a multilingual environment. Thus, translanguaging practises are observed in all the settings described here, regard-less of whether they are officially sanctioned in the policy. In Chap. 3 Ishikawa discusses pedagogic approaches which introduced students to key concepts in EMF

(English as a multilingua franca), transmodality and transcultural communication. He reports how such practices enabled the students to reflect further on multilingualism and multimodality in communication and their own translanguaging practices both inside and outside of the classroom. Ishikawa concludes with the importance of including EMF and translanguaging in teacher education so that teachers can incorporate it into their classroom practices. Chapters 5 (Kao et al.) and 6 (Zhang and Wei) zoom in on instructors' classroom discourse and translanguaging practices. Based on their data from EMI classrooms in Taiwan Kao et al. identify two main types of translanguaging strategies employed by instructors: instructional and interactional. Instructional translanguaging strategies refer to translation and paraphrasing in the L1 (Chinese) to support student comprehension of content. Interactional strategies typically involved shuttling between the L1 and English to maintain fluency, undertake classroom management, engage students and create a lively atmosphere. However, interactional strategies did not involve translation and paraphrasing and there was recognition from the instructors that this could exclude international students. Hence, this strategy was not used in content delivery. Kao et al. propose that EMI instructors would benefit from training in the use of these different strategies. Zhang and Wei analysed classroom discourse from an EMI programme in China in which all the participants shared an L1. Four translanguaging strategies emerged: adopting L1 for domain-specific knowledge, complementing English with L1, L1 recast, and utilizing L1 for localized knowledge. Zhang and Wei emphasise that these translanguaging practices were typically not employed as a compensation for students' perceived lack of English proficiency. Rather they were a deliberate pedagogic decision to enhance teaching through making use of students full linguistic repertoire as well as non-linguistic knowledge and experience, for instance when drawing on local knowledge. They suggest that policy in EMI programmes needs to recognise the value of these translanguaging practices, challenging an "English only" approach.

Turning to students, in Chap. 7 Ngo investigates the classroom practices of students in an EMI programme in Vietnam. Ngo documents the different practices and perceptions of students in a class where translanguaging was sanctioned in students' presentations by the teacher and another class with an English-only policy. In the former class the focus of students' work and assessment was on content and there was no obligation to use English exclusively. Observations showed the students using both their L1 and English across spoken and written work to construct meaning and understanding for others, for example having PowerPoint slides in English and explaining them in Vietnamese. In contrast, in the English-only class, the lack of space for L1 impeded meaning-making and understanding, for instance students "mechanically" reading out rehearsed presentations with little comprehension from classmates. However, as discussed under the section on agency (A), the students resisted this monolingual policy by preparing for class in their L1 with other classmates, for example agreeing in advance on a set of questions and answers for a presentation. Ngo argues that whether or not the teacher made space for translanguaging practices, the students used their full linguistic repertoire "to participate", "to elaborate ideas", and "to raise questions" (García & Li, 2014, p. 103). While classroom practices and discourse are not the focus of Humphries and Yashima's chapter, their participants did discuss the development of their linguistic repertories over the course of study abroad in Taiwan both inside and outside of the classroom. In particular, they reported on increasing translanguaging patterns with their different languages supporting each other and their development of a multilingual identity. Huang's study of local and international students in a Taiwanese EMI programme also illustrated the importance of translanguaging spaces and strategies for students. She reported positive perceptions of instructors' use of translanguaging including from international students who were interested in learning and using Chinese. Students also made use of their own various L1s alongside English in group work, student to student interaction in class, and social conversations at break times. As previously discussed under agency (A), the findings highlight the importance of translanguaging practices and spaces in empowering students and developing agency in their studies through making use of their full linguistic repertoire and encouraging further translanguaging practices. It is important to note that alongside making use of their full linguistic repertoire, Ngo and Huang's studies also illustrate how other multimodal resources such as images (PowerPoint slides) and gestures are used by students (see also Ishikawa). Like the chapters on teacher practices, all of the student-focused chapters propose that based on the practices and process reported it is crucial for pedagogy and teacher education to incorporate translanguaging perspectives and teaching strategies in EMI.

Internationalisation and glocalisation (ING) is another dimension that is a feature of all the chapters here in that they deal with EMI as an aspect of and response to internationalisation of HE at the university and government policy level. However, within EMI programmes the responses vary from recruitment of international students and staff to "internationalisation at home" with local students and teachers. Moreover, given that a number of the settings described are Chinese L1 speaking it also perhaps not surprising that the role of Chinese as an international language also comes up (Humphries and Yashima, Chap. 8). Nonetheless, the main discussion of internationalisation and glocalisation appears in the first part of this book dealing with EMI theory and policy. Tsou (Chap. 1) directly addresses glocalisation and EMI in Asia and cautions against adoption of English-only approaches that imitate Anglophone academic norms which may be unsuited to Asian education settings. As an alternative, she proposes translanguaging as a glocalising strategy better suited to EMI in Asia. Drawing on work by Lin (2020), Tsou argues that translanguaging offers a scaffolding strategy in bilingual/multilingual education that utilises learners' and teachers' full linguistic and semiotic repertoire. However, she also notes that an in-depth understanding of learners and their environment is needed in order to be able to use all the linguistic and other semiotic resources present and, hence, translanguaging pedagogy must also be localised. In relation to internationalisation, Baker (Chap. 2), suggests that in parallel with translanguaging EMI classrooms should also be viewed from a transcultural perspective. He argues that just as linguistic borders are blurred and transcended in translanguaging practices, so too are traditional notions of communities and cultural borders which need to be approached as equally dynamic and porous in EMI policy and practices. Similar ideas are put forward by Ishikawa (Chap. 3) who proposes that given the international nature of academia, greater awareness of EMF (English as a multilingua franca), transmodality and transcultural communication is needed at all levels of EMI from government and university policy, to teachers and students. In particular, he proposes EAP and ELT classes as a suitable setting to introduce these ideas. Ra and Baker's (Chap. 4) consideration of government and university policy in Thailand highlights the regional dimension of EMI. Many of the policy documents they examined position EMI as a response to increasing regional integration through the ASEAN community. However, as previously outlined in language management (M), they also note the approaches to English are still based on monolingual Anglophone ideologies, rather than regional ELF uses.

By way of summing up, it must be underscored that although each of the six ROAD-MAPPING dimensions is presented separately in practice they are closely interlinked as illustrated in Fig. 1 and underscored by the overlapping discussions of the chapters with many chapters appearing in multiple dimensions. Thus, the role of English and other languages is influenced by classroom practices and processes, which in turn is dependent on agents. At the same time, there is a two-way bottom-up and top-down relationship between the agents and language management with agents both implementing and being influenced by management practices. Moreover, language management is in itself also influenced by wider concerns of internationalisation and glocalisation.

4   Conclusion

A central theme throughout the chapters in this book and the subsequent synthesis through the ROAD-MAPPING framework is that in EMI in Asia English functions as a lingua franca in a multilingual environment in which translanguaging practices are always present. Based on the chapters presented here this appears to be the case regardless of whether there is an "English-only" or bilingual policy in EMI classrooms. This volume, thus, makes an original contribution in focusing on a translanguaging perspective in EMI, as well as adding to the growing body of evidence that EMI is a multilingual phenomenon (Baker & Hüttner, 2017, 2019; Barnard & Hasim, 2018; Bradford & Brown, 2018; Fenton-Smith et al., 2017; Jenkins & Mauranen, 2019; Murata, 2018; Tsou & Kao, 2017) and underlining the importance of conceptions of EMI, such as EMEMUS, that emphasise this multilingual dimension (Dafouz & Smit, 2020). However, like the previously cited research, the studies collected here show that this dynamic use of English as part of translanguaging practices in EMI classrooms is not recognised in official policy. Examinations of policy documents suggest that they are still predominantly underpinned by a monolingual and standard language ideology in which languages are strictly separated and English is approached from an Anglophone native speaker perspective. As discussed both in the chapters here and previous research (e.g. Jenkins & Mauranen, 2019; Murata, 2018), a focus on Anglophone English in academia and the marginalisation of multilingual resources and translanguaging practices can have a detrimental impact on the linguistic and academic practices of the majority of EMI stakeholders for whom English is an additional language. Nonetheless, and despite a lack of support from official policy, many of the chapters here illustrate positive attitudes towards ELF, multilingualism and translanguaging practices in EMI from both teachers and students, who at times also actively resisted "English-only" policies, indicating that bottom-up changes to monolingual ideologies may be possible. Furthermore, the descriptions in these chapters of the translanguaging practices and strategies employed by instructors and students, provide empirical support for proposals for pre and in-service teacher education in EMI that incorporate ELF and translanguaging perspectives. Additionally, the findings here suggest that ELT and EAP also need to move into a more central position in EMI in preparing and supporting students for the multilingual and transcultural reality of EMI (see also Dafouz & Smit, 2020; Doiz & Lasagabaster, 2020; Galloway & Rose, 2020).

There are a number of limitations to the collection of studies presented here that must be acknowledged. Firstly, although a range of settings in both East and South East Asia are covered in this volume, these are just two regions in Asia and far from representative of all of the huge diversity of Asia, let alone other regions in which EMI is prominent. Secondly, the settings are all ones that would traditionally have been regarded as expanding circle settings (Kachru, 1998) and no Asian post-colonial settings such as India or Malaysia are included. While the rapid expansion of ELF over the last few decades has problematized simplistic distinctions between the circles (Jenkins, 2015), it is, nonetheless, important to be aware of potential differences in attitudes and approaches towards English and EMI in post-colonial settings which have a long and complex history of both EMI and English use. Thirdly, within the settings investigated two important sets of voices are missing; that of management and administrators. Administrators are on the "frontline" of EMI and involved in key support roles for both students and staff, as well as often serving important roles in admission processes and policy formation. However, their perspectives have been largely absent from EMI research (see Dafouz & Smit, 2020; Poole, 2018 for exceptions). While management policies are investigated in some detail here, it would be a mistake to make simplistic correlations between policy documents and the beliefs and attitudes of management, who like other agents respond to and are influenced by a range of factors. Although it is unrealistic to expect one collection of studies to address all these areas, we hope that future research will turn its attention to these often neglected areas. Finally, despite the limitations, we hope that the richness and diversity of the studies presented here and the links to the wider body of EMI research through the ROAD-MAPPING framework offer a valuable resource for both researchers and practitioners in the relatively new but rapidly expanding field of EMI studies.

References

Baker, W., & Hüttner, J. (2017). English and more: A multisite study of roles and conceptualisations of language in English medium multilingual universities from Europe to Asia. *Journal of Multilingual and Multicultural Development, 38*(6), 501–516. https://doi.org/10.1080/01434632.2016.1207183

Baker, W., & Hüttner, J. (2019). "We are not the language police": Comparing multilingual EMI programmes in Europe and Asia. *International Journal of Applied Linguistics, 29*(1), 78–94. https://doi.org/10.1111/ijal.12246

Barnard, R., & Hasim, Z. (Eds.). (2018). *English medium instruction programmes: perspectives from South East Asian universities.* Abingdon: Routledge.

Bradford, A., & Brown, H. (Eds.). (2018). *English-medium instruction in Japanese higher education: Policy, challenges and outcomes.* Clevdon: Multilingual Matters.

Dafouz, E., & Smit, U. (2020). *ROAD-MAPPING English medium education in the internationalised university.* Cham, Switzerland: Palgrave Macmillan UK.

Doiz, A., & Lasagabaster, D. (2020). Dealing with language issues in English-medium instruction at university: a comprehensive approach. *International Journal of Bilingual Education and Bilingualism,* 1–6. https://doi.org/10.1080/13670050.2020.1727409.

Fenton-Smith, B., Humphreys, P., & Walkinshaw, I. (Eds.). (2017). *English medium instruction in higher education in Asia-Pacific: From policy to pedagogy.* Berlin: Springer.

Galloway, N., & Rose, H. (2020). English medium instruction and the English language practitioner. *ELT Journal,* 75th Anniversary Celebratory Issue (In Press).

García, O., & Li, W. (2014). *Translanguaging: language, bilingualism and education.* Basingstoke: Palgrave Macmillan.

Jenkins, J. (2015). *Global Englishes: A resource book for students* (3rd Ed.). London: Routledge.

Jenkins, J., & Mauranen, A. (Eds.). (2019). *Linguistic diversity on the EMI campus: Insider accounts of the use of English and other languages in universities within Asia, Australasia and Europe.* Abingdon: Routledge.

Kachru, B. (1998). *English as an Asian language.* Retrieved May, 2006, from www.bib.uab.es/pub/linksandletters/11337397n5p89.pdf.

Lin, A. M. Y. (2020). Cutting through the monolingual grip of TESOL traditions—The transformative power of the translanguaging lens. In Z. Tian, L. Aghai, P. Sayer, & J. L. Schissel (Eds.), *Envisioning TESOL through a translanguaging lens.* Switzerland: Springer.

Murata, K. (Ed.). (2018). *English-medium instruction from English as a Lingua Franca perspective: Exploring the higher education context.* Abingdon: Routledge.

Poole, G. (2018). Administrative impediments: How bureaucratic practices obstruct the implementation of English-taught programs in Japan. In A. Bradford & H. Brown (Eds.), *English-medium instruction in Japanese higher education: Policy, challenges and outcomes* (pp. 91–107). Clevdon: Multilingual Matters.

Scott, P. (2011). The university as a global institution. In R. King, S. Marginson, & R. Naidoo (Eds.), *The handbook of globalisation and higher education* (pp. 59–75). Cheltenham, UK: Edward Elgar.

Spolsky, B. (2004). *Language policy.* Cambridge: Cambridge University Press.

Tsou, W., & Kao, S.-M. (Eds.). (2017). *English as a medium of instruction in higher education: Implementations and classroom practices in Taiwan.* Singapore: Springer.

Will Baker is an Associate Professor of Applied Linguistics and Director of the Centre for Global Englishes at the University of Southampton, UK. His research interests are English as a Lingua Franca, Intercultural and Transcultural Communication, English medium instruction, Intercultural education, Intercultural Citizenship and ELT, and he has published and presented internationally in all these areas. His current research projects have focused on the links between Intercultural Citizenship, Internationalisation of HE and EMI including the recently completed

"From English language learners to intercultural citizen" https://www.teachingenglish.org.uk/art icle/english-language-learners-intercultural-citizens. Recent publications include: Baker, W., and Ishikawa, T. *Transcultural Communication through Global Englishes.* (2021, Routledge), co-editor of the '*Routledge Handbook of English as a Lingua Franca*' (2018), author of the monograph '*Culture and Identity through English as a Lingua Franca*' (2015, DGM), and co-editor of the book series '*Developments in English as Lingua Franca*' (DGM).

Wenli Tsou is a Full Professor in the Department of Foreign Languages and Literature, and currently Director of the Foreign Language Center at National Cheng Kung University, Taiwan. She received her Ph.D. in Foreign and Second Language Education from the State University of New York at Buffalo, US. She is the project leader of the National Cheng Kung University ESP and EMI programs. She is also the leading figure of the bilingual education in Taiwan, helping with its teacher training and curriculum design. Her research interests include teacher training, ESP, English as a Lingua Franca, Content and Language Interacted Learning and English as a Medium of Instruction. Her current research projects have focused on the links between transdiciplinary teaching and translanguaging of bilingual education and EMI. She chairs the 13th International Conference of English as a Lingua Franca and has co-edited the following books: "*English as a Medium of Instruction in Higher Education: Implementations and classroom practices in Taiwan*" (2017, Springer), "*Exploring CLIL: A Resource Book*" (2018, Bookman) and "*Resources for Teaching English for Specific Purposes*" (2014, Bookman).

Printed in Great Britain
by Amazon

43016327R00119